Film, History and
Cultural Citizenship

Routledge Studies in Cultural History

Film, History and Cultural Citizenship

Sites of Production

**Edited by
Tina Mai Chen and
David S. Churchill**

Routledge
Taylor & Francis Group
New York   London

Routledge
Taylor & Francis Group
711 Third Avenue
New York, NY 10017

Routledge
Taylor & Francis Group
2 Park Square
Milton Park, Abingdon
Oxon OX14 4RN

First issued in paperback 2011

ISBN13: 978-0-415-77117-7 (hbk)
ISBN13: 978-0-415-51464-4 (pbk)

Library of Congress Cataloging-in-Publication Data

Film, history and cultural citizenship : sites of production / edited by Tina Mai Chen
   and David S. Churchill.
      p. cm. -- (Routledge studies in cultural history ; 3)
   Includes bibliographical references and index.
   ISBN 978-0-415-77117-7 (hbk. : alk. paper)
      1. Motion pictures--Social aspects. 2. Motion pictures and history. I. Chen, Tina
Mai. II. Churchill, David S.

PN1995.9.S6F47 2007
302.23'43--dc22   2006035814

Visit the Taylor & Francis Web site at
http://www.taylorandfrancis.com

and the Routledge Web site at
http://www.routledge.com

Contents

Acknowledgments

This project began in collaboration with our friend and scholar Thomas Lahusen. Over the past three years, Thomas has been a mentor and critical intellectual model for this volume. Started as a lecture series on film and global imaginaries organized at the University of Manitoba by the Interdisciplinary Research Circle on Globalization and Cosmopolitanism, this collection has benefited from Thomas's direct involvement and his enthusiastic support.

Many people and organizations have made significant contributions to *Film, History and Cultural Citizenship: Sites of Production*. The Social Sciences and Humanities Research Council of Canada provided funding for the workshop from which this volume emerged. Additional funding was provided by the Office of the President as well as Richard Sigurdson, Dean of Faculty of Arts, and the Department of History at the University of Manitoba. For her commitment to the work of IRCGC since its founding and to this specific project, we would like to thank Mary Kinnear.

In addition we would like to extend our appreciation to Diana Brydon for providing helpful commentary on parts of the manuscript, Katy Hunt and Sandra Ferguson for their administrative and technological assistance, Andrea Vidal for her design and maintenance of the website, and Carl Klassen for his meticulous editorial assistance.

We would also like to recognize the outstanding efforts of the contributors and their willingness to embrace our vision of a collective research project. Finally, we need to thank Frank, Steven, and Cecilia for their patience and for reminding us that watching movies is also about fun.

1 Introduction

Tina Mai Chen and David S. Churchill

In July 2003 *The Washington Post* ran an article outlining the work of a French-organized, internationally funded initiative to provide mobile cinemas to Afghanistan (Pitman 2003). Supported by the United Nations, the European Union, and other donors, the French group AINA oversaw the screening of films produced by the Ministry of Information and Culture on the topics of Afghan artists, cultural heritage, and girls' education. The films were shown in Badakhashan, Kandahar, Jalalabad, Mazar-e-Sharif, Barniyan, Paktia, Herat, and the capital of Kabul. Western reporting such as that offered by Pitman drew upon dichotomous frameworks that positioned Afghans (represented by Afghan women and girls) as the victims of an oppressive Taliban that denied access to modernity, education, and film. This discourse of underdevelopment perhaps explains the international funding and the use of a UN spokeswoman for the news release; it also makes relevant the references to the lack of electricity and communication with the outside world in the "rugged Asian nation filled with remote mountain villages," and justifies the reclaiming of Afghan culture and heritage through film. The language of orientalism and developmentalism through which the work of the NGO AINA was characterized brings into sharp relief the overlapping historical moments of colonialism and Cold War modernization through which the present, and film as a technology of the modern, acquire meaning.

AINA, an organization with programs "developed to support democracy in Afghanistan through the development of media and cultural expression," works, in part, by training male and female camera operators and video journalists (http://www.com/filmcatalog/makers/fm658.shtml, accessed 26 June 2006). The ethos behind the program is seemingly informed by scholarly and political concerns with agency in representation. This is an ethos that pervades the work of NGOs and scholars who provide to communities cameras, video, and other media alongside technological knowledge in the hope of enabling marginalized and "othered" peoples to participate in the construction of their identities and social situations.

The films produced by AINA include *Afghanistan Unveiled* (2003), a film that premiered at a Washington fundraiser and then was screened at various international film festivals. Not surprisingly given the intended audience for the film, the promotional materials for *Afghanistan Unveiled* unselfconsciously present the mobility of AINA-trained filmmakers and film itself as delivering modernity and light after the darkness of the Taliban. Neither reviewers nor reporters pause to consider the politics of place and history so clearly expressed in the broad operation of film and modernity in this context. Rather, there is an easy comfort with the cosmopolitan subject position that the newly trained Afghan filmmakers are called upon to occupy alongside international activists, and for the entertainment/education of international viewers. But what if we were to think more carefully about the social and political operation of film in this case and the place of film as a site of production of history and cultural citizenship?

With this question in mind, *Film, History, and Cultural Citizenship* investigates the relationship of film to history, power, memory, and cultural citizenship. We are concerned with three central issues: one, the participation of film and filmmakers in articulating and challenging projects of modernity; two, the role of film in shaping particular understandings of self and other to evoke collective notions of belonging; and, three, the combination of film industry, text, and viewing practices in structuring modes of everyday political life and subjectivities. The contributors to the volume begin from the position that film is a powerful medium that transmits ideological narratives of nation, affiliation, everyday life, identity, and psychological experience. It is then the aim of the volume collectively to investigate the complexity of the historical dynamics that situate modern subjects in cultural frames formed by governments, corporations, the imaginations of filmmakers, and those that view films.

BEYOND FILMIC FACTICITY

There is a danger whenever historians approach film criticism that their analysis will focus on the absence of historical accuracy and nuance. Though such criticisms are important—particularly when considering the ideological operation of film and its ability to generate a popular understanding of the past, place and people—this collection seeks to engage film and history beyond the realm of fact. As such, the contributors to *Sites of Production* engage film scholarship and history across disciplines such as anthropology, sociology, literary studies, media and cultural studies, and history, as well as across film genres including documentary, independent shorts and features, Hollywood features, state-sponsored films, historical films, and popular-scientific productions. This collection's critical approach embraces textual workings, archival renderings, and the public operation of film. Though diverse in approach, all contributors take seriously the social and historical contexts of film, as well as the more textual relationship between the film and its audiences. Indeed, the multiplicity of audiences, be they dramatically different groups of people in one or more national locales or transnational audiences engaging films on a global scale, is a key concern for many of the authors.

In this volume, the contextual social and historical field refers to the broader socio-political and economic structures in which film is produced, circulated, and viewed, the aesthetic conditions and conventions, as well as the epistemological structures. Because we understand film and those associated with film industries at all levels to be involved in knowledge production, we directly locate our studies of film and history not only within the texts of film and the practices of history, but also within the discourses of film and history. Rudy Koshar argues that, while having its uses, an approach to film that either sees it as secondary illustrative material or a document to be read as archival material is too narrow because of the ways in which it diverts our attention away from understanding film as a way of constructing pasts (Koshar 1995: 155). Koshar draws upon Hayden White's notion of *historiophoty*, "the representation of history and our thought about it in visual images and filmic discourse" (White, cited in Koshar 1995: 57) to argue that "the 'constructedness' of film, its placement in a studio 'reality' far away from the historical reality to which it gestures, could be used by historians as a springboard for considering the strategies, advantages, and shortcomings not of the film but of previous historical narratives, filmic and written."

This book takes up White and Koshar's challenge to see film as historiography. In this manner, this book understands the past to be a contentious domain mediated by memory, politics, and the particularities of the archival record. What is at stake, in our minds, are the ways in which film and history produce each other in historically specific and contingent contexts as narrative texts. Yet, we agree with Rebecca Karl (2001) that we must avoid facile observations in the study of either film or history that simply conclude that changing times demand changing uses or interpretations. In the specific contexts of revolutionary and post-revolutionary China, Karl insists that we consider the competing filmic visions of the Opium War produced in China in 1959 and 1997 within "the time-space of a contemporary Chinese cinematic and historical imaginary, particularly by opening a discussion on the problem of 'historical burdens' or 'burdens of history' as a central topos of Chinese discourse on modern history" (231). This call to think through cinematic and historical visions in relation to specific formulations of history and historical problems as political and literary motifs of space-based modernities informs many of the chapters in this book. The problematic of burdens of history shapes the shared concern of the contributors with the ways in which films engage with historical moments in their narrative and visual texts within and against the available imaginaries of their moments of production and circulation.

As discussed by John Mowitt (this volume), we are concerned not only with film as historiography, then, but also with film as historicity. That is, to use Philip Rosen's formulation, "the particular interrelations of the mode of historiography and the types of construction of history related to it" (Rosen 2001: xi). For us this is a productive site of tension because it leads us to consider cinema and historiography as social and cultural operations as well as technological and epistemological structures. Contra Rosen, however, we choose not to undertake this through readings of historicity in film theory or specific films but rather by historicizing the specific social and cultural operations of film and historiography across global space and time. Film, like history, is an epistemological form of knowledge production and is often in narrative structure and production linked to projects of national modernization. But if we confine this observation to the study of historical film (Landy 2000) or the New History film (Rosenstone 1995), we privilege analytic frameworks that address the questions of how we can understand history in the visual media, and how the visual media writes histories. Excellent scholarship from precisely this perspective exists. But because we are interested in understanding how film and historiography operate as technological and epistemological forms in relation to projects of national modernization—and challenges to them—this volume takes a different entry point into the relationship between film and history than those works with which it shares a similar theoretical positioning. Rather than focus on the structures of visuality through which film mobilizes and enacts particular historical narratives and moments, we are concerned with the intersecting sites of production of film and history.

By highlighting sites of production we call attention to the multiple registers through which film, representation, and meaning operate. Without creating hierarchies of production, we want to emphasize the embodied craft of film production. This includes the communities of directors, actors, writers, camera operators, sound technicians, editors, and the like who make films (Buddle, Kulchyski), as well as the particular places of production (Hayashi, Naghibi). In addition, the practices and locales of screening and the contexts in which films are viewed/consumed (Chen, Gómez-Barris) also represent sites of historical production that are part of modern social practice and collective experience (Jancovich et al. 2003: 16). Another site of production stressed in this collection is the political economy of film production and its relationship to corporate, national and international networks of funding and development (Churchill, Austin-Smith, Stewart, Hoad). Finally, the representational operation of film and its ideological and historical use by various actors represents a site of production in its ability to generate meaning and agency within a cultural field (Mowitt, Crowe, Dueck). What all the contributors point out is that in the production of meaning and connection, film across these various sites has served cumulatively as a site for the praxis of modernity, a place where meaning and connection are mediated, cultural publics are generated, and the theories and ideologies of the modern are played out and experienced.

As film scholar Miriam Hansen has argued, "whether we like it or not, the predominant vehicles of public memory *are* the media of technical re/ production and mass consumption" (Hansen 1996: 310). Film in its public and collective nature is a particularly powerful medium of memory, of popular history, and historiography. Thus, film is also a classic product of modernity—a modernist form that is simultaneously a response and reaction, even a site of resistance, to the profoundly transforming, shattering, and dislocating effects of modern life. Critical scholarship of film in this register represents the historicization of what we are calling the "lived experience of modernity," a method of scrutinizing modernity(ies)'s "plurality and complexity" as well as its multiple operations (Hansen 1995; Jameson 2002; Berman 1988: 91; Mitchell 2000; Das 2000). In addition, the focus on *site*, on the physical and social location of film, as well as the productive realm of ideology, representation, and affect is part of this project of historicization. Though strategies of close textual reading and analyses of form are employed, the ultimate concern of this collection is on the contextual social field and the actors who produce, consume, and utilize film.

Forefront in the lived experience of modernity and the contextual social fields of film is the place of memory, even though history—as a critical epistemological practice—is too often forgotten. Here distinctions need to be made between what is meant by memory as well as the reasons we feel that distinguishing it from history is of importance. Memory has both subjective and collective meanings. On an individual level, common usage of the term *memory* encompasses the personal recollection of experiences, recalling lived experience and even bearing witness. Yet, personal memories of individuals can be collected and archived to provide an assemblage of experiential memory and a set of documents with which to reconstruct the past. Such an approach has been central to grassroots historians, human rights investigators, and documentary filmmakers. As such, memories can become an evidentiary base for history through an interweaving of mediated experiences with collective identity. In the early decades of the twentieth century the French sociologist Maurice Halbwachs developed the notion of "collective memory" to understand the ways in which memory is historically situated and particular. "Every collective memory," he wrote, "requires the support of a group delimited in space and time" (Halbwachs 1980: 48). Halbwachs's formulation is useful in that it is a call to historicize memory and to position it within social and political contexts. In so doing, we are reminded that the interpretation of memory—the afterlife of an event—is imbricated with identity and social class (Ross 2002).

Halbwachs's attention to the connection between collective memory and groups delimited in space and time, as well as Ross's attention to the afterlives of event, directly informs the focus of this volume on sites of production of film, history, and cultural citizenship. This book joins recent scholarship that works to understand the spatial and temporal histories within which film and cinema circulate and acquire meaning. Such approaches include a focus on the legal histories of cinematic spaces and their relationship to the city (Liang 2005), geographies of filmic communities and their lived identities (Widdis 2003), and the representability of time in photographic and cinematic technologies (Doane 2002). Along with these studies, this book emphasizes the relationship between the people who live in the times and spaces crosscut by cinema and the lived experiences of modernity mediated by cinema. Our approaches to this relationship range from studies of personal historicity as related to a specific film (Austin-Smith), to specific filmmakers' mobilization of international funding, audiences, and transnational textual imagery (Stewart, Churchill, Gómez-Barris), to collectivities enabled through film production and circulation (Buddle, Chen, Kulchyski). Moreover, the studies and their specific conclusions underscore our belief that once we begin to analyze spatial and temporal histories of cinema as experiences of modernity we are also drawn into the terrain of states, citizens, and lived identities. We have chosen to think about how issues of state, citizen, and lived identity intersect with film and history through the conceptual framework of cultural citizenship.

CULTURAL CITIZENSHIP'S RELATIONSHIP TO FILM AND HISTORY

Many of the essays in this volume explore the public culture of private emotion and affect. Often posited in geographically national or local spatial realms, the feelings of community, collective identity, cultural citizens, and subjects are nonetheless articulated through the technological production and viewing of films, and in relation to state formations. Within its shifting local, national, and transnational contexts film has served—and at times has been utilized instrumentally—to prevent what political theorist Chantal Mouffe has identified as liberalism's tendency to "reduce citizenship to a mere legal status" (Mouffe 1992: 227). That is, film can provide a key investment in the cultural capital of citizen/subjects, be they remotely situated rural spectators or cosmopolitan viewers in a modern metropolis. This power of film, and its role as an epistemological technology of knowing and of providing simultaneously shared and profoundly intimate experiences of viewing, is part of what gives film historical significance.

For us, then, the concept of cultural citizenship invokes notions of political citizenship and rights, but highlights the cultural frameworks through which citizenship acquires meaning as lived experience. The state–citizen relation is therefore only one component; and as we demonstrate from a broad set of geographical and historical locations it is a relation oft refracted through media systems and cinematic sites. We are thus concerned with the multiple forms of subjectivity that converge around the state–citizen nexus and that are brought into being through both speech and visual acts.

Because we recognize, along with organizations like AINA, that film provides a medium through which new subject positions can be enacted to alter socio-political conditions, this book elucidates the precise conditions of subjectivity that are mobilized in different historical and geographic moments. Despite the range of methodological approaches, the contributors to this book share a commitment to thinking through the processes of power and inequality within social fields, and to how politics of sameness and difference can render questions of citizenship cultural. Yet, contra much of the scholarship on cultural citizenship (Flores and Benmayor 1997; Rosaldo 2003), we are not only concerned with claims that citizens make against the state through cultural projects; we examine the range of cultural practices through which citizenship as political and affective affiliation is enacted. This means that while some contributors to this volume focus on cultural citizenship as alternative communities to nation–state histories and discourses, others draw out how nation–state projects mobilize cultural citizenship alongside political citizenship.

PRODUCING NATIONAL AND TRANSNATIONAL IMAGINARIES

The first section of this book locates questions of film, history, and cultural citizenship at the nexus of the national and transnational. Our attention to the *sites* of production results in a foregrounding of the multiple locales that give places meaning through mobilizations of film and history. In this respect we are concerned with how geocultural and geopolitical entities have been constructed through discourses of film/history, and the forms and theories of subjectivity that animate these discourses. This means that we challenge the presumed naturalness of geopolitical units by drawing out the speech and visual acts that constitute these units within politicized settings. Our focus on the imaginary of the geopolitical is informed by scholars who have demonstrated that such an approach is fundamental to making sense of, and transcending, historiographical and filmic fascination with the national (Saldhana-Portillo 2003; Renda 2001; and Klein 2003). This often means analyzing the negotiations across and between newly legitimate and delegitimated discourses and practices such as nationalism and imperialism, and how they operate in and through film and the film industry (Jaikumar 2006).

The chapters by Hayashi, Churchill, Naghibi, Chen, and Gómez-Barris all share a concern with the relationship between discourses of nation, imperialism, and transnationalism. To this end, they do not reject the national framework but collectively advocate for a radical rethinking of the national as an analytic. For these scholars, any consideration of the national must take seriously the specific ways in which the national is imbricated in the pasts, presents, and futures of nationhood, colonialisms, imperialisms, and other global processes. In this regard, Hayashi, Churchill, and Naghibi foreground the relationship between filmmakers' national imaginaries within, and against, forces of imperialism. Hayashi attends to these dynamics in the context of Japanese empire in the 1930s and 1940s. Through readings of Shimizu Hiroshi's road films, Hayashi highlights the challenges to national ideology presented by Shimizu as he refused to reproduce normative familial and hierarchical subjectivities, and instead focused on the margins of the nation-state embodied in migrant labor and alternative children's subjectivities. Hayashi's attention to the ways in which Shimizu counters dominant nation–state discourses by disrupting the very geography of the attendant imperialist vision suggests to the reader the productive potential of thinking through subjectivities on the borders of empire.

Churchill and Naghibi take up this line of inquiry with an eye toward the contemporary moment and the operation of film and history within the context of twenty-first century US imperialist visions. Through an analysis of Michael Moore's vision of Canada as an alternative to mainstream US politics, Churchill argues that Moore remains committed to an American left-nationalist politics that cannot realize an internationalist vision. Even as Moore regularly crosses the US–Canadian border in both text and practice, Churchill demonstrates that Moore reifies the border for the purpose of a simplified critique of corporate America that ultimately characterizes transnational or international complicity as the actions of 'dupes of America.' In so doing, Churchill locates Moore's cultural work within the broader historiography of left-nationalism in the United States and Canada. This draws our attention to the ways in which the national framework can operate to the detriment of a full analysis of transnational and international economic processes.

Naghibi is also concerned with moments of complicity between hegemonic visions produced in the Euro-American world and the ways in which they frame their others. Naghibi analyzes Saira Shah's documentaries *Beneath the Veil* and *Unholy War* in light of their mass circulation following the terrorist attacks of 11 September 2001, and the preoccupation of CNN with making meaning of, and for, Afghanistan. Like Churchill and Hayashi, Naghibi locates her study in terms of historicized epistemological exercises that inform subjectivities available for political mobilization. Naghibi argues that Saira Shah operates within a tradition of colonial feminist discourse about veiled Muslim women awaiting liberation as delivered by the West. Through a close reading of Shah's films alongside the intertextuality introduced by CNN news tickers across the bottom of television screens, Naghibi provides an analysis of the flipside of the dynamics highlighted by Churchill. That is, Churchill shows how Moore's apparent internationalism is overdetermined by a nationalist imaginary; Naghibi demonstrates the imperialist and international epistemological frameworks through which Afghan as nation (presumably the focus of Shah's work) acquires meaning.

Taking up the national, international, and transnational as historicized constructs, Chen and Gómez-Barris consider the relationship between national liberation and filmic spaces of resistance to specific forms of colonialism and oppression. Chen examines how film as a modern technology and cultural enterprise was central to the national and socialist imaginaries of Maoist China. Through an analysis of the overlapping textual communities and communities in practice associated with film, Chen argues that the Chinese nation-state was configured through simultaneously circulating national, colonial, and internationalist historical and filmic discourses. The remapping of China as a modern socialist nation therefore entailed envisioning the nation in relation to the films/histories of other struggles for socialism, namely those of the Soviet Union and Korea. While Chen encourages us to consider the materialization of internationalist imaginaries through local and national filmic practices, Gómez-Barris considers how the specific history of Chile under Pinochet created the conditions for filmic expressions of exile subjectivity that contested silenced historical memories of the nation. Gómez-Barris carefully analyzes Patricio Guzmán's *The Pinochet Case* to draw out the transnational dimensions through which collective identities can be forged at the intersection of the film text and the audiences who watch film. Guzmán's desire to produce empathetic attachment is central to Gómez-Barris's analysis; yet Gómez-Barris reminds us that the collective attachments can be located within Chilean national/transnational communities or within human rights networks. In each instance, the transnational stakes of film as memory work and historiography are evident.

HISTORICAL FEELING IN THE SITES OF PRODUCTION

The chapters in the second section of the book deal with the affective power of film and its place as historical narrative, document, and emotional archive. Hoad, Crowe, Kulchyski, and Austin-Smith examine the intimate relationships of film and the engendering of personal and collective forms of meaning. In particular the contributors explore the cinematic representations of trauma, violence, and their affective operation on an array of subjects. As film scholar Kirby Farrell argues, trauma in contemporary culture has become a ubiquitous mediating technique to deal with the aftermath of radical historical change and rupture. In his view, the "post-traumatic" condition is "psychocultural because the injury entails interpretation of the injury" (Farrell 1998: 7). Themes of loss—be they of homeland, loved ones, or collective and individual autonomy—are productive sites not only for filmmakers and scholars but also for popular commemoration and collective memory (Kaplan 2005). As LaCapra argues, it is the intimate connection through which we "invest trauma with value and make its reliving a painful but necessary commemoration or memorial to which one remains dedicated or at least bound" (2001: 22). Reconciling the tension between individual and collective emotions, acts of violence and shattering loss, and shared historical experience has been a persistent project of filmmakers and video producers.

In Neville Hoad's contribution, the place of national historical trauma—the legacy of apartheid and the crisis of the HIV/AIDS pandemic in South Africa—is central to his close reading of Darrel Roodt's IsiZulu language film *Yesterday*. Hoad shows how the national historical drama of health-care crisis, tied to the political economy of migrant labor and an ineffective post-apartheid state, are told through the perspective of a rural Zulu family. As such, Hoad questions Roodt's utilization of family melodrama as a national allegory and raises questions about the politics of representation, as well as the political effect of cinematic storytelling.

The representation of trauma is also central to the innovative chapter by Roewan Crowe. For Crowe, the Hollywood Western is generative of a mythic but nonetheless embodied landscape of the Western, which is experienced and ultimately contested through the field of historically situated social relations and the practice/production of art. Utilizing fiction as well as a critical analysis of her own video production—*Queer Grit*—Crowe challenges the doxa generated by the inter-subjective reality of the Law, Father, and John Wayne that shapes masculine conventions in contemporary North America, particularly for the rural communities of the United States and Canadian Prairies. Recasting the West as a place of possibility and self-creation, Crowe explores the ambiguity of violence, particularly in relation to alternative genders and sexualities, as well as the racist history of colonialism.

Kulchyski's provocative essay on the Zacharias Kunuk film *Atanarjuat* (The Fast Runner) also takes up the theme of violence. Kulchyski's analysis of violence moves from a subtle reading of murderous action within the film, to the symbolic and representational violence perpetrated by mechanical production, to what he terms non-alienated communities—be they represented, idealized, or embodied. In recognizing Kunuk's remarkable aesthetic, and as Kulchyski suggests more problematically, Kunuk's historical/ethnographic achievement, Kulchyski theorizes the idea of affective community and authenticity in these multiple registers.

Kulchyski, Crowe, and Hoad, along with Austin-Smith, all explore how films can form what literary scholar Anne Cvetkovich has so evocatively called an "archive of feeling" (Cvetkovich 2003). The films themselves—whether the Western, the independent film of Isuma Productions, or the Hollywood studio melodrama—provide emotional and representational narratives, which operate at the most intimate levels of everyday life. Austin-Smith's point of entry into the intimate operation of film is an exploration of the way that the Bette Davis vehicle *Now, Voyager*—a classic representative of a "women's weepie"—could occupy a complicated place in the personal transnational history of a particular viewer. Situating the film within the tradition of Fordist studio production, as well as the broader context of the Second World War and the post-war decades, Austin-Smith reveals the way that the emotional affect of the film plays an abiding role in the personal history of a British immigrant woman to Canada. Here the transnational dynamic of cultural exchange, embodied representation, and gesture are constituent parts of a modern subjectivity mediated by an intimate reading of the film.

THE CULTURES OF FILM AND THE PRODUCTION OF HISTORY

Cultural historians, film scholars, and filmmakers often recognize that films are integrated in gendered political–social formations, even as they remain alert to the need to understand films to be individualized artifacts of cultural and personal memory. Further developing the analyses offered in the first two sections of the book, the final section's focus on the cultures of film and the production of history takes up work by leading cultural historians such as Mary Renda (2001), Stephanie Donald (2000), and Poshek Fu (2003). These scholars analyze the larger cultural milieus that allow film-viewing publics to make sense of government policies and historical events. To this end, Fu advocates for historical interpretations that are attuned to the institutional and industrial contexts as well as the specific circumstances of production, screening, and debate. As Fu insists, we need to consider cinema as "a cultural practice that by its nature is soaked through with the social conditions of its making" (xv). In following this formulation, the analyses presented in this book encompass, but are not limited to, aesthetic issues as they seek to understand how film transcends national frameworks (part I), invokes affective and historicized feelings (part II), and produces history along multiple axes (part III).

The papers in the final section pay particular attention to the social conditions, cultural practices, and politics of film production and screening. Each of the contributors asks how historical structures, memory, and possibilities are expressed in relation to these conditions and politics. Buddle convincingly argues that the performative act and expressive practice of filming is, for female Native directors in Canada, aimed at reconfiguring the social dynamics of the worlds these women inhabit. Buddle's focus on community filmmaking as activism highlights the ways in which Native women's documentary production re-envisions womanhood and female subjectivity against domesticized narratives of "traditional womanhood." In the process, filmmaking as praxis becomes a mode of challenging historical structures and narratives that naturalizes particular racial and gendered hierarchical structures, and proposes alternative historical possibilities for Aboriginal womanhood.

The radical potential of filmmakers to challenge unequal power relations reinforced by historical narrative, events, and geopolitics is also addressed by Stewart in her analysis of Abderrahmane Sissako's films. Stewart begins by analyzing how the structure of African filmmaking has been shaped by the history of national cultural policies in France and various African states. She then interweaves this analysis with close readings of Sissako's films, with a focus on the themes of the ethics of listening and exile subjectivity. Stewart suggests that Sissako's filmmaking (as text and practice) is both constrained and enabled by the conditions of its production and screening. Despite funding preferences for narrative film by French funding agencies, Sissako makes historical contingency central to his work and resists the national allegory film that dominated African national cinema in the 1970s and 1980s. His own mobility, past and present, produces a vision of a grounded 'world citizen' that makes Sissako and his work both fitting for, and a challenge to, European funding that favors transnational filming and production for largely European audiences. This is because Sissako is also able to enunciate a transnational exile subjectivity that problematizes rather than elides or simplistically reverses the unequal power structures constitutive of colonialism, neo-colonialism, and independence that are inherent in the various national and historic formations that shape his filmmaking.

Mowitt and Dueck also interrogate the transnational socio-cultural conditions of film, but unlike Stewart who foregrounds the movement of a filmmaker across space and time, Mowitt and Dueck are concerned with the ways that directors or agencies of the state move film and history over national borders. In her study of the two filmic versions of *Jacob the Liar*, one produced in the German Democratic Republic in 1974 and the other by an America-based company in 1999, Dueck highlights the importance for the final product and its success of the memory cultures within which Holocaust films are produced. Dueck argues that these films serve a function common to the Holocaust industry in that each film is invested in the founding myths of the countries in which they were produced. Through close textual analysis of the two films, Dueck highlights how the different relationships to the historical memory of the Holocaust result in filmic interplay between truth and imagination in the GDR version, and an overarching insistence on authenticity in the US version. In the former, hope and the myth of anti-fascism dominates while in the latter the myth of individual freedom overdetermines the filmic text and its possibilities.

Mowitt is also concerned with cultural conditions of film viewing in the United States as he considers Pontecorvo's iconic film *The Battle of Algiers*. Mowitt takes as his point of departure for a broader inquiry into the relationship between film and historicity the question of why this film has been screened by the US State Department for training purposes in the current war on terrorism. Mowitt echoes Dueck's claims about authenticity and US memory culture as he analyzes the pedagogical function assigned to *The Battle of Algiers* in both its use by the State Department and its championing by radical historians as a teaching tool for anti-colonial history.

Despite the disclaimer Pontecorvo inserted at the beginning of the film to clarify that none of the footage in the film was drawn from French television, Mowitt demonstrates that the radicality of the film is not appreciated because of the modalities of study through which it has been presented and viewed. That is, Pontecorvo's disclaimer calls on the viewer to reflect on what constitutes evidence and the realness of the past, and to what extent cinema acts as a documenting medium. Yet, as Mowitt argues, when viewed through a lens in the contemporary United States in which *The Battle of Algiers* is presumed a priori to represent evidence and the realness of the past, this radical framework is undermined, as are questions of how history, film, and representation adjust themselves to one another.

In sum, this collection of essays on film, history, and cultural citizenship provides an interdisciplinary and global approach to film history, film as historical experience of modernity, and film as a site for the production of historiography and historicity. We illustrate how questions about the relationship between film and history can be considered outside of the genres of historical and documentary film, while simultaneously recognizing the importance of these genres to historical representation and popular understandings of the past. We provide examples of alternative analytic formulations of historic encounters with film/filmic encounters with history that foreground the multiple sites of production through which film and history acquire personal and collective meaning. Moreover, we hope that this volume provides critical tools that will widen our discussions of film and history to include sustained consideration of questions of subjectivity and affective identities as key components of the operation of film and history as practices and discourses. It is our belief that by looking at such questions we can better understand the social, cultural, and political dimensions of film, history, and cultural citizenship as interrelated frameworks that are intimate yet embedded within local, national, and global technological and epistemological structures, and that are materialized in specific historical and geographic conditions.

REFERENCES

Berman, M. (1988) *All That Is Solid Melts Into Air*, New York: Penguin Books.

Cvetkovich, A. (2003) *An Archive of Feelings: Trauma, Sexuality and Lesbian Public Culture*, Durham, NC: Duke University Press.

Das, V. (2000) "The Making of Modernity: Gender and Time in India Cinema," in T. Mitchell (ed.) *Questions of Modernity*, Minneapolis: University of Minnesota Press.

Doane, M. (2002) *The Emergence of Cinematic Time: Modernity, Contingency, the Archive*, Cambridge, MA: Harvard University Press.

Donald, S. (2000) *Public Secrets, Public Spaces: Cinema and Civility in China*, Lanham, MD: Rowman & Littlefield.

Farrell, K. (1998) *Post-traumatic Culture: Injury and Interpretation in the Nineties*, Baltimore: Johns Hopkins University Press.

Flores, W. and Benmayor, R. (1997) *Latino Cultural Citizenship: Claiming Identity, Space, and Rights*, Boston: Beacon Press.

Fu, P. (2003) *Between Shanghai and Hong Kong: The Politics of Chinese Cinema*, Stanford, CA: Stanford University Press.

Halbwachs, M. (1980) *The Collective Memory*, Trans. Francis J. Ditter, Jr. and Vida Yazdi Ditter, New York: Harper and Row.

Hansen, M. (1995) "America, Paris, the Alps: Kracauer (and Benjamin) on Cinema and Modernity," in L. Charney and V.R. Schwartz (eds) *Cinema and the Invention of Modern Life*, Berkeley: University of California Press.

——(1996) "*Schindler's List* is Not *Shoah*: The Second Commandment, Popular Modernism and Public Memory," *Critical Inquiry*, 2.2: 292–312.

Jaikumar, P. (2006) *Cinema at the End of Empire: a politics of transition in Britain and India*, Durham, NC and London: Duke University Press.

Jancovich, M., Faire, L. and Stubbings, S. (2003) *The Place of the Audience: Cultural Geographies of Film Consumption*, London: BFI.

Jaumeson, F. (2002) *A Singular Modernity: Essay on the Ontology of the Present*, London and New York: Verso.

Kaplan, E.A. (2005) *Trauma Culture: the Politics of Terror and Loss in Media and Literature*, New Brunswick, NJ: Rutgers University Press.

Karl, R. (2001) "The Burdens of History: *Lin Zexu* (1959) and *The Opium War* (1997)," in X. Zhang (ed.) *Whither China? Intellectual Politics in Contemporary China*, Durham, NC and London: Duke University Press, pp. 229–62.

Klein, C. (2003) *Cold War Orientalism: Asia in the Middlebrow Imagination*, Berkeley: University of California Press.

Koshar, R. (1995) "Hitler: a film from Germany," in R. Rosenstone (ed.) *Revisioning History: Film and the Construction of a New Past*, Princeton, NJ: Princeton University Press.

LaCapra, D. (2001) *Writing History, Writing Trauma*, Baltimore, MD: The Johns Hopkins University Press.

Landy, M. (2000) *The Historical Film: History and Memory in Media*, Newark, NJ: Rutgers University Press.

Liang, L. (2005) "Cinematic Citizenship and the Illegal City," *Inter-Asia Cultural Studies*, 6.3: 366–85.

Mitchell, T. (ed.) (2000) *Questions of Modernity*, Minneapolis: University of Minnesota Press.

Mouffe, C. (1992) "Democratic Citizenship and the Political Community," in C. Mouffe (ed.) *Dimensions of Radical Democracy: Pluralism, Citizenship, Community*, London and New York: Verso, pp. 225–39.

Pitman, T. (2003) "Mobile Cinemas Showing Films to Afghans," *The Washington Post*, 27 July, Online. Available HTTP: <http://www.washingtonpost.com/wp~dyn/articles/A53618-2003Jul27.html> (accessed 28 July 2003).

Renda, M. (2001) *Taking Haiti: Military Occupation and the Culture of U.S. Imperialism, 1915–1940*, Chapel Hill and London: The University of North Carolina Press.

Rosaldo, R. (2003) *Cultural Citizenship in Island Southeast Asia: Nation and Belonging in the Hinterlands*, Berkeley: University of California Press.

Rosen, P. (2001) *Change Mummified: cinema, historicity, theory*, Minneapolis: University of Minnesota Press.

Rosenstone, R. (1995) *Revisioning History: Film and the Construction of a New Past*, Princeton, NJ: Princeton University Press.

Ross, K. (2002) *May '68 and Its Afterlives*, Chicago: University of Chicago Press.

Saldhana-Portillo, M. (2003) *The Revolutionary Imagination in the Americas and the Age of Development*, Durham and London: Duke University Press.

Widdis, E. (2003) *Visions of a New Land: Soviet Film from the Revolution to the Second World War*, New Haven and London: Yale University Press.

Part I
Producing national and transnational imaginaries

2 Negotiating mobile subjectivities
Costume play, landscape, and belonging in the colonial road movies of Shimizu Hiroshi

Sharon Hayashi

Shimizu Hiroshi directed an astounding 163 films during his lifetime (1903–1966). Despite his status as one of the Shochiku studio's top prewar directors, Shimizu and his oeuvre remain in relative obscurity next to the so-called masters of Japanese cinema: Ozu, Mizoguchi, and Kurosawa. In the field of national film studies and the international circuit of film festivals, the measure of a director's "Japaneseness" determines the attention his or her work receives. During the war, cultural conservatives latched onto Mizoguchi Kenji's historical dramas and cinematic style as the incarnation of Japanese beauty. Shimizu's films, meanwhile, were criticized for their lack of seriousness in representations of Japanese imperialism. His formalist play and playful treatment of serious subjects, such as national identity and mobilization for war, invited the ire of cultural conservatives. In the postwar period Shimizu made low-budget independent films about travel, utopia, and children's subjectivity—themes that were unlikely to gain him recognition abroad as a "Japanese" film director or popularity at home.

Shimizu Hiroshi's films made from 1936 to 1942 raised questions about what it meant to be Japanese during the expansion of the Japanese empire into Asia. His road movies were enabled by the great structural changes in first domestic and then colonial travel and transportation taking place in the expanding Japanese empire. Shimizu's interest in travel and landscape, although exaggerated, was not just a personal preference but rather reflected the structural changes in transportation. The theme of landscape increasingly used by filmmakers from the mid-1930s was in part made possible by developments in the travel and tourism industry, such as the establishment of the Japan Travel Bureau by the Ministry of Railways in 1920. Shimizu used the genre of the road movie to focus on the plight of migrant labor, social outcasts, and imperial subjects, positions outside normative roles within the family and nation.

His formalist filmmaking style as well as the recurrent theme of play in his films could be interpreted as questioning the prescribed roles of the nation-state family system and national identity. In 1936 the director Itami Mansaku praised Shimizu's use of symmetry and play, which he described as a "stylization not only in the visual field, but of the position of the characters, the environment, and the plot" (Itami 1961: 361). Formalism, especially when it mocked serious subjects, was frowned upon in the late 1930s and early 1940s by conservative film critics. *Star Athlete* (Hanagata senshu), filmed right after the outbreak of the war with China in 1937, portrayed student troops being mobilized for the war. Although the film is about military training, the athletes are shown lounging around or simply running up and down a road. In its playfulness on the level of plot and character position, the film is anything but a serious representation of soldiers preparing for war.

Shimizu's contemporary Ozu Yasujiro was also a formalist, but because his formalism was considered artistic rather than comic, it did not come under the same criticism during the war. Shimizu came under attack for using comic formalism when addressing serious themes, or for not making films with appropriately serious themes that supported nationalism and the military. A politics of play pervades Shimizu's films from this period and the labor depicted in his films was never overtly aligned with national mobilization for the war.

In 1939 a prohibitive film law was passed and films that touched upon the unflattering lives of soldiers were discouraged or simply not made after 1939. Yet in 1941 Shimizu shot a film entitled *Ornamental Hairpin* (Kanzashi) in which a wounded soldier from the front is shown convalescing at a hot spring resort. Already suffering from a foot injury from battle, the soldier accidentally steps on the hairpin of the title while bathing. There are no heroic portrayals of soldiers at the battlefield and the bulk of the film is comprised of lengthy scenes of rehabilitation seen from the comical viewpoint of children.

Although a very small number of filmmakers or film critics were jailed for their political beliefs, most filmmakers, like most liberals, did not go through the renunciation of Marxist views demanded by the state. The process of political conversion is much more difficult to trace in the film world than that of the literary world. While writers were usually affiliated with specific journals or groups that had a definable political orientation and usually wrote as single authors, filmmakers worked collectively, and their politics were less well defined. Oftentimes the contributions of leftist filmmakers who ended up supporting the national war effort took the form of national policy. Their films were filled with images of rationalized labor processes in service of the national effort: factory scenes showed workers making airplane parts for the nation with clock-like precision under great duress while domestic spaces were rationalized in order to become more efficient for the national effort. The allure of rationalization of labor and its promise for a better life, and the ideals of social improvement attracted many leftist documentary filmmakers to the national cause. The rationalization of work in many documentary films of the late 1930s and 1940s soon became part of an assembly line in the production of national propaganda as the process of work became aligned with and eventually subsumed to the national cause. Shimizu's politics of play during the war can be read as a refusal to portray industrious workers offering their labor to a national and imperial cause.

THE ROAD MOVIE

Shimizu's films are particularly helpful in charting the way travel and migration transformed the film world as both a theme and a condition of production. By the mid-1930s the portability of film equipment and the development of railways had made shooting on location possible. Being on the road for Shimizu meant a kind of liberation, not only from the confines of the studio and the star system but also from the normative roles of the petty bourgeois family drama.

In the 1930s the prominent film critic Kishi Matsuo often commented that the road was the "stereotypical ideology of Shimizu's filmmaking" (Kishi 1938: 131). Not only did the road function literally as a protagonist in many of his films, but also in bringing the film on the road Shimizu was able to portray a whole section of society that had been for the most part neglected in cinematic representations of the time. Many directors at this time turned their cameras on the landscape, and Shimizu in particular was interested in using the landscape to show the plight of migrant labor. Shimizu was especially fond of portraying mistresses and traveling prostitutes, characters who did not fit into prescribed roles of the naturalized family known as the nation–state family. In the 1890s, when the emperor was restored to rule after living in obscurity to head the newly created nation-state, the nation began to be represented as a family, in which the imperial household and the people were bound together as a family and the righteousness between the ruler and his subjects was equated with the intimacy between father and child. This stable and hierarchized unit of the family provided the model for the nation and became the ground on which the state was naturalized. Images that questioned the naturalized and stable family were therefore questioning the stability of the nation.

In Shimizu's films, women who reject or are rejected by the naturalized family often became part of new temporary communities formed on the road. His images of travelers were a direct rejection of the normative and oppressive bourgeois household that functioned as the building block of the nation. Many of his films depicted the injustice of patriarchal households for mistresses and illegitimate children. Shimizu is the only Japanese director of his time who consistently made films featuring single mothers and orphaned, handicapped, and delinquent children. At the height of Japanese wartime nationalism in the 1940s, Shimizu went to extremes and chose to make a film about an orphanage. Most films that took up children's subjectivity at this time portrayed the innocent child as the ideal citizen of the state, hard-working and willing to sacrifice himself or herself for the good of the community. Yet the children of the orphanage and the children presented in Shimizu's films in general are often delinquent, sometimes mentally handicapped, and their efforts are expended in play rather than in mobilizing for the national effort. Almost all of Shimizu's films portray a kind of self-selecting community of migrants and outcasts rather than naturalized communities based on family or an attachment to land. In this way the films avoided reproducing the family-state ideology that conveniently collapsed notions of the family into the national community.

Portraying fluid communities in transit was also a way of addressing the very real social problem of migrant labor in Japan during the depression era of the 1930s. In 1936 Shimizu made one of the first road movies in Japan. The film, *Mr. Thank You,* is based on a three-page short story by the noted writer Kawabata Yasunari. The simple story describes a mother from the countryside bringing her daughter by bus over a mountain pass to a train station in order to sell her into prostitution in the big city, and then returning home. Shot completely on location, the film takes place entirely on the bus, steered by a bus driver nicknamed Mr. Thank You who courteously shouts out his thanks to all the travelers on the road who move aside to let the bus pass. The symmetrical structure of the narrative is echoed by the visual symmetry of the comic interactions between the travelers. Two similarly attired male passengers twiddle their mustaches in union and become visual patterns on the screen. This comic visual moment is connected to the landscape of dire economic depression navigated by the bus and its passengers when it is suggested that one of the men has sold his own daughter into labor. The roads are filled with day laborers returning from the city after being laid off from factories, and with young women being sold into labor or prostitution in the cities. The film uses both comic and melancholic portrayals of the landscape to narrate the plight of migrant laborers from the countryside, and is an example of the hybrid genre of the pre-war period which included a variety of styles that are now associated with specific and separate genres. Geographically, this is a film that takes place neither in the city nor the countryside but rather in the intermediate space of travel, and the most noticeable travelers are young migrant working women. The instability, motion, and uprootedness that characterize these travelers are major themes of Shimizu's films.

The short story focuses on the plight of a 17-year-old girl being sold into prostitution, but Shimizu adds another, slightly older prostitute to the film version, a cheeky, whiskey-slugging, hard-smoking woman who harasses the male riders that step out of line on the bus. The traveling prostitute is a recurrent theme in Shimizu's oeuvre and can be traced to his early films of the 1930s such as *Japanese Girls at the Harbor* (Nihon minato musume, 1933), which follows the wandering lifestyle of harbor girls, including a young woman who sets off to China to become a prostitute. Unlike the stationary prostitutes portrayed in the films of his contemporaries like

Mizoguchi Kenji, the traveling prostitute in Shimizu's films does not sacrifice herself for love of a man but rejects subordination to both place and men. The itinerary of young women travelers in Shimizu's films reflects the changes in the flow of gendered labor throughout the empire. The exportation of Japanese prostitutes into the empire until the mid-1930s is reversed to include the importation of Korean migrant laborers by 1936.

Mr. Thank You was one of the first films in Japan ever to be shot completely on location and not in a studio; the landscape is used to express the melancholy of the young woman about to be sold into prostitution. As the bus approaches the train station, the young girl looks forlornly out of the bus window. The camera cuts between shots of her forlorn face and the magnificent passing scenery. The melancholy of the girl is projected onto the landscape itself.

Shimizu, however, doesn't just use the road as a vista on the landscape or as a path to show the migration of labor; instead, he indicates how the road itself is the product of migrant labor. While hunting for locations for *Mr. Thank You*, Shimizu came upon a Korean road construction crew and decided to weave their story into the plot. He incorporated actual documentary footage that he had shot of the crew at the time. Korea was annexed by Japan in 1910 and the land reform policies carried out by the Japanese in the colony created conditions so dire that many Koreans were forced to migrate to Japan to work in mines and on road construction crews such as the one that appears in this film.

The road functions as the real protagonist of many of Shimizu's films providing not only a theme or backdrop but serving as the organizing spatial and narrative configuration of the films themselves. When filming the road, Shimizu almost always placed the camera in the centre of the road, which creates a "head on" perspective that gives the viewer a sense of the infinite expanse and possibilities of the road. In *Mr. Thank You*, the camera takes the perspective of the bus as it navigates through the mountainous pass. When the bus approaches pedestrian travelers on the road, we see the travelers in front of us as if we are seeing the road from the perspective of the bus driver. What makes this film unique, however, is that instead of cutting to the bus driver, or continuing to show his point of view, the image dissolves into a view shot from the back of the bus. A moving shot approaching the pedestrian travelers from behind dissolves into a shot moving away from the pedestrian travelers walking forward. The camera moves from the front of the bus to the back of the bus creating the illusion that the bus has passed right through the travelers. This technique makes it seem as if the pedestrians are made of air and the road stretches into infinity.

As a rule Shimizu chose to film the road head-on both because he felt that "you can sense things best when viewed straight on," and because placing the camera beside the road and filming would create a road only as wide as the dimensions of the frame (Kishi 1941: 52). While filming the Korean laborers in *Mr. Thank You*, however, Shimizu decided to film the

Korean laborers who appear in the film from the side of the road so that they are seen walking across the screen, as opposed to walking into, or emerging out of, the depths of the screen. Shooting the laborers crossing the screen suggests the restricted movement of the laborers and their difference from the other Japanese travelers on the road.

Up until this point in the film, the landscape is filtered through the melancholic eyes of the young Japanese girl. Suddenly, even her position as future indentured labor reveals her different relationship to home and homeland that is denied the Korean laborers. Along with the documentary footage of the Korean laborers he shot while location-hunting, Shimizu also added the character of a young Korean woman laborer to the film. During the construction of the road, the Korean laborer's father dies and since she must move on to the next job, she asks Mr. Thank You to look after her father's grave. In this scene she looks off-screen towards the landscape. As he follows her gaze, she turns to the mountains and says, "I'm leaving my father here; can you leave flowers and water his grave once in a while?" The mountains become not only a site of melancholy but of mourning. She must, however, ask Mr. Thank You to perform the labor of remembering her father, because her own labor forces her to move on to the next remote mountainous region.

The two young women trace two distinct paths through the mountains of Japan. Near the end of the film, the bus driver convinces the mother not to sell her daughter into prostitution or factory labor, and mother and daughter return to the countryside together, following the symmetrical structure of the short story. As with many impoverished workers from rural villages who found temporary work in the cities, only to be laid off and forced to return to the countryside, the young girl's trajectory is from the country to the city. In the film version this trajectory is juxtaposed with the uncertain path of the migrant Korean laborer who continues to move on to wherever the next job takes her, which means leaving her father behind. The different relationship to the road occupied by each of the characters shows how Shimizu's ideology of the road is not only a rejection of normative notions of family but also a depiction of the breakdown of the colonial family due to migrancy and labor that are experienced differently according to national subject positions in the empire. While the Japanese laborers go back and forth between the countryside and the city, the Korean laborer has left Korea for Japan and may never return. She will probably repeat the fate met by her father.

The disjunction in status between the Korean and Japanese women is further underlined by national costume. In this scene the young Korean laborer, whom Mr. Thank You has frequently passed on the road during the construction, approaches the bus to announce the completion of the road. She is dressed in a *chogori*, a Korean national dress, but reveals her desire to wear a Japanese kimono. "I always wanted to put on a Japanese kimono and ride your bus," she says, equating the act of wearing national clothing, of putting on a kimono, with the privileged pleasure of viewing the landscape and the privileges of Japanese modernity built on and by colonial labor. In the next shot the Korean laborers pass silently across the winding road. The privilege of enjoying the road, which is a product of their labor, is reserved for the Japanese passengers of the bus. The landscape made accessible by the group of Korean laborers is denied to them as travelers. The landscape becomes a place of loss and discrimination—the site of both the political act of mourning as well as the place that exposes national and class hierarchies.

Why is labor projected onto the landscape in Japanese cinema of the mid-1930s? Technological advances in portable equipment had made shooting on the road possible, but more significantly, the increasing censorship of the government on cinematic portrayals of labor unrest and labor organizing made the direct depiction of labor movements impossible. In the early 1930s the government shut down labor movements, and socialist and Marxist writers were forced to convert to the national cause. This process of coerced conversion included not only a renunciation of their so-called misguided Marxist beliefs but also a pledge of allegiance by converters to the goals of the state.

Even after their conversion, many Marxist or proletarian writers continued to write about labor organizing. In 1938 Shimizu planned to make a film based on Mamiya Mosuke's *Raw Metal* (Aragane, 1937–38), a conversion novel about impoverished workers at a coalmine that included a scene of labor unrest. The Ministry of the Interior warned Shimizu that scenes representing the organization of laborers would be censored. The film was never made.

Given the tightening censorship on the representation of labor movements, the projection of melancholy and mourning onto the landscape became an effective way to portray the situation of these laborers. It is understandable then that Shimizu's laborers are shown *passing through* the landscape rather than toiling in the land or in factories. In *Land of Freedom* (Jiyu no tenchi), a no-longer extant film that Shimizu also shot in 1936, young Japanese women being sold into prostitution are juxtaposed with Korean laborers, but this time in a train rather than a bus. The young Japanese women sing merrily, but as the train passes their hometown, they burst into tears. Landscape here is used in a similar way to *Mr. Thank You*. The injustices of the class and patriarchal system which force the young woman to be sold as indentured labor are not directly criticized but sublimated into the landscape as melancholy. The passing view of the landscape triggers an emotional reaction in the women while the pimp accompanying them remains expressionless.

The presence again of the Korean laborers, however, expands the critique beyond one of domestic Japanese patriarchy. When the Korean laborers board the train, the geographical boundaries of the empire become evident. The trajectory of the Japanese women from countryside to city is contrasted to the ambiguous path the Koreans will take. They are boarding a train in search of the "Land of Freedom." It is unclear whether they are headed for the coalmines and construction sites of rural Japan, or whether they are headed back to Korea, which, when called the land of freedom, would imply a radical support for Korean independence. Nostalgia for the Japanese hometown is juxtaposed with longing for a return to one's home country, Korea, or for another utopia that neither the Japanese prostitutes nor the Korean laborers will find in Japan.

It is the specific relationship of the characters to the road that marks these different positions in society. In *Mr. Thank You* the disparity between different groups is indicated not only by national costume but also by the different speeds at which the groups traverse the road. The road acts as an intersection between the travelers on the bus, a young urban couple in a car, and the itinerant laborers and entertainers who travel the road by foot. These travelers exist in different temporalities that are layered on the same road. Yet the convergence of temporal layers on the space of the road reveals divergences in trajectory as well. The bus heads back and forth as part of the journey from country to city and back, connecting the small mountain villages with the train headed towards the city. The Korean laborers who construct the paths between the city and country do not go back and forth between the city and country; instead, they circulate endlessly, opening up, but never using, new roads into the mountainside.

These two films are an example of how landscape was used to depict the situation of migrant labor in Japan where migrant labor is defined both as gendered labor in depression-era 1930s Japan as well as colonial labor in the Japanese empire. Korean laborers are never shown to form a politicized community. It is not until the late 1950s and 1960s that Korean identity in Japanese cinema is explored. Shimizu is no exception. His films never present well-developed characters. In fact, he likens characters in his film to props or sets or as part of the landscape. When he portrays Korean laborers, he does not depict characters so much as a subject position within society. He treats characters as formal elements that he could play around with. According to Itami Mansaku, Shimizu's use of symmetry of dialogue, composition, and formalist play made possible a sophisticated critique of the family and of hierarchies. In *Mr. Thank You*, costume play extends the critique to national hierarchies. It is a film that uses kimono and chogori, national clothing, to identify subject positions that point out the privileges of being Japanese or Korean. The desire to don the kimono reveals the contradictory promise of entering Japanese modernity as a colonial subject. In the end, wearing the kimono and being fully assimilated into the empire is shown to be an impossibility and the young Korean laborer rejects the privilege of riding the bus, choosing instead to walk together with her fellow countrymen.

IMPERIAL TRAVEL AND THE COLONIAL ROAD MOVIE

The outbreak of the Sino-Japanese War in 1937 instigated a travel boom to which the Japan Travel Bureau responded by expanding operations to the colonies and China. The war on China was the motivation for most film directors and the general population to take trips abroad, and the Japanese empire was the destination. The relative proximity of the contiguous empire made imperial travel easier and so many Japanese filmmakers traveled throughout the empire at any given moment that it would be difficult to call the film industry Japanese at this time. As one of the nation's most prominent filmmakers and an avid traveler, Shimizu was quickly chosen to make films in the Japanese empire. In 1938, two years after using landscape to depict both Japanese and colonial migrant labor in *Mr. Thank You*, Shimizu traveled to China with the head of the Shochiku Film Studios. A year later, the popular film journal *Kinema Jumpo* organized a trip of Japan's most established directors to the studios of the Manchurian Motion Picture Association, the Japanese-run film studios in the Japanese puppet state of Manchuria in Northeast China. Justifying Japan's empire to its Japanese audiences and colonial populations was one of the main functions of this studio. The most effective strategy used was geopolitical allegory or films that portrayed Japan's relationship with China as a romance, almost always as a romance between a Japanese man and native woman. The most popular films shot at the studios cast the Japanese romantic lead Hasegawa Kazuo with Ri Koran (also known as Li Xianglan, Yamaguchi Yoshiko, or Shirley Yamaguchi), a Japanese actress who passed as Chinese because she had grown up in Manchuria and spoke fluent Chinese. The films starring this Japanese-'Chinese' pair met with such acclaim that the theme song performed by Ri Koran in *China Night* (Shina no yoru, 1940) became an overnight hit and Ri Koran became an instant star. This film is an overt geopolitical allegory that casts the dashing Hasegawa as a caring Japanese engineer who wins over the Chinese girl (Ri Koran) with acts of great kindness. He is so successful at this endeavor that she rallies her fellow countrymen into supporting Japanese military efforts to build roads that will benefit the Chinese people. In *Song of the White Orchid* (Byakuran no uta, 1939), Hasegawa plays a bureaucrat in the employ of the Manchurian Railway Company. When the railway that he is helping to construct to provide a lifeline to the Japanese military is about to be attacked, Ri Koran's character comes to his side and informs him of the impending attack. The two die valiantly protecting the railway, literally sacrificing their lives for the Japanese empire.

Although the Manchurian film studios were run by a right-wing Japanese officer, the studios were also home to Japanese filmmakers who had been jailed for their radical and socialist political views. After being released from jail in Japan, the Marxist film critic Iwasaki Akira was given a job at the Manchurian film studios, and he invited Shimizu to make films at this new center of Japanese film production for imperial consumption. In 1941 Shimizu was commissioned by the Japanese colonial government of Taiwan and the Manchurian Film Studios to make a film set in Taiwan with the same popular actress Ri Koran. The script, entitled *Sayon's Bell*, traces the real-life story of a woman of the Takasago tribe named Sayon who fell in love with a Japanese policeman. In her enthusiasm to see her lover off in service of the Japanese empire, she drowns in the river. She was memorialized by the governor-general of Taiwan who presented her family with a commemorative bell.

The romance that the film was intended to memorialize—Sayon's love for a Japanese policeman—receives little attention in the narrative, and the majority of the film is devoted to Sayon's relationship to a group of children. As the caretaker of the village children, infants, and animals, Sayon is simple and sympathetic. Ri Koran plays her as a slightly infantilized young woman, as she does in her many other 'colonial subject' roles. Although the film does present colonial subjects woodenly declaring their allegiance to the empire, the typical civilizing discourse and the emphasis on the romantic male lead are almost absent in Shimizu's film. Instead of focusing on the melodramatic relationship between the Japanese police officer and the Takasago woman, *Sayon's Bell* (Sayon no kane, 1943) is almost entirely about Sayon's everyday life as guardian of village children as they wander up and down the roads of the village. The staple stage for melodrama, the family and its intricate relations played out in domestic space, are as absent as the formal technique of close-ups meant to elicit sympathy or to portray romance. There are no soft-focus kiss scenes or teary-eyed women. The failure of *Sayon's Bell* to depict a romantic allegory as in Ri Koran's other films contributed to the film's failure. The infantilized colonial subject portrayed by Sayon held appeal neither for the Japanese audiences in the colonies or at home, nor for colonial subjects who were being represented. In its denial of the pleasures of the romantic allegory, the film refuses to fulfill the dictates of celebrating a war hero. The film ends with Sayon's funeral procession on the road that Shimizu amusingly portrays as a parade of animals and children. *Sayon's Bell* was intended to commemorate Sayon's diligent service to the Japanese stationed in Taiwan and pay homage to the governor-general's gift of a bell to Sayon's family. Shimizu, however, replaces the solemn procession of a hero with marching pigs, exemplary of his penchant for using play to subvert authority.

Evocative landscapes that were used in *Mr. Thank You* to depict colonial and migrant labor disappear in *Sayon's Bell* in favor of a focus on national costume. Shimizu originally wanted to film *Sayon's Bell* in an area that was deemed too dangerous by the Japanese authorities and was left with no other choice but to find inspiration in national costume. In *Mr. Thank You*, national costume—donning the kimono—represented the complicated desire for belonging in the Japanese empire. In 1943 in *Sayon's Bell*, national costume is used to signal difference but also fluidity between nationalities in the empire. Throughout the film costume, rather than a racialization of features, is used to depict national difference. When difference merely involves donning an outfit, however, the essentialization of ethnicity disappears and reveals the anxieties of passing, assimilation, and race in the Japanese empire. In one complex and illustrative scene Sayon (Ri Koran) weaves through a crowd of Takasago. It is a moment of double passing: a Japanese actress passing as a Chinese actress playing a Taiwanese native. The recourse to national costume to signal difference was also due in part to the erasure of linguistic difference that formed part of the cultural assimilation policies of the Japanese empire. Beginning in the mid-1930s colonial languages were banned and Japanese became the sole language of education in Korea and Taiwan. In an attempt to erase the national sovereignty of Japan's colonies, the languages spoken in these countries were no longer classified as national languages. By 1935 Taiwanese and Korean were officially re-classified as regional dialects of the standard Japanese spoken in Tokyo. These linguistic policies ensured that after 1939 films produced in Korea and Taiwan were made in Japanese. Difference represented through language was no longer possible.

The classification of language was similarly mirrored in the categorization of colonial films. Films produced in Korea were usually called Korean films (*Chosen eiga*) until the mid-1930s when Korean films suddenly became known as "peninsula films." Similarly, films shot in China were referred to as "continental films." Korea, formerly considered a separate country, albeit a protectorate and then a colony of Japan, was evacuated of political meaning and reduced to a geographical term, a peninsula off the coast of Japan. Titles such as *Peninsula Dancer* (Hanto no maihime, 1936) explicitly indicated this lexical turn to a new geopolitical conception of Japan and Korea's relationship.

It was against this backdrop of tightening restrictions on the film world in terms of locations and languages that Shimizu began making films in the colonies. Shimizu's turn to national costume was a product of these transformations. The use of national costume in Shimizu's colonial films reflected what was possible in a context of changing national and imperial policies.

Several years before *Sayon's Bell*, in 1940, on the way back from his visit to Manchuria, Shimizu stopped off in Korea to do location-hunting for the film *Friends* (Tomodachi, 1940), a short two-reel educational documentary for children that describes the relationship between a Japanese and a Korean boy. In the early 1940s government policy promoted more cultural contact with the colonies and the Shochiku studios planned its first "peninsula culture film" (*hanto bunka eiga*). Since Shimizu was well known for his love of travel, he was sent to the Korean peninsula to direct *Keijo* (Seoul), Shochiku's first venture in documentary filmmaking. Just as the appellation 'peninsula' rather than the name of the country Korea (*Chosen*) signaled the political subordination of Korea to Japan, the title of the film also signaled Japan's geographical rewriting of territory. Keijo, now present-day Seoul, was the name used for Korea's capital by the Japanese colonial government in Korea. The film never made it to the Japanese screen, only playing briefly in Seoul. In contrast, *Friends* received a recommendation from the Japanese Ministry of Education to be shown in Japan as a documentary film for a 14 and under audience. The film was shown so widely throughout Japan that the only extant print is too badly damaged to be screened.

Friends, which charts the relationship between a Japanese boy and a Korean boy, is meant to be read as a geopolitical allegory of the relationship between Japan and Korea. The formal symmetry used in Shimizu's earlier films to disrupt the seriousness of national mobilization is used in *Friends* as a means to make the boys equals. While Yokoyama chases the Korean boy Lee after school, they exchange playful banter:

Lee: Why are you chasing me?
Yokoyama: Why are you running away?
Lee: Because you're chasing me.
Yokoyama: I'm only chasing you because you're running away.

The symmetrical nature of the dialogue serves to place the boys firmly as equals rather than as one superior to the other. After they get into an arm-wrestling deadlock they both agree that they are equally strong.

The Japanese boy Yokoyama has just moved to Korea from Japan, and distracted by the unusual nature of the Korean clothes of his classmate, makes mistakes while reciting in class for which he is scolded by his teacher. The Korean child Lee is embarrassed about his Korean clothes and thus prohibited from playing with the other Japanese children. Yokoyama, however, convinces Lee that there is nothing wrong with his clothes and even goes so far as to exchange his own clothes for them. They then both agree that their new clothes suit them well.

Through costume, the film becomes a short parable about the equality and interchangeability of Koreans and Japanese. Although the film does not directly portray the colonial subordination of Korea by Japan, it does suggest through allegory that Japan and Korea are equal. Both the visual and vocal symmetry of the boys and the interchangeability of their positions through clothing point to their equality. In *Mr. Thank You*, the kimono functions as a marker of Japanese privilege that makes the *inequality* of the Korean laborer's situation apparent. In *Mr. Thank You* it is the enjoyment of a road that has been built by Korean labor, and in *Friends* it is the enjoyment of the company of other children without being discriminated against. If wearing national clothing endows a person with the privilege associated with those clothes, difference is marked only by clothes and not ethnicity or socially constructed racial categories. In these two colonial films Shimizu showed how hierarchy and ethnicity could be erased by a simple change of costume. He used clothing to show the equality of Korean and Japanese but also the inequality of their situation.

The circumstances of costume play, however, vary drastically between the two films. The portrayal in *Mr. Thank You*, made in 1936, of donning the kimono as an unfulfilled desire that exposes the contradiction of belonging in the empire, is strikingly different from the facility of clothing exchange in *Friends*, made four years later. The carefree ease with which clothing is exchanged by the boys reveals the ways that costume play falls in line with assimilationist propaganda of the state. The suppressed gendered desire of the colonial Korean laborer for Mr. Thank You and the generational suffering imposed by colonialism disappear in the representation of colonial "friendship" represented by the boys.

In the 1930s, the road movie and the rejection of the nation–state family and romantic melodrama allowed Shimizu to portray the lives of migrant laborers and social outcasts outside normative family roles. When the Sino-Japanese war expanded the Japanese film world into the colonies and China, Shimizu rejected using the romantic melodrama as a form of geopolitical allegory. Instead, he used the trope of the national costume to question the hierarchy and boundaries between nations and to show the equality of people and the inequality of their situations. Shimizu's films show both the possibilities of critical costume play as well as its increasing difficulty in the face of changes in colonial policy. In the end, the interchangeability of characters didn't endow them with a political subjectivity but allowed Shimizu to make a critique of their positions in society and the category of national identity itself.

REFERENCES

Itami, M. (1961) "Shimizu Hiroshi shi no kingyo," *Itami Mansaku zenshû*, vol. 2, Tokyo: Chikuma Shobô, pp. 361–366.
Kishi, M. (1938) "Kyo no hito, asu no hito," *Nihon Eiga*, 1: 131.
———(1941) "Shimizu Hiroshi no enshutsu shuho 1," *Shin Eiga*, 3: 52–55.
Tanaka, M., Kimata, K. and Sato, C. (2000) *Eiga Dokuhon: Shimizu Hiroshi*, Tokyo: Firumu aatosha.

3   Moore's utopia
Canada in the cinematic imagination of Michael Moore

David S. Churchill

In the days before the 2006 Canadian election, US filmmaker Michael Moore published an open letter to Canadians imploring them not to vote for the Conservative Party led by Stephen Harper. Moore's appeal was made in his casual mix of incredulousness, joking familiarity, and authenticating gestures of cultural knowing and understanding. "Oh, Canada" he begins riffing on the national anthem "you're not *really* going to elect a Conservative majority on Monday, are you? That's a joke, right?" (Moore 2006). Indeed, it is the supposedly ironic Canadian sense of humor cultivated and fed by a cold climate and the even colder comfort of the asymmetrical relationship to the United States that animates Moore's letter. The specter of Canada with its "stand against the war in Iraq," its declaration that "gay people have equal rights," as well as its giving "native peoples their own autonomy and their own territory" is after all a progressive counterpoint to the United States. Moore's imagining and historical framing of Canada is a seductive and flattering image that plays on difference and national autonomy. For Canadians to "elect a guy who should be running for the governor of Utah" must be an absurdist farce. Moore's epistle is quick to martial the language of nationalism, appealing to anti-American sentiments and a vague Canadian patriotism, he argues that Canada needs to remain distinct from its southern neighbor:

> C'mon, where is your Canadian pride? I mean, if you're going to reduce Canada to a cheap download of Bush & Co., then at least don't surrender so easily. Can't you wait until he threatens to bomb Regina? Make him work for it for Pete's sake.

Here Moore articulates one of his central political themes—that corporate conservatives, of the Bush & Co. variety, have hijacked the United States. Canada, with its enviable array of public policy alternatives (anti-war, pro-gay, and self-government of indigenous peoples), is a place where American citizen consumers can window shop and dream of a utopian alternative. Such a place for Moore's and America's dreaming can only take place if Canada utilizes a protective nationalism to resist assimilation—or, as Moore puts it in technological parlance, "downloading."

Moore's letter garnered some attention in the days leading to the Canadian vote, making the rounds of left/liberal e-mail lists, and being posted on websites such as that of the left nationalist periodical *Canadian Dimension* (where it got mixed though generally favorable comments). Moore's comments on Canada and Canadian politics were nothing new. Prior to the 2004 election Moore was equally blunt in his hope that Canadian voters would reject the Conservative Party:

> I have spent a lot of time convincing Americans that Canadians are smart people and you're going to make me look really bad (chuckles), if you do not make sure Mr. Harper doesn't take over. Why would you want to be like us? ("Michael Moore Premiers Film in Canada," 2004)

Instead, Moore is quick to argue that the United States needs to be Canadianized, that Canadian political culture needs to work its way into the consciousness of Americans. Speaking at an award show for documentary filmmakers on 10 December 2004 Moore implored Canadians to "Infiltrate America: We need a Canadian in every church basement, every town meeting infecting us with such dangerous thoughts as the crazy notion that when people get sick they should have a doctor!" (Kanegis 2005).

This chapter explores Michael Moore's envisioning and utilization of Canada as a nation and as a political cultural realm. More specifically, I trace how Moore's own patriotic and American left-nationalist discourse dovetails with his promotion and celebration of Canada as a useful alternative to mainstream US politics. I argue that Moore's seeming promotion and celebration of Canada does not represent an internationalist perspective, but rather is an expression of his own American left-nationalism—a nation-building project of economic and social justice within a nation–state framework—one which ultimately is in conflict with the very sorts of political tendencies he finds praiseworthy amongst Canadians. For Canadian left-nationalists Moore's conceptualization of Canada as a liberal haven conforms to the reassuring vision of the nation as a progressive alternative—one which is a victim of American hegemony, rather than a complicit agent and beneficiary.

NATIONALISM AND WORKING-CLASS PATRIOTISM

Much of Moore's work is suffused with the language of authenticity and estrangement. In the opening of his 1989 documentary film *Roger & Me*, Moore situates himself as a genuine product of post-war America, an individual raised in the midst of Midwestern industrial affluence. The movie begins with a series of Moore's own home movies, showing a healthy and a seemingly loving family, celebrating holidays, birthdays, and outings. These jumpy, amateur bits of Super 8 film are augmented by newsreel footage of Flint, Michigan, Moore's hometown, to create a seamless image of social and economic contentment. In this representation the family, Moore's own family, is the embodiment of the economic success and bounty of the United States during the 1950s and 1960s. Moore further personalizes the domestic images and stock footage through his voiceover commentary. He intones, in his casual and intimate way, that "We [the citizens of Flint] enjoyed a prosperity that working people around the world had never seen before." He compliments this rosy image of post-war consensus by adding that he remembers his childhood as a place "Where every day was a great day." Moore's utilization of a "Happy Days" national fantasy plays on existing notions of US history invoking what Lauren Berlant has termed an "intimate public sphere." Berlant argues that, "contemporary nationalist ideology recognizes a public good only in a particularly constricted nation of simultaneously lived private worlds" (Berlant 1997: 5). Here the patriotic space of the nation is the normalized domestic space of Moore's childhood, a vision of the nation that could easily conform to the social conservative framework of the likes of James Dobson and *Focus on the Family*. Rather than challenging this sort of patriotic doxa, one which historian Elaine Tyler May famously termed "domestic containment," Moore celebrates it, wedding it to a naturalized and mythic history of the American heartland. The very divisive realities of the 1950s and 1960s around McCarthyism, racial segregation, and the war in Vietnam are lost in this historical recounting.

Moore's evocation of place—Flint of the mid-twentieth century—is a powerful symbol in the political discourse of deindustrialization in the United States as well as Canada. Indeed, Moore's narrative in *Roger & Me* is a classic example of "the community abandonment thesis" articulated by Barry Bluestone and Bennet Harrison in the early 1980s (Bluestone and Harrison 1982). In Bluestone and Harrison's work and similar critiques of the deindustrialization of the 1980s, the interests of communities (often dominated by a single industry) and their workers, were subordinated to those of capital in which politicians and in many cases union hierarchies failed to act in the interest of citizens and members. In privileging community and family, Moore articulates a patriotic vision of the American nation in which protecting the national interest means protecting the families of GM workers, and their community, from economic hardship. The national injury of plant closures in Flint, Michigan, in Youngstown, Ohio, Gary, Indiana, or other industrial towns was thus a twin failure of economic and domestic containment—a failure to keep "heartland communities" and their attenuated traditional families safe, secure and prosperous.[1]

Moore's film *Roger & Me*, with its poignant images of economic collapse, unemployment, and corporate indifference, nonetheless plays on the fear of foreign competition and the willingness of corporate executives to move production to countries such as Mexico. As historian Dana Frank has shown, the protest movements that rose against these plant closures were inflected with often racist and nativist sentiments. In the auto industry this meant overt hostility to foreign made or owned cars. During the 1980s, protests by autoworkers included the smashing of Toyota vehicles and the burning of the Japanese flag. Resentment against so-called imports became so acute that a sign was posted for a time in the UAW parking lot in Detroit that read "UAW PARKING RESERVED FOR US AND CANADIAN VEHICLES ONLY. PLEASE PARK IMPORTS ELSEWHERE" (Frank 1999: 162). Moore's film, with its focus on the local and exclusively US-based impact of deindustrialization and globalization never deals with the plight of these newly employed Mexican workers in the regions that would come to be known as the *maquiladora*. At least in the overt narrative of the film working-class solidarity is not a theme Moore advocates or even mentions.

Interestingly enough, Moore's use of the Canadian alternative works well within the left-nationalist paradigms of both countries. Moore's interventions to Canadian audiences are often framed as warnings about becoming too American, losing the distinctive Canadian cultural and political sensibility so generative of supposed national difference. In this way, Moore's American left-nationalist aspirations can find inspiration and example in Canada. Though Moore has at times argued that Americans should be more like Canadians, the effect of such a position re-inscribes nation-state solutions to global economic predicaments. Thus, the US should adopt policies, regulatory laws and statutes, as well as social programs, similar to those in Canada. Such national economic policy would protect "American" jobs and maintain the "American Dream." As such, Moore's own economic nationalism and his criticism of American corporations and capital, is similar to Canadian left-nationalist critiques.[2] In particular, generations of left-nationalist critics have lamented the branch-plant status of Canadian capitalism, often utilizing a developmental narrative of arrested economic and political sovereignty.[3] Canada in this analysis is a subordinated, even a neo-colonial province, of the American empire.[4]

Left-nationalism in Canada has a long tradition, one that is too broad to be comprehensively treated in this paper. Nonetheless, as a movement and critique of US influence it has had a major impact on both major centre-left political parties as well as sites of more radical left opinion and activism. The core analysis of left-nationalist thought is that the Canadian economy is an extension of the US economy, that Canada as a nation is in a dependent economic and thus political relationship to the United States, and that this gross asymmetry means that there is no genuine autonomy or sovereignty for Canadians. Historian Steven High's comparative work on deindustrialization in the United States and Canada provides support as well as critical points of departure for the left-nationalist thesis of foreign ownership. Contra to Canadian nationalist assertions, High (2003) found that the process of plant closures, layoffs, and outsourcing was more dramatic and extensive in the United States than it was among similar industries in Canada. The reasons for this are diverse, some having to do with the internal migration of jobs and factories from states in the Northeast and Midwest to the South and Southwest. Such movement allowed companies to leave heavily unionized parts of the United States for so-called right-to-work states where there were weaker labor laws, allowing the corporations to radically reduce the wages of workers. Equivalent factory and job migration in Canada, where there are comparatively uniform labor laws, was simply not feasible. In addition, the economies of industrial manufacturing regions of Canada, principally along the Great Lakes and St. Lawrence River Valley, were much more diversified than those found in many industrial towns of the so-called Rust Belt. As a consequence, plant closures in the United States had a disproportionate impact on the economies of the communities.

Though invested in different national geographies, Moore and many left-Canadian nationalists shared a vision of US corporate capital as a threat to the public interest of the nation. Where Canadians have seen the United States as a neo-colonial economic power, Moore argues that many of the same neo-liberal initiatives such as plant closures, deregulation, and outsourcing are problems internal to the United States. Corporate America is thus not only a threat to foreign and dependent nations but it is primarily a threat to the American nation itself. Here American capitalists, and much of the American government itself, fail the test of patriotism, operating in their own elite class interest rather those of the country and its citizenry.

Where High does identify successes and benefits of nationalist industrial strategy, something that Moore seems to yearn for in the United States, is in the ability of local, provincial, and even federal levels of government to ameliorate the impact of deindustrialization. High writes that Canadian workers "were able to marshal nationalist claims as rhetorical weapons against plant shutdowns and lobbying tools" while their US counterparts were "unable to save factories from closing or to soften the blow of displacement" (High 2003: 11–12). Yet, the ability of Canadian workers, as well as other concerned parties, to politically mobilize to save jobs in Canada, seems to be something that is particular to the country and the dynamic of US/Canada relations. US workers' appeals to patriotism proved insufficient or ineffective, while Canadians were able to mine the deep political vein of nationalism, even anti-Americanism, to secure jobs and lessen the impact of deindustrialization.[5] Moreover, the use of such nationalist political strategy in a US context, seemingly free from a broadly based left political tradition, runs dangerously close to reactionary xenophobic and anti-foreign sentiments. After all, conservatives such as CNN commentator Lou Dobbs and Republican Presidential candidate Pat Buchanan routinely utilized protectionist language, leavened with patriotic economic nationalism. Though Moore is no conservative, his populism, his selective use of patriotic language, and his fondness for the resistive parts of Canadian political culture do not seem to suggest a broader class based solidarity of workers, be they across the Canada/US border or internationally. Moreover, Moore seems to have no notion of political solidarity that works outside of the citizen worker model and as such perpetuates what sociologist Nandita Sharma has evocatively termed a "global apartheid" that denies the vast majority of migrant workers legal status, protections, and rights. Such restrictions on migrants create a vast, vulnerable class of workers inside nations such as the United States and Canada—workers whose conditions don't fit easily into nationalist dreams (Sharma 2006: 145).

THE DREAM WORLD OF *CANADIAN BACON*

Moore's association with Canada is of long standing. Canada, after all, was the setting of his first feature film *Canadian Bacon*, a political spoof in which a US President (played by Alan Alda) attempts to boost his popularity by declaring war on its northern neighbor. Following in the wake of the first Gulf War, and concerns that the US government was pursuing military options to boost domestic popularity, Moore's film is a convoluted narrative of American paranoia, military defense contracting corruption, venal politicians, and patriotic but foolish US citizens. Utilizing his characteristic tone of mocking flattery, Moore presents Canada as a cloyingly sweet dream world of social democratic values, a utopian alternative for American political consumers. Canadian earnestness and patriotism are matched to references of the largess of the Canadian welfare state. A conspiracy spouting CIA official, heading the Canadian desk, declares, "We think they are a little strange with the socialized medicine stuff but did you know that they provide free college to anyone, free trains, free eye-glasses, free condoms!" Here is a set of state services, programs, and initiatives for the citizen consumer to daydream about—health, education, mobility, clarity of sight, and sexual liberation. This is the Canada of left fantasy rather than neo-liberal reality.

In a scene at a hockey game between a Canadian and American team, the Canadian announcer reminds the crowd not to use profanity or to litter. This civil and placid milieu is however ruptured by the comments of American Sheriff, Bud B. Boomer (played by the late Canadian actor John Candy), who loudly declares, "Canadian beer sucks"—setting off a mass riot. Canadians, it turns out will indeed fight, at least over important issues. Canadians in the film are characterized by their extreme politeness: near the end of the film Sheriff Boomer roughly pushes his way through a crowd of Canadians at the base of the CN Tower, who immediately apologize for their clumsiness and for being in his way. Moreover, Canada as a spatial locale is presented either as a glittering modernist realm, of clean and polished glass or a pastoral landscape of rustic cottages. Both modern and traditional, Canada is a utopia of clean, efficient technology as well as a sublime Acadia. Again the phantasmagoric and enchanted qualities of Canada are contrasted against the imminent sites of America—the local bar, the bowling alley, and the rusting factory.

In contrast, the United States is a land of decaying industrial landscapes and closed factories, populated with people who seem to have endless access to firearms. Moore's image of the United States is similar to that portrayed in *Roger & Me*. Both films deal with the corrosive effects of plant shutdowns, job loss, and deindustrialization in the auto industry. In *Canadian Bacon* Moore shifts from Flint, Michigan to the border town of Niagara Falls, New York. As with the Sheriff in Flint who evicts people on Christmas Eve, Sheriff Boomer and his friend are former employees at the local plant. As such, they are economic victims of the peace that supposedly came with the end of the Cold War. Indeed, it is this crisis of peace that animates Moore's humor and plot. In the vacuum created by this secession of hostilities, politicians have neither a convenient enemy nor ready justification for military expenditure. Similarly, generals and soldiers have little justification for their existence or the massive infrastructure of bases and weapons systems. Finally, corporations who have long benefited from lucrative Defense contracts are faced with the loss of business. As Moore's film illustrates, this peculiar architecture of the American state demands the existence of a perpetual enemy. Without a constant threat to national security, the very structure of the US government falls into crisis.

Moore's choice of Canada as the foil to this martial logic is premised on a set of stereotypes. These comforting narratives of national identity often appear in the public culture produced by agencies of the Canadian state. Foremost of these is the representation of Canadian peaceability and Canada as an international peacemaker. Moore perpetuates this flattering image of Canadians for his own instrumental reasons. The "peace, order, and good government" of Canada is of course a useful contrast to the militaristic traditions of the United States of the "Wild West," Civil War, and numerous foreign invasions throughout the twentieth century. Such a representation of Canada, however, is a flawed historical gloss.

The strongest illustration of this revisionist historical narrative is Moore's use of the so-called Mounties—Royal Canadian Mounted Police Officers (RCMP)—throughout *Canadian Bacon*. Indeed, the scarlet tunic RCMP officer is one of the few icons of Canada that reaches beyond the nation's own borders. Playing with this popular symbol, Moore populates his film with proper, pedantic, though ultimately ineffectual RCMP officers, characters familiar to Americans from the Dudley Do-Right cartoon. Here are police officers without menace or for that matter corruption. Indeed, the righteousness of the Mounties is underscored by the fact that they have a suit and tie wearing corporate executive in jail. Yet, the RCMP and its predecessors were instrumental in the so-called North West Rebellion of 1885, which saw the end of Métis and First Nations sovereignty on the Canadian prairies.

Far from being a benign organization, the RCMP is a para-military force with a long history of surveillance, domestic espionage, and use of force against protest movements such as the disruption of the "On-to-Ottawa Trek" during the Depression, spying on the Nationalist movement in Quebec, and the infiltration of various labor and left political organizations.[6] Despite Moore's sanguine assessment of same-sex marriage in Canada, the RCMP launched an extensive campaign against homosexuals during the Cold War. As sociologist Gary Kinsman has shown, by 1968 the RCMP had collected a list of over 9,000 homosexual persons, as part of its national security initiative (Kinsman 1995: 133; Maynard 2001). Moreover, the contention that Canada has an admirable record in its historical relations with First Nations peoples is a case of wishful thinking on Moore's part. The relations between First Nations peoples and the British and French colonial settlers, and later the Canadian government, have been marked by a persistent racism, violence, paternalism, forced assimilation, and abuse.[7]

In addition, Canada's international profile as a neutral peacekeeper, an image constantly fostered by the Ministry of External Affairs and generations of Canadian governments, masks the very close military ties between Canada and the United States through organizations such as NATO and NORAD. Rather than being an alternative to American militarism, Canada has been a partner and supporter throughout the Cold War and continues to be so through its current involvement in Afghanistan and in Haiti.[8] The dream of a peaceful Canada is a comforting one for Canadians, and a useful one for Moore, but it creates a false dichotomy between US imperialism and hegemony on the one hand, and on the other hand Canadian innocence and neutrality.

Dreams and awakening are central to Moore's film. One of the subplots follows Sheriff Boomer's Deputy "Honey" (played by Rhea Perlman). After accidently being left behind enemy lines in Canada, Honey is arrested for littering by the RCMP. Awakening in a clean and modern hospital room, surrounded by stuffed animals and get-well cards Honey is greeted by two impossibly sweet (and rather dim) hospital workers who inform her she can stay in the hospital for up to two years based on Canada's universal healthcare system. Honey, horrified by the treacle tones of the young, ever smiling, blond hospital workers quickly makes her escape—all with the help of her ever handy automatic weapons. Yet, Honey's real awakening comes later, only after nuclear war has been diverted, and she and Deputy Boomer head back across the border. Upon seeing the familiar and comforting image of a smoking industrial factory, the pair awaken to the reality of their American everyday, and joyously celebrate their return home to "the good old U.S. of A." For Moore, however, the moral economy of *Canadian Bacon* lies in another awakening, not of Boomer and Honey, but of the American audience/electorate in the theatre. Here there is the political hope that upon seeing "the closest, tritest, most obvious" aspects of American life, US citizens will finally understand the history of their nation, and recognize the need to awaken to its political realities (Benjamin 1999: 388–89). As Walter Benjamin muses in his *Arcades Project*, "The imminent awakening is poised, like the wooden horse of the Greeks, in the Troy of dreams" (Benjamin 1999: 392). Nevertheless, where Benjamin—the German exile in the city of modernity—rejects nation and nationalism, Moore's historical awakening maintains at least the utopianism of the social democratic nation-state or at least an expansive system of welfare. Canada is thus the fulfillment of a more complete Great Society, the liberal road not taken by the United States, but still an option for enlightened modernization.

THE DIFFERENCE OF UNLOCKED DOORS

In more recent years Moore's association with Canada has moved from parody to counterpoint, particularly in his award-winning documentary *Bowling for Columbine*. The film is Moore's attempt to understand the killing of 12 Colorado high school students, and the wounding of 24 others, at the hands of two of their classmates. In what is Moore's most explicit use of Canada as a political alternative, the movie follows Moore on a trip to two Canadian border cities, Sarnia and Windsor, as well as to its largest metropolis, Toronto. In a series of interviews, Moore presses people on what the differences are between Canadians and Americans. His subjects are quick to contrast the social reality as well as sensibilities of the two countries. After a certain amount of prompting from Moore a group of Canadian high school students explain that Americans are more hateful and violence prone than their Canadian counterparts. Thus, Moore flattens out economic class, social context, and cultural particularity into national distinctions, all supported by anecdotal testimonials.

Moore interviews a number of Canadian gun owners asking them how many, and what types of guns they own. In a nation of about 30 million people Canadians own about 7 million guns. In one scene Moore goes into a Canadian Wal-Mart store and buys live rounds of ammunition, thus illustrating that lethal weaponry is available north of the border. Though bullets may be relatively easy to purchase, the guns to propel those bullets are much harder to purchase. In explaining why there is a supposed difference in attitudes about personal safety between the two countries, Moore resurrects a gag from his feature film *Canadian Bacon,* in which Canadians never lock doors. Walking down a street in Toronto, Moore walks up to a number of houses finding their front doors to be unlocked. The explanation for this is that Canadians are less fearful than Americans. One Canadian explains that Americans believe that locking a door is a way of "keeping people out of your place. We as Canadians see it more as when we lock the door we are imprisoning ourselves inside." Here again Moore advances comforting myths about peaceable Canadians, living without the specter of fear driven by a tabloid media culture and alarmist politicians.

Moore uses an interview with Sarnia Mayor Mike Bradley, a member of the centrist Liberal Party of Canada, to revisit the constellation of social and economic programs that are the hallmark of difference between the two countries. Framing the Mayor's comments with the voiceover cue "their politicians talk kind of funny" Moore emphasizes the concern for public welfare in Canada. Bradley goes through a list of programs that are hallmarks of "how you build a good society." Bradley asserts that governments need to be:

> ...making sure they [citizens] have proper day-care, that they have assistance for their parents when they're elderly and need to be in an old-age home, that they have proper health-care that ensures they won't lose their business or house because they can't afford their medical bills.

Here again the "good" goods of social democracy are placed on display for potential American consumption.

Moore explores the social geography of the Canadian welfare state by asking a man in a bar where one can find "indigents in the city." Shrugging and explaining, "We don't have that problem here really" he supposedly points Moore to a Canadian slum. Moore's cameras film scenes of the J.S. Woodsworth Co-op in Toronto, a mixed-income housing complex financed through government supported mortgages. Though the co-op movement is a progressive housing initiative, started in large part during the 1970s, it represents only a fraction of subsidized housing units in Toronto. Moore does not go to any of the City's public housing projects such as St. James Town, Regent Park, or Moss Park, which are similar in architectural style and design to Housing and Urban Development (HUD) projects in large American cities. Moreover, homelessness and poverty are severe problems in Canada, something that Moore in his utopian dreaming wishes to or needs to ignore. A 2003 report on housing and homelessness in Toronto found that 31,985 different people stayed in an emergency shelter at some point in 2002. The waiting list for social housing in the city stood at over 71,000.[9]

In Moore's fantasy image of Canada there exists an alternative political ethic, in which there is a more expansive and collective political sensibility. Released from the "culture of fear," Canadians have supposedly been able to reject the pervasive culture of what C.B. Macpherson called "possessive individualism."

> I believe that if we were able to get rid of all the guns in America and have strong gun control laws that we would still have the central problem—the central problem of being afraid of the other. And being manipulated so easily by politicians, by corporations, and the media as they appeal to our baser instinct. We need to change our ethic...and be more Canadian like. What is the Canadian ethic? The Canadian ethic

is "We are all in the same boat. We are all Canadians." We don't have that ethic in America. Our ethic is "It's everyman for himself and to hell with you! Me, me, me, me, mine, mine, I, I, I, I! Pull yourself up by your bootstraps."[10]

Here Moore explicitly laments the lack of a functional national fraternity in the United States, a lack of the sort of broad horizontal sense of community belonging that supposedly animates Canada's functional nationalist polity. Two years later Moore utilizes almost exactly the same language in relationship to the possible election of a Conservative government in Ottawa and Canada's potential contribution to the US led occupation of Iraq.

As an American looking north I've spent a lot of time saying we should be more "Canadian-like" and we would be better as a people. Our government is "Every man for himself" and "Pull yourself up by your own boot straps"…me, me, me, me. To let those people in your country, who have that American ethic, take over – to take that thing which makes you wonderfully Canadian away, this must be resisted on June 28. I can't imagine anybody wanting to join this coalition and send your sons and daughters over there to die. ("Michael Moore Premiers Film in Canada," 2004)

As two Canadian critics of *Bowling for Columbine*, Joseph Heath and Andrew Potter, have pointed out, Moore's adherence to the "culture of fear" thesis reifies difference between the two countries. In Moore's view it is US culture itself, its tabloid media obsessed with crime, its legacy of colonial conquest of indigenous peoples, and ultimately, the fear and racism generated by the legacies of slavery and segregation, that are responsible for the high rates of violent gun death. In cleaving to this cultural explanation, rather than more pragmatic explanations such as the impact of Canadian gun control legislation, Moore seems to be questioning the very efficacy of politics (Heath and Potter 2004: 142–43). Though Moore does not explain this, there is extensive gun control legislation in Canada: the 1995 Firearms Act created a national registry of all guns and their owners. Not only has it been necessary for all handguns to be registered firearms since 1934, they are restricted weapons with limits on where they can be used (such as for target practice in gun clubs) and by whom they can be used. All fully automatic weapons have been illegal since 1977. The guns used in the Columbine massacre, along with almost all handguns and semi-automatic weapons are illegal in Canada.

When Moore has been challenged on the question of differing gun laws, as he was at the Cannes Film festival by a Canadian film critic, he has consistently pointed to a cultural, even material difference, between the citizens of the two countries. Utilizing reductionist and essentializing language, Moore responded to his Canadian critic:

That's very Canadian of you. You believe because you don't have the temptation, you don't kill. But I believe that there is something different about you and American DNA. If you get sick in America: fuck you! If you are poor in America: fuck you! We're about beating you down when you are down. State-sponsored terrorism. It's not because you don't have handguns in Canada that you don't kill each other. (<http://www.geraldpeary.com/interviews/mno/moore.html> , Accessed 5 March 2006).

Here Moore posits a dystopian vision of American exceptionalism, based on a seemingly immutable historical and cultural particularism of the United States. For Moore US citizens have an inherent possessive individualism bred in the bone, which prevents them from thinking and acting in a communitarian manner. Such gross generalization and totalizing notions of cultural difference, which reify historic actors into national types, seems to leave little place for cultural change, or room for political struggle. Nor do they account for the moments of communitarian political action that Moore nostalgically celebrates at the beginning of his film *Roger & Me*. In Moore's dreaming of Canada he seems to engage in convenient acts of historical forgetting.

MADE IN CANADA

For a number of years Moore has had a working relationship with the Canadian production company Salter Street Productions. After the NBC network canceled his first foray into television *TV Nation*, Salter Street produced his subsequent television show, *The Awful Truth*. Salter Street and their partner Alliance/Atlantis would go on to produce Moore's *Bowling for Columbine*. During much of the promotion for *Fahrenheit 9/11* Moore's ubiquitous baseball cap read "Made in Canada." This bit of Canadian nationalist sloganeering, a Canadian parallel to the "Buy American" campaign, was not a rejection by Moore of his own US-centered focus, or even an example of cultural outsourcing, but rather an ironic statement about the failure of the United States to provide a home for contentious political filmmaking. Nor was Moore a cultural and artistic exile forced to leave the United States to make films, produce television shows, or write books, because *Fahrenheit 9/11* did receive industry support for its production. Initially, Moore's project was to be funded by Icon Productions, an independent film studio owned by actor Mel Gibson. When Icon backed out of the project in 2003, the boutique Hollywood studio Miramax bought the distribution rights for the film. Once *Fahrenheit 9/11* was complete, however, Miramax's parent corporation, the Walt Disney Company, prevented its subsidy from distributing Moore's film in the United States.

In a letter to *The New York Times,* Disney President Michael Eisner defended his company's decision not to distribute the film as an exercise in choice rather than a violation of free speech. The controversy, however, played into Moore's hands, allowing him to utilize a number of rhetorical strategies that situated him as a populist defender of free speech, a patriotic defender of the Bill of Rights, and once again the little guy fighting the corporate giant. The controversy also allowed Moore's film to receive an enormous amount of free publicity. Eventually Miramax founders, Bob and Harvey Weinstein, were able to buy back the film from Disney/Miramax and distribute the film themselves through a third company, Fellowship Adventure Group (Waxman, 2004: E1). Though Moore's baseball cap read "Made in Canada," he was ultimately able to navigate the contours of an American corporate system and get his film funded and distributed. Moore's strategic use of Canada as realm of cultural exile is an instrumental and symbolic migration that seeks to shame his US critics, rather than embrace the possibility of transcending the border and embracing a politics, which was not limited to the country of his birth.

CONCLUSION

Moore's phantasmagoric vision of Canada, filled with the commodities of social democracy, and its sweet—if at times painfully naïve and innocent populace—serve him as a useful foil in his critique of the dysfunctional political culture of the United States. Though such attention to the supposed strengths of Canadian society have been welcomed by some Canadian commentators, it is important to recognize that Moore's use of Canada is ultimately instrumental. Moore's romance with Canada is never about leaving the United States, or for that matter about transcending borders in an attempt to reinvigorate progressive internationalism. Rather, Canada is a political tool for Moore, to cleave away at US corporations, government, and culture. Yet as a tool, Canada must be fashioned in particular ways, which often efface the historical particularity of the nation. Moore's Canada is ultimately a fictive space—which would not necessarily be a troubling thing if it were not for the dramatic and seemingly inviolable notions of national difference. This calcified political vision seems most troubling and one can only wish that such a progressive public figure as Moore had a more genuinely utopian ambition and sensibility, one that at least entertained the notion of historical transformation and change rather than pessimism. In his essay on the writer Edmund Wilson, political theorist Marshal Berman reminds us of the importance of the historical imaginary, writing: "we can use it to teach ourselves how to keep the dreams alive in the present, and maybe even, in the future, how to make the visions real. It can help us learn to create ourselves" (Berman 1999: 63).

Utopian thinking is a type of dream work, a wish for a better society, a hope for what social life could be (Harvey 2000: 255). In Michael Moore's films and in his political commentary, Canada has served as a dream world, an alternative vision of North American society. Though Moore's romantic and idealized depiction of Canada is troubling, what is of even greater concern is the seeming immutable quality of US politics. In contrasting US political pathology with supposed Canadian normalcy, Moore laments the state of the Union, diagnosing US political malady, without embracing a curative praxis to change and transformation. Though Moore claims that he would like to see the United States be more like Canada, his reified notions of national difference, as well as his commitment to an authentic working-class Americanness, belie the possibility of transcending national interests. If Michael Moore really wants to change US politics he must first dream that it is in fact transformable, and not something that is a fixed ethic and character.

NOTES

1. This reading of nationalism is indebted to historian Claudio Lomnitz's critique of Benedict Anderson and the ways that nations can be imagined not as a broad horizontal community but rather as "a community that is conceived of as a deep comradeship among full citizens, each of whom is a potential broker between the national state and weak, embryonic, or part citizens who he or she can construe as dependent." See C. Lomnitz, *Deep Mexico, Silent Mexico: an anthropology of nationalism* (Minneapolis: University of Minnesota Press), pp. 12–13; B. Anderson, *Imagined Communities*, 2nd ed., New York: Verso, 1994.
2. For recent popular critiques of Americanization and US economic and political influence see: M. Barlow, *Too Close for Comfort: Canada's future within fortress North America* (Toronto: McClelland and Stewart, 2005); M. Hurtig, *The Vanishing Country: is it too late to save Canada?* (Toronto: McClelland and Stewart, 2002).
3. Classic works in this genre are: D. Godfrey and M. Watkins, *From Gordon to Watkins to You, A Documentary: the battle for control of our economy* (Toronto: New Press, 1970); K. Levitt, *Silent Surrender: the multinational corporation in Canada*, (Toronto: Macmillan, 1970); A. Rotstein, *The Precarious Homestead: essays on economics, technology and nationalism* (Toronto: New Press, 1973). See also: I. Lumsden (ed.) *Close the 49th Parallel etc: the Americanization of Canada* (Toronto: The University of Toronto Press, 1970); G. Teeple (ed.), *Capital and the National Question*, (Toronto: University of Toronto Press, 1972); R.M. Laxer (ed.), *Canada Ltd: the political economy of dependency* (Toronto: McClelland and Stewart, 1973). For a discussion of economic nationalism in Canada during the 1960s and 1970s see: S. Azzi, *Walter Gordon and the Rise of Canadian Nationalism* (Montreal: McGill/Queen's University Press, 1999); W. Clement and G. Williams (eds) *The New Canadian Political Economy*, (Montreal: McGill Queen's University Press, 1989).
4. Economic nationalism is far from a consensus in Canada. During the 1970s, Marxist critics argued that Canada should not be seen as a colony of the

United States but as an imperialist nation itself or at least a willing partner in American imperialism. See S. Moore and D. Wells, *Imperialism and the National Question in Canada* (Toronto: Better Read Graphics, 1975); C. Heron (ed.) *Imperialism, Nationalism and Canada: Essays from the Marxist Institute* (Toronto: Between the Lines, 1977).

5. High argues that US workers should have utilized a strategy that utilized nationalist rather than community based rhetoric to help lessen the impact of deindustrialization. In light of Dana Frank's observations about nativism, and at times anti-foreign protests, US nationalism did inflect these movements. Moreover, the efficacy of Canadian nationalism was aided by the presence of a powerful labor movement that provided a rallying point for oppositional organizing and resistance, something that US workers in rust-belt industrial towns did not have (High 2003: 166).

6. On the Northwest Rebellion and the 'On-to-Ottawa Trek' see: G. Friesen, *The Canadian Prairies* (Toronto: University of Toronto Press, 1987), pp. 227–36, 398–400. For a history of the RCMP and internal espionage see: S. Hewitt, *Spying 101: The RCMP's Secret Activities at Canadian Universities, 1917–1997* (Toronto: University of Toronto, 2002); G. Kinsman, D.K. Buse, and M. Steedman (eds) *Whose National Security? Canadian State Surveillance and the Creation of Enemies* (Toronto: Between the Lines, 2000); L. Hannant, *The Infernal Machine: Investigating the Loyalty of Canada's Citizens* (Toronto: University of Toronto Press, 1995); R. Cleroux, *Official Secrets: The Story Behind the Canadian Security Intelligence Service* (Montréal: McGill-Queen's University Press, 1990).

7. P. Kulchyski, *Like the Sound of a Drum: Aboriginal Cultural Politics in Denendeh And Nunavut* (Winnipeg: University of Manitoba Press, 2006); J. Milloy, *A National Crime: The Canadian Government And the Residential School System*, (Winnipeg: University of Manitoba Press, 1999); R.J. Brownlie, *A Fatherly Eye: Indian agents, government power, and Aboriginal resistance in Ontario, 1918–1939* (Toronto: University of Toronto Press, 2003).

8. For a critique of Canadian Peacekeeping practices see: S. Razack, *Dark Threats and White Knights: the Somalia affair, peacekeeping, and the new imperialism* (Toronto: University of Toronto Press, 2004). On Canadian support of the US war effort in Vietnam, see: V. Levant, *Quiet Complicity: Canadian involvement in the Vietnam war* (Toronto: Between the Lines Press, 1986).

9. *The Toronto Report Card on Housing and Homelessness, 2003*, Online. Available HTTP: < http://www.toronto.ca/homelessness/pdf/reportcard2003. pdf> (accessed 12 March 2006).

10. Interview from the *Toronto International Film Festival*, Disc Two, *Bowling for Columbine*, DVD.

11. <http://www.geraldpeary.com/interviews/mno/moore.html> (Accessed 5 March 2006).

REFERENCES

Benjamin, W. (1999) *The Arcades Project*, Cambridge, MA: Harvard University Press, pp. 388–89.

Berlant, L. (1997) *The Queen of America Goes to Washington City*, Durham, NC: Duke University Press.

Berman, M. (1999) *Adventures in Marxism*, New York: Verso.

Bluestone, B. and Harrison, B. (1982) *The Deindustrialization of America: plant closings, community abandonment, and the dismantling of basic industry*, New York: Basic Books.

Dobbs, L. (2004) *Exporting America: why corporate greed is shipping American jobs overseas*, New York: Warner Business Books.

Frank, D. (1999) *Buy American: the untold story of economic nationalism*, Boston: Beacon Press.

Harvey, D. (2000) *Spaces of Hope*, Berkeley: University of California Press.

Heath, J. and Potter, A. (2004) *The Rebel Sell: why the culture can't be jammed*, Toronto: Harper/Collins.

High, S. (2003) *Industrial Sunset: the making of North America's rust belt, 1969–1984*, Toronto: University of Toronto Press.

Kanegis, A. (2005) "The Worst of Times Are the Best of Times: the explosion of documentary films and Michael Moore," *Scene4 Magazine*, (January).

Kinsman, G. (1995) "'Character Weaknesses' and 'Fruit Machines': towards an analysis of the anti homosexual security campaign in the Canadian civil service," *Labour/Le Travail*, 35 (Spring): 131–61.

Lomnitz, C. (2001) *Deep Mexico, Silent Mexico: an anthropology of nationalism*, Minneapolis: University of Minnesota Press.

Maynard, S. (2001) "The Maple Leaf (Gardens) Forever: sex, Canadian historians, and national history," *Journal of Canadian Studies*, 35: 70–105.

"Michael Moore Premiers Film in Canada," *Catholic New Times* (4 July 2004).

Moore, M. (1995) *Canadian Bacon* [DVD] Santa Monica, CA: MGM Home Entertainment Inc.

—— (1999) *Roger & Me* [DVD] Burbank, CA: Warner Brothers. Entertainment Inc.

—— (2003) *Bowling for Colombine* [DVD] Santa Monica, CA: MGM Home Entertainment Inc.

—— (2006) "Michael Moore Statement on Canadian Election," 20 January, Online. Available HTTP: <http://www.michaelmoore.com/words/message/index.php?messageDate=2006-01-20> (accessed 10 March 2006).

Sharma, N. (2006) *Nationalism and the Making of 'Migrant Workers' in Canada*, Toronto: University of Toronto Press.

Waxman, S. (2004) "Moore's Film Is Held Up By Questions about Rights," *The New York Times*, 25 May, E1.

4 Seeing *Beneath the Veil*

Saira Shah and the problems of documentary

Nima Naghibi

Saira Shah's *Beneath the Veil*, a documentary on Taliban-controlled Afghanistan, filmed by Hardcash productions for Britain's Channel Four, CNN, and CNN International in February 2001, was shown in heavy rotation on *CNN Presents* in the weeks after 11 September 2001. The relentless screening of the documentary on CNN was presumably intended to disclose the evils of the Taliban regime, most obviously exemplified by their brutal oppression of women, and to provide some insight into the minds of those who were believed to have launched the 9/11 attacks. *Beneath the Veil* thus became a central part of the propagandist machinery of CNN that worked to justify the US war against Afghanistan. *Beneath the Veil* and Shah's follow-up documentary, *Unholy War*, filmed shortly after 9/11 illustrate the complicated ways in which documentaries work as narratives that claim to make historical interventions by disclosing concealed "truths" while simultaneously working to shape their audience's perception of those truths. These documentaries also demonstrate the potential of the genre to work towards social and political change as they can "instruct through evidence [and] pos[e] truth as a moral imperative" (Rabinowitz 1994: 18).

It is no secret that before the events of 9/11, the West was not particularly interested in Afghanistan or the Taliban. Part of Shah's motivation for filming *Beneath the Veil* was to make the world care about the sufferings of Afghan peoples.[1] The world did not remain indifferent for long. After 9/11, the documentary was shown on a loop on *CNN Presents*, transforming it from a potentially interventionary political document (albeit with Orientalist biases) to one complicitous with and co-opted by hawkish neo-conservative US rhetoric advocating the bombing of Afghanistan. One of the ways in which the repetitive screening on CNN of *Beneath the Veil* reorients the film is through the relation of the news ticker at the bottom of the screen to the documentary itself. The continuous 9/11 updates in the crawler contribute to the mounting anxiety in the United States about the sanctity of its borders; the ticker and the documentaries thus work in an intertextual and self-referential way to reinforce the climate of fear and panic in a post-9/11 America. This panic is effected through representations of, predictably, oppressed veiled women; the two most famous moments in the documentary are the secretly-shot footage of a woman's public execution in Kabul's infamous football stadium, and Shah's disturbing interview with three little girls in the village of Mawmaii (both are discussed at further length below). These two moments epitomize not only the problems associated with the ethnographic documentary, but the persistence of a colonial discourse that aims to reveal the hidden truths of the East.

Beneath the Veil begins with the camera focused on Shah travelling in a truck with an armed Afghan soldier. Her voiceover informs us: "I'm trying to find out more about one of the most repressive and mysterious places in the world: Afghanistan." To this point, the Western viewer is faced with a familiar image: that of an intrepid woman traveller who dares to venture alone to the Orient in order to expose its mysteries and disclose what *really* lies beneath the veil. Since at least the eighteenth century, Western women have participated in figuratively unveiling Muslim women, arguing that because of their gender, they have privileged access to the women's quarters, and thus to the heart of the Orient (Ahmed 1992; Burton 1994; Grewal 1996). They positioned themselves as independent, agential figures against which their Muslim sisters were portrayed as objects-to-be-rescued. The subjection of veiled women achieves the status of established "truth" through a universalizing colonial discourse which sets up the oppressed, captive woman against the liberated, unfettered woman: "the declaration of an emancipated status for the Western woman is contingent upon the representation of the Oriental woman as her devalued Other, and this enables Western woman to identify and preserve the boundaries of self for herself" (Yeğenoğlu 2002: 87).

This discursive "truth" in the history of colonial feminist discourse about the subjugated, veiled Muslim woman awaiting liberation manifests itself through repetition and difference in Shah's documentary. Her impulse to unveil Afghanistan and its women for the viewing pleasure of a Western audience is a familiar one, but she is quick to produce a trump card at the very beginning of the film, one that makes her narrative different from and more "authentic" than that of intrepid Western women travellers before her:

> For me, this is personal. I was raised in Britain but my father was an Afghan. And I grew up with a very different vision of Afghanistan. He used to tell me stories of my family's homeland: a place called Paghman. He described gardens and fountains, a kind of Eden. I've never been to Paghman. Now I'm trying to get there. I'm hoping my journey will help me understand what's happening to my father's country.

This confessional account situates Shah on the border between otherness and sameness, between East and West. As a Western journalist, Shah aligns herself with the Western viewer by mobilizing a long history of representations of the East and of its women; by doing so, she represents herself as an outsider looking in on a foreign culture. At the same time, she invokes her "insider" status by mentioning her Afghan father and heritage, thus establishing her perspective as culturally authoritative. Shah cannot be uncomplicatedly placed in the same category as Western women travellers, and it is not my intention to do so here; rather, what interests me is the way in which Shah participates in and perpetuates colonial feminist representations of Muslim women by echoing familiar views of the veil as unequivocally oppressive (Ahmed 1982; Hoodfar 1993/1997; Naghibi 1999).

The subject of *Beneath the Veil* is, at times, difficult to discern: its declared focus, Afghanistan, and more specifically, the plight of Afghan women under the Taliban, is often in competition with the centrality of Saira Shah and her autobiographical quest; this, too, is a typical feature of travel narratives by "intrepid adventuresses" whose putative subject, the foreign country and its people, tend to be displaced by the author's self-representation as heroic and adventurous.[2] In *Beneath the Veil*, the crew's first stop in Afghanistan is Kandahar, and Shah alerts us: "I'm now getting closer to Paghman, the family home I've never seen." The documentary is peppered throughout with reminders that this trip is a form of "spiritual homecoming" for Shah, a reconnecting with the ancestral homeland described to her in her father's stories. While the intrepid adventuress persists in underscoring her own significance in her travel writings, the lionization of the filmmaker is also a central feature of what Bill Nichols calls the "participatory documentary": "[t]he filmmaker's presence takes on heightened importance, from the physical act of 'getting the shot'...to the political act of joining forces with one's subjects" (Nichols 2001: 117).

As the van rumbles along the streets of Kandahar, the camera builds up an atmosphere of suspense and fear, panning over sinister looking men in turbans and veiled women; at the same time, the news ticker reminds us of the encroachment of this lawless world on the security, the stability of "our" world: "Government Allocates Millions to help NY and DC-Area Schools and Students Affected by Terrorist Attacks; Money can pay for counselling, substitute teachers, clean up, added security and long-term crisis planning." And again, "U.S. Flags at White House, Capitol Return to Full Staff for First Time Since Sept 11 attacks." The growing threat of the Muslim world to the free and democratic West is thus further cemented in the mind of the (Western) viewer, leaving her open to Bush's imperatives about the United States being under siege. This is a valuable illustration of the failure of intentionality to determine a text's meaning and the material effects of discourse and representation. The timing of the film's release and its repetitive screening on CNN, the colonialist gestures in the documentary which decry the abjection (and advocate the liberation) of Afghan women, combined with an overdetermined discourse in the West about a growing Islamic threat to the "free" world, all contribute to transforming a film concerned with social justice into war propaganda for the

United States.[3] Thus, the content of Shah's documentary combined with the contexts in which it was circulated allowed for the cultural and political uses to which the film was put.

The documentary also consolidates a history of Western liberal feminist collusion with the project of colonialism. This unfortunate history reproduces itself as post 9/11 debates around Afghanistan hijack the language of feminism in the service of neo-colonial interests. Two months after 9/11, Laura Bush used her husband's weekly radio address to the nation to lend her support to the "war on terror," invoking familiar colonial justifications for military invasion in the interests of rescuing women.

> Because of our recent military gains in much of Afghanistan, women are no longer imprisoned in their homes. They can listen to music and teach their daughters without fear of punishment. Yet the terrorists who helped rule that country now plot and plan in many countries. And they must be stopped. The fight against terrorism is also a fight for the rights and dignity of women. (17 November 2001)[4]

US concerns for the well-being of women dovetails nicely here with their military fervour; Bush's speech is a crystallization of how feminist discourse and military goals are deployed in the name of progress and emancipation. Judith Butler puts it succinctly:

> The sudden feminist conversion on the part of the Bush administration, which retroactively transformed the liberation of women into a rationale for its military actions against Afghanistan, is a sign of the extent to which feminism, as a trope, is deployed in the service of restoring the presumption of First World impermeability. (Butler 2004: 41)

Beneath the Veil participates in this colonial feminist discourse by focusing its lens on the abject female subject. The introductory preamble in the documentary shows images of the Taliban meting out their particular form of justice in Kabul's football stadium while Saira Shah's voice-over describes and interprets the scene for us:

> Veiled women hunched in the back of a pick-up truck. The football stadium in Afghanistan: A place of entertainment turned into an execution ground. Secret pictures showing scenes the country's rulers want to keep hidden. We are trying to uncover the truth behind Afghanistan's veil of terror.

The shot ends with a frozen image of a soldier pointing the barrel of a gun to the back of the head of a crouching veiled woman. Immediately, the viewer recognizes that she has been provided access to something forbidden. These "secret pictures," as Shah calls them, were recorded with hidden cameras by members of the feminist opposition group, RAWA (Revolutionary Association of the Women of Afghanistan). It is clear that we are getting illicit access to these pictures, and the use of the hidden camera heightens the viewer's sense of danger and pleasure. Indeed the desire to know converges here with a sadistic pleasure in looking at what lies beneath the veil, as the images we see appear to confirm what the West has always imagined to lie at the heart of Orient: the brutalized female subject.

The horrifying footage of public executions filmed by RAWA is partly responsible for catapulting the Afghan feminist organization to fame. In *Beneath the Veil*, RAWA's footage is interspersed with shots of Shah standing in the notorious football stadium; she narrates and interprets the events recorded by RAWA's secret camera, pointing to the specific places in the (now empty) field that are captured on film. Meanwhile, the crawler at the bottom of our television screens urges us to log on to the CNN website: "Inside Osama Bin Laden's Organization: An Overview of Al Qaeda on CNN.Com." This widely recognized scene in *Beneath the Veil* demonstrates the ways in which the film works with multiple layers of text: Shah's narration, RAWA's secretly captured footage, and the news ticker are superimposed on each other, reconsolidating Western discursive representations of Islam as a religion of terror, and the Taliban and Al-Qaeda as its prophets. The self-referentiality of this scene in which the three texts refer back to each other in a continuous loop buttresses colonial representations of the Muslim world as backward, violent, and in need of Western intervention. These representations reach their apogee in the figure of the veiled woman who is seen as simultaneously oppressed and sexualized, an object to be pitied and rescued, as well as an object to be desired. Further, Shah's own interpretation of this scene combined with CNN's news ticker at the bottom of the screen in effect "sandwich" RAWA's documentation of events and determine, or direct our view of the footage and its possible meanings.

Shah's showcasing of RAWA is also worth examining. RAWA has strong connections to mainstream Western liberal feminists such as Eve Ensler and organizations such as the Feminist Majority Foundation, of which Mavis Leno (the wife of talk-show host, Jay Leno) is a vocal member. The organization is famous for its commitment to the plight of Afghan women under the Taliban even before it was in vogue, in other words, before 9/11. However, one of their controversial, albeit well-meaning, campaigns involved the selling of swatches of mesh fabric, ostensibly from authentic burqas, to American women who wore them on their lapels in solidarity with their oppressed Afghan sisters. The unquestioned "truth" of the abjection of the veiled body is one of the pitfalls of the organization; indeed, as Minoo Moallem writes in *Between Warrior Brother and Veiled Sister*:

> [T]he Western trope of the Muslim woman as the ultimate victim of a timeless patriarchy defined by the barbarism of the Islamic religion, which is in need of civilizing, has become a very important component of Western regimes of knowledge…it is under the sign of a veiled woman that "we" increasingly come to recognize ourselves not only as gendered and heteronormative subjects but also as located in the free West, where women are not imprisoned. (Moallem 2005: 19–20)

RAWA is guilty of enforcing this binary of oppressed veiled woman and her liberated unveiled counterpart in a most spectacular way by its participation in the $1000 a ticket celebrity production of Ensler's *The Vagina Monologues* at Madison Square Garden in February 2001. After Oprah Winfrey's reading of Ensler's monologue, "Under the Burqa," at this event, a veiled woman stepped onstage, and Oprah slowly lifted her veil to thunderous applause. The woman was Zoya, a member of RAWA, and author of one of the now ubiquitous life narratives about oppression under the veil, *Zoya's Story: An Afghan Woman's Struggle for Freedom*. This public unveiling is fraught with colonial and imperial significations as Oprah, the iconic figure of emancipated, triumphant, and successful American womanhood, benevolently lifts the veil off her sister's face; this moment underscores "the presumption of the truth and naturalness of the unveiled body that the discourse of colonial feminism is predicated upon" (Yeğenoğlu 2002: 92).[5]

In both *Beneath the Veil* and *Unholy War*, Shah plays out a long-held Western fantasy of access to the forbidden by literally going "beneath the veil" and taking us with her. In the first film, she explains her decision to wear the veil thus: "So far, I've been an outsider here. Now I want to get inside the world of ordinary Afghans…I'm going undercover. From now on, I'll live the life of an Afghan woman." The scene in which she puts on the *burqa* is particularly fascinating: it is shot at night under low light conditions with (again) ominous sounding Eastern music, all contributing to a growing sense of excitement and intrigue. In her autobiographical book, *The Storyteller's Daughter: One Woman's Return To Her Lost Homeland* (2003), which capitalizes on the success of *Beneath the Veil* by basically re-telling the story of the documentary as well as of her family heritage, Shah confirms Western stereotypes about the practice of veiling as a form of women's oppression:

> I am choking under the *burqa*, the pale blue veil, which begins in a cap upon my head. It covers my face, my body, my arms and my legs, and is long enough to trip me up in my muddy plastic shoes. A crocheted grille obscured my vision. A grid of black shadows intersects trees, fields, and the white road outside. It is like looking through prison bars. (2003: 7–8)

For the Western reader and viewer, then, what makes Shah so palatable is that she is an authentic other who delivers to the West comfortable notions of what it means to be an oppressed Afghan woman. She claims that her disguise enables her to see Afghanistan through the eyes of an Afghan woman, and what she "authentically" sees is what we already knew was there: the abject, imprisoned, suffering Eastern woman; she provides her audience with the same vantage point as we follow her gaze through the hidden camera.

Shah takes pains to remind us again of the risks involved in this enterprise; in the documentary, she tells us that she will have to leave her crew behind in order to travel with members of RAWA deep into the heart of Afghanistan by posing as an Afghan woman, and ensures that her audience appreciates the danger she faces: "As an Afghan, I'll have no protection at all. But I can enter the Kabul foreigners don't see." This statement is particularly appealing to the Western viewer because it underscores the dangers involved and makes a tantalizing promise that we, too, can see the city "foreigners don't see" since we, too, are looking through Shah's "crocheted grille" (2003: 7). One of the places we visit via Shah's hidden camera is, as she describes, "the most subversive place of all—a secret beauty parlour." Inside, we see grainy footage of women (with their faces blurred to prevent identification) having their makeup done; Shah tells us: "If they're caught, these women will be imprisoned. But they still paint the faces they can never show in public." Immediately, a pop-up text box swoops across the screen, and hovers over an anonymous woman's face: "Restrictions imposed by the Taliban. CNN.com/Presents." The pop-up as intertext contributes again to a reconsolidation of dominant Western discourse; the invitation to visit CNN.com is an invitation to get authoritative information on the subjects and their experiences of victimization portrayed here.

In *The Storyteller's Daughter*, Shah revisits her experience as a "secret operative," emphasizing once again the risks she has taken:

> As a Westerner, if I am caught, I may be imprisoned and accused of espionage. If the Taliban discover my family history and decide I am an Afghan, then I share the same risks as the Afghan women who are helping me: torture, a bullet in the head or simply disappearing in Pul i Charki, Kabul's notorious political prison.(2003: 8)

Like other Western women before her, Shah ironically chooses to veil herself in order to unveil Afghanistan and its women for a Western audience. The motif of disguise runs through both documentaries. *Unholy War* begins with Shah and her crew in Pakistan, determined to cross the closed border into Afghanistan. They decide to sneak across the border in disguise, drawing on a Western tradition of paradoxically revealing the "truth" at the heart of the Orient through disguise and deceit. Shah informs viewers that they are disguising themselves as Afghans, and cuts to a shot of the director, James Miller, putting on a burqa, masquerading as an Afghan woman. The decision to get "inside" Afghanistan by "going undercover" participates in another Western tradition of cross-dressing or wearing some form of disguise in the Orient. In the nineteenth century, Jane Dieulafoy travelled through Persia, and Isabelle Eberhardt through North Africa dressed as men; in the twentieth century, T.E. Lawrence "went native" and cross-dressed in the Orient; in the 1970s, Sarah Hobson went to Iran disguised as a man; in the 1990s, Geraldine Brooks "disguised" herself as a belly-dancer in Egypt, and the list goes on. In the days and months after 9/11, there was a revival of Western desire to access the "truth" of the Orient through deception. Several international journalists, the first among them, BBC journalist John Simpson (for whom Shah has expressed great admiration), stole across the border into Afghanistan disguised as women in burqas.[6]

In Western discourses, the Orient has been often configured as a place where disguise and deceit are not only possible, but indeed necessary. It is a place to which one cannot simply travel. It is a place of danger and desire, of darkness and mystery, of sexual repression and sexual license. These contradictory representations continue to inform Western narratives about the Middle East, and Shah participates in perpetuating these representations. The Western desire to look beneath, beyond, or under the veil has, I have been arguing, a long colonial history; this prurient interest in what lies "beneath the veil" has roots in Enlightenment oculocentrism: the privileging of rendering visible as the means of understanding and controlling a subject. This scopophilic desire to unveil the Muslim woman is also spurred by epistephilia, or a desire to know, which Nichols identifies as central to documentary filmmaking (2001: 40). Documentary film often seeks knowledge of the other through unveiling "truths"; this is a desire it shares with an Orientalist discourse which seeks the unveiling of such mysteries of the East as the veiled woman. If the figure of the abject veiled woman inspires the impulse to emancipate, it also inspires a sadistic desire to (forcibly) unveil, to strip away the protective layers, and expose her in her vulnerable state.

The history of Western desire to look beneath the veil is thus intertwined with a colonial impulse to categorize, to possess the colonized other. In her work on Western representations of veiling, Yeğenoğlu has argued: "this metaphysical speculation or mediation, this desire to reveal and unveil is at the same time the *scene of seduction*. The metaphysical will to know gains a sexual overtone" (1998: 45). In this case, *Beneath the Veil* and *Unholy War* participate in the unveiling of the Orient by partaking of a colonial and eroticised project to unveil and thereby to know and to control the ethnographic other. As Zillah Eisenstein observes:

> Veils, like any piece of clothing or drapery, cover over; they create both
> fantasy and fetish at the same time. All clothing is used to cover over

desire—to repress it by putting it out of sight. But the covering also is always a reminder of what is covered, of the desire itself. The denial of desirous pleasure remains always unstable; to repress is to simultaneously expose it. (Eisenstein 2004: 170–71)

Western documentaries that promise a glimpse into the Muslim world (and invariably the closed, forbidden world of women) are fascinating because always behind this colonial impulse to "lay bare" the native subject for a scopophilic Western audience is the desire to be thwarted in the act. Behind the plurality of Western documentaries, articles, and books on the secret, veiled world of Muslim women, each of which promises that this will be the last, the ultimate act of unveiling, lies another promise of deferral and displacement. Thus the desire to look "beneath the veil" resides in the repetition of the promise of unveiling, and not in the final act of unveiling itself.

Both documentaries focus their look "beneath the veil" disturbingly on the figures of the three little girls in the village of Mawmaii. In the first film, Shah discovers the grief-stricken girls and their father in the courtyard of their family home. In her book, she describes them in the highly clichéd language of female captivity:

> Sitting in a row, hunched in their veils—pink, yellow and blue—the girls looked like broken birds. All I could see of them was [sic] their huge dark eyes. Slowly, from the corner of one eye a tear appeared and quivered for a moment before it burst and flowed. I could not even imagine from what deep well of suffering this single drop had escaped. (2003: 215)

The girls' mother was murdered by the Taliban who proceeded to stay in the house for three days; although there is no explicit mention of rape, the implication is clear. This scene, one of the most famous in the documentary, highlights some of the problems inherent to the genre and to the impulse and motivation to see "beneath the veil." It is an extremely disturbing moment because it shows us the brutality of the Taliban. It is also unsettling because it asks us to consider the politics of witnessing a Western reporter insist on painful testimony from three clearly traumatized Afghan girls. The discursive context here is already, as Nichols has observed, "overdetermined" by the structure of the interview that "testifies to a power relation in which institutional hierarchy and regulation pertain to speech itself" (1991: 50).

The hierarchical relations and power inequalities exposed in the interview are further compounded by unstated, complex cultural codes of behaviour. As their elder and as someone in a position of authority, Shah's questions demand an answer. But the answer conflicts with cultural codes of modesty and "saving face" that would not allow the girls to articulate what they experienced at the hands of the Taliban. Shah describes the interview in further detail in her book:

> How long did the men stay in the house with them, while their mother's body lay in the yard? The old man turned away. No other Afghan father would have allowed me to ask such a question. But he was impotent: he had not been there when the soldiers came. The men had stayed alone with the girls for two days. What did the soldiers do to them during that time? At this point, the eldest girl, Amina, covered her face and began to weep. Fairuza had an unquenchable spirit. She looked at her sister, then tilted her chin at me and said, in that clear voice: "They asked for food and water. What could we do? Our mother was dead. We had to do whatever they told us."(2003: 215)

This is a troubling scene in which Shah exploits her multiple positions as a Western reporter, as a woman, and as an Afghan to assert her authority and ask questions otherwise forbidden in this cultural context. As a Western reporter, she draws on her authoritative position to demand an answer for her probing questions. As a woman, she can ask direct questions that would be otherwise difficult for a male reporter. As an Afghan, she can reach out and connect with the girls, speaking to them in Dari, making them feel as though they are speaking to one who understands them and shares their culture and experience. But at the same time, as an Afghan woman, Shah knows that she is participating in rendering the father impotent. She is divesting him of his authority and respectability: he couldn't prevent the violation of his daughters at the hands of the Taliban. He can't prevent their further violation at the hands of Saira Shah. She is well aware of this and yet she persists in her interrogation. At the same time, the girls' refusal to provide her with the answer that she wants can be read as a renunciation of Shah's imperialist gestures; their silence on the subject of rape and their response through the language of hospitality—they provided their visitors with food and water—re-codes them as dutiful Afghan daughters who conduct themselves through culturally sanctioned behaviour.[7] It also refigures them as agential subjects who repudiate the label of victim and upset the colonial narrative of salvation and protection.

Shah has expressed discomfort with the way the barbarism of the Taliban became epitomized for viewers by the figure of the three girls, particularly in the United States; she even had offers to adopt the three girls in a valiant attempt to rescue them from their plight:

> After 11 September, *Beneath the Veil* was shown again and again on CNN. Although we had made the film before the attack on the World Trade Center, Western politicians on all sides had used the faces of the three girls in Mawmaii to further their own ends. The girls' suffering was used both as an argument for bombing Afghanistan and for delivering aid to it. (2003: 216)

Although she appears uncomfortable with the way the girls' cause is championed by self-serving Western politicians, she too, uses them for her own ends; their situation becomes the motivation for her second film, *Unholy War*: "We had decided to try to return to Mawmaii and find the three girls. I had convinced my editors that the fate of Amina, Fairuza and Fawzia was the perfect metaphor for the plight of Afghanistan" (2003: 217). Just as *Beneath the Veil* began with Shah's declaration of the personal and filial nature of her motivations, *Unholy War* begins with a personal statement:

> For me, there's also a personal quest. Six months ago I met three young girls. The Taliban shot their mother in front of their eyes. Now their village is on the front line. I want to find them. I want to know if they're safe.

Here, Shah claims the story of the three girls as part of her own personal history just as she does the stories of Afghanistan told by her father. There is a proprietary quality to both these cases as she makes other people's stories her own, and a self-referentiality as all stories about Afghanistan refer back to Saira Shah.

After an excruciating journey on foot through smugglers' routes and the punishing terrain of the Hindu Kush during which Shah, the fearless adventurer once again, suffers from frostbite and exhaustion, they arrive in Mawmaii. They find the girls and their father still in the same house. They are extremely poor; the father cannot work because the girls are terrified of being left alone. Shah interviews the girls again, wanting desperately to "rescue them" as she puts it in her book:

> I asked [Fairuza] what she needed and, again, I heard that clear, melodic voice: "We have lived through a war and a revolution. We just want our country to be at peace." She looked sadly at her two sisters. "Until then, we will continue to suffer in silence. We just suffer in silence." (237)

In the course of her interview with the girls, Shah determines that what they really want is to go to school. She is delighted to discover a girl's school about a day's walk from the village, but finds that the father is resistant to the idea as he is afraid to leave his home. Shah makes several efforts to convince him that enrolling his daughters in this school would be the best thing for them all, and even tells him that the television company will pay for their relocation. He remains intransigent on the subject of his daughters' education, but suggests he might reconsider if they are willing to buy him a new wife (2003: 246). Shah finally has to concede defeat and returns to England having ultimately failed in her efforts at salvation and personal redemption.

Beneath the Veil and *Unholy War* share a colonial impulse to posit themselves as pioneering and as culturally authoritative perspectives on Afghan
women. Both provide surreptitious glimpses "beneath the veil" in order to
show the sufferings of Afghan women. These documentaries foreground
the problematics of the scopophilic and epistephilic impulses of the colonial
gaze in documentary film. Shah does seem to want to accomplish something different in *Unholy War*, but the film suffers a curious contradiction
as it takes pains to remind viewers of its prequel by interspersing footage
from the first film throughout. Thus, while Shah claims unease with the
repetitive screening of the film on CNN, she contributes to its "looping" by
including in her second film the most emotionally evocative scenes from the
first (such as her interview with the three girls).

Unholy War, however, is not as sensational a film as *Beneath the Veil*,
most probably because of the timing of its filming and release; even the
information in the news ticker is not as apocalyptic this time around.[8]
Nevertheless, elements from the first movie remain present, such as, for
example, Shah's posturing as an intrepid adventuress. This is now coupled
with a missionary impulse as the story is built around the heroic "rescue"
of the three girls. While the missionary persona may appear to be a departure from the figure of the intrepid adventuress, they both operate from
within colonial discourse. It bears mentioning, however, that there appears
to be in this second film, albeit momentarily, a recognition that Western
quick-fix solutions do not work. This recognition disrupts, again momentarily, the Western narrative of colonial salvation and rescue—indeed, the
very narrative underpinning justifications of the war in Afghanistan and
in Iraq. Shah ends *Unholy War* by expressing her concerns about Western
intervention in Afghanistan: is the West committed to doing the hard work
of rebuilding or will Afghanistan be forgotten? We know now, of course,
that it has been forgotten, displaced by the fiasco of Iraq, and the looming
threat of military attacks against Iran.

In her book, Shah confesses: "I had failed. Afghanistan had confounded
me, just as it has always confounded the West" (2003: 246). While *Beneath
the Veil* ends with a shot of Shah standing with her back to the camera, legs
astride, feet firmly planted on the ground surveying the majestic mountainous view, very much the intrepid adventuress, the second film ends disqui-
etingly with the unsmiling face of an Afghan girl in a refugee camp gazing
defiantly into the camera. The colonial gaze in *Unholy War* is thus briefly
disrupted by an Afghanistan that has consistently resisted colonial interference. While CNN used *Beneath the Veil* for basically propagandist purposes in the days immediately following 9/11, the irresolution in *Unholy
War*, the obvious failure of Shah's stated purpose "to use the documentary
as an instrument to rescue those three girls" works, at least momentarily,
as a refusal, and as a challenge to the West (2003: 217).

ACKNOWLEDGMENTS

I would like to thank Tina Chen, David Churchill, and all the participants at the Film, History, and Cultural Citizenship workshop in Winnipeg who provided me with invaluable feedback on my paper. I am grateful, as always, for Andrew O'Malley's thoughtful criticism.

NOTES

1. In an online interview with Nermeen Shaikh of AsiaSource, Shah states that in making "Beneath the Veil," her goal was to attract Western attention to a corner of the world that she felt had been forgotten:
   "What I would say is that *Beneath the Veil* was very much a product of its time. In the context in which we made this documentary, there was basically a complete lack of interest in Afghanistan.... So *Beneath the Veil* was a cry. We made the strongest film we could possibly make to try and get attention. Having said that, there was journalistic rigor; we did not make anything up. Everything we put in was true. The passion you see in the film came from just the frustration of seeing this kind of suffering and knowing that people did not care about it." (Shaikh 2003: 4–5)
2. For a discussion of the "intrepid adventuress" in feminist criticism, see S. Mills, Discourses of Difference: an analysis of women's travel writing and colonialism, London: Routledge, 1991.
3. Examples of inflammatory information in the news ticker include: "FBI seeking 230 People for Questioning in Terror Investigation"; "11 People Being Held in Britain and France for Possible Involvement in Anti-American Terrorist Attacks"; "Pres. Bush Places Bounty on Terrorists Behind Attacks. Nearly $25 Million Set Aside to Reward People Who Provide Information Leading To Arrests."
4. My thanks to John Mowitt for directing my attention to this speech.
5. For a wonderful analysis of this moment, see G. Whitlock, "The Skin of the Burqa: recent life narratives from Afghanistan," Biography, 28.1: 54–76.
6. The enthusiasm for this practice waned with a growing number of arrests by the Taliban, including British and French journalists Yvonne Ridley and Michel Peyrard, and Japanese photojournalist Yanagida Daigen.
7. My thanks to Tina Chen and David Churchill for suggesting the possibility of resistance here.
8. An exception would be: "Nat'l Security Adviser Rice About Osama Bin Laden: 'We are putting a net around him, and eventually we are going to get him.'"

REFERENCES

Ahmed, L. (1982) "Western Ethnocentrism and Perceptions of the Harem," *Feminist Studies*, 8.3: 521–534.
—— (1992) *Women and Gender in Islam: historical roots of a modern debate*, New Haven, CT: Yale University Press.
Burton, A. (1994) *Burdens of History: British feminists, Indian women, and imperial culture, 1865–1915*, Chapel Hill: University of North Carolina Press.

Bush, L. (2001) "Radio Address by Mrs. Bush," *The White House*, Online. Available HTTP: <http://www.whitehouse.gov/news/releases/2001/11/20011117.html> (accessed 1 June 2006).

Butler, J. (2004) *Precarious Life: the powers of mourning and violence*, London: Verso.

Eisenstein, Z. (2004) *Against Empire: feminisms, racism, and the west*, London: Zed Books.

Grewal, I. (1996) *Home and Harem: nation, gender, empire, and the cultures of travel*, Durham, NC: Duke University Press.

Hoodfar, H. (1993; 1997) "The Veil in Their Minds and on Our Heads: Veiling Practices and Muslim Women," in L. Lowe and D. Lloyd (eds.) *The Politics of Culture in the Shadow of Capital*, Durham, NC: Duke University Press.

Moallem, M. (2005) *Between Warrior Brother and Veiled Sister: Islamic fundamentalism and the politics of patriarchy in Iran*, Berkeley: University of California Press.

Naghibi, N. (1999) "Bad Feminist or Bad-*Hejabi*? Moving Outside the *Hejab* Debate," *Interventions: International Journal of Postcolonial Studies*, 1.4: 555–71.

Nichols, B. (1991) *Representing Reality: issues and concepts in documentary*, Bloomington: Indiana University Press.

—— (2001) *Introduction to Documentary*, Bloomington: Indiana University Press.

Rabinowitz, P. (1994) *They Must Be Represented: the politics of documentary*, London: Verso.

Shah, S. (2003) *The Storyteller's Daughter: one woman's return to her lost homeland*, New York: Knopf.

Shaikh, N. (2003) "The Storyteller's Daughter: An Interview with Saira Shah," *AsiaSource: A Resource of the Asia Society*, Online. Available HTTP: <http://www.asiasource.org/news/special_reports/shah.cfm> (accessed 29 March 2006).

Yeğenoğlu, M. (1998) *Colonial Fantasies: towards a feminist reading of orientalism*, Cambridge: Cambridge University Press.

—— (2002) "Sartorial Fabric-ations: Enlightenment and Western Feminism," in L. Donaldson and K. Pui-lan (eds) *Postcolonialism, Feminism and Religious Discourse*, New York: Routledge.

5 Textual communities and localized practices of film in Maoist China[1]

Tina Mai Chen

In Soviet director Mark Donskoy's 1947 film *Village Schoolteacher*, the young teacher Varenka makes her way down the main street of a remote village where she has recently arrived. She walks through the snow on her way to the schoolhouse with a globe cradled in her arm. The children stare with expressions of potential interest while their parents comment on "city folk," displaying a general resistance to her presence. The schoolhouse is empty with the exception of the custodian but Varenka is not deterred. She sets the globe on the desk and insists that children will come. Children do not arrive on this day, but in future days begin to fill the schoolhouse after Varenka establishes herself in the village by challenging the local tyrant who is on the verge of publicly assaulting his wife. In each of these scenes, Varenka embodies enlightenment, a way of thinking that in the opening scenes of the film has been linked to revolutionary thought through the conversations between Varenka and her love interest, a Bolshevik partisan, Sergei.

On Varenka's first day at the school, the custodian, Igor Petrovich, is curious about the globe. Varenka explains the globe depicts the world and shows him how it rotates. Petrovich is later seen surreptitiously touching and contemplating the object. The globe continues to feature prominently throughout the film and the unfolding of Varenka's career as an educator over three decades. Along with the school clock and bell, the globe is a recurring motif that marks the start of each school day. Through this imagery, Varenka literally delivers the world to rural children who symbolize the Soviet future. Importantly, the delivery of the world to rural youth is contingent upon an education linked to the revolutionary resolve and projects that inspire Varenka, and to an internationalist imaginary. Donskoy's *Village Schoolteacher* takes the Russian social movement of populist-inspired "going to the people" as the historical context against which to develop narratives of revolutionary sacrifice and commitment that highlight the interpenetration of global to local as revolutionary praxis.

We could analyze production of knowledge and consciousness at the nexus of global and local as developed on screen in this popular late-Stalinist era film, but let us step back from the screen and text to consider the

Figure. 5.1 Varenka's arrival at the schoolhouse where only the custodian, Igor Petrovich, is present. *Village Schoolteacher* (1947).

possible mise-en-scène of the screening of *Village Schoolteacher* in 1950s or 1960s China. A couple of generic possibilities exist. First imported into China and dubbed in Chinese by the Shanghai Studio of the China Film Company in July 1950, the film was distributed for urban and rural viewing. In the urban setting, *Village Schoolteacher* would have appeared in cinemas with capacities of approximately 1,000 and for which tickets could be purchased for a fee roughly equivalent to bus fare. Those in attendance would largely be high school students and regular filmgoers who attended the range of urban international film festivals. They arrived on foot or by bus with friends or colleagues and would leave in similar manner. In workplaces and rural areas, the film screening was more of an inclusive event. For rural screenings, a film projection unit generally composed of three or four youth would arrive in a village, perhaps once a month or in more remote areas once a year. The projection unit would set up a white sheet as the screen, explain the film projector and generator to anyone who was interested in the technology, discuss the film plot, and when nightfall arrived, begin the outdoor screening. Peasants from neighboring areas would walk to the village following a day's work and the audience composed of children, parents, and grandparents would sit on all sides of the screen, watching the images and listening to the film dialogue. Spectators would also be guided by the interjections of the film projectionists designed to ease comprehension for the numerous first-time viewers. On occasion, the film projection unit would be accompanied by photographers and journalists who reported on film screenings in remote areas for provincial and national media. These stories explained the importance of the new film culture and technology to China and linked the presence of film in rural areas to the delivery of socialism and a new global consciousness (Chen 2003, 2004).

In both the text of *Village Schoolteacher* and Chinese Communist Party (CCP) film praxis, remote areas appeared as sites of transformation within newly emerging national and international units. This chapter focuses on the spatio-temporal dimensions of film in Maoist China to interrogate the multiple levels of community at work on the screen and in the practices of film screening in Maoist China. I am interested in exploring the interplay between, on one hand, international and national textual communities and, on the other hand, practices of community in localized spaces. I begin by examining how film projection workers occupied liminal spaces between these different forms and levels of community. From here I move to consider the ways in which Chinese and Soviet films that were steeped in (global) revolutionary historical narratives acquired meaning in Maoist China through distribution and screening practices, as well as through narrative constructions of history. In this regard, I focus on how film projectionists functioned as modernizing agents of a nation–state project even as they participated in decentralizing initiatives and articulated global discourses and subjectivities for popular consumption.

Multiple levels of community are evident in the texts, discourses, and practices of film in sources from 1949 to 1966, as well as commemorative texts referring to this period. In 2001, to celebrate the 50th anniversary of the China Film Company (Zhongying gongsi), the company published *Fifty Years of China Film* (Tong 2001). The opening paragraph concluded as follows:

> Over the last fifty years, Chinese film has entered into the remote corners of the country, entered into the hearts of hundreds of millions of audience members; when Chinese films have been sent out of the country, to the world, the China Film Company has realized the goals it pursued. In celebrating these fifty years, every film worker must be filled with emotion and deep pride. (Tong 2001: 6)

In these two sentences four levels of community are invoked: the Chinese nation-state (linked to claims over the geographical spaces of China reached by film), the Chinese people (considered as audience members), the international community (of which China is a member through film import and export), and the film workers (who have enabled these communities to come into being). *Fifty Years of China Film* frames the different levels of communities in terms of the practices of film work; but these also need to be analyzed alongside the textual communities that film workers disseminated and embodied. Together these forms of community were integral to the CCP-directed socio-political project of producing collective consciousness. It is in the collective consciousness of overlapping communities that Maoist thought and CCP praxis located the potential for agency, progress, and revolutionary transformation; in short, the realization of History.

TRANSACTIONAL LOCATION OF FILM WORKERS: MULTIPLE LEVELS OF COMMUNITY

From its founding in 1921, the Chinese Communist Party identified film as a powerful medium through which it could invoke a socialist national community. Rooted in the left-wing cinema and realism of the 1920s and 1930s, the CCP viewed film as a medium that consolidated national consciousness by harnessing emotional responses to the visual rhetoric of film. This was accomplished through the narrative structure of the films as well as the articulation of the medium and content of film to the unfolding history of the Chinese nation. With Mao Zedong's 1942 *Talks on Art and Literature*, there emerged in the liberated areas a commitment to using film to serve the worker, peasant, and soldier (Ding 1998: 138–75). Mao's insistence that film should serve worker, peasant, and soldier was an explicit recognition that cultural products and their circulation could produce 'the people' of a new China. In the late 1940s, the people were served through film by having their struggles and victories showcased, in sharp contrast to the plots and characters of dominant films in circulation elsewhere in China. CCP-produced films of this period included the feature film *Bridge* (Qiao, 1949) and the documentary *Democratic Northeast* (Minzhu Dongbei, 1949).[2]

The visual and narrative filmic texts reveal the forms of subjectivity encouraged by CCP film and were part of the textual basis of the newly envisioned communities and their attendant spatio-temporal configurations of History. *Bridge* takes as its namesake the bridge over Songhua River, which required repairs in the winter of 1947 to ensure the successful advance of Communist forces. The film champions the leadership role of the proletariat and indicates that historical progress rests with workers' ingenuity and commitment. This is achieved by using a classic separation between the intellectual class and the workers. The Chief Engineer doubts the feasibility of the project but the enthusiasm and innovation of worker-hero Liang Risheng inspires other workers and they complete the task before the spring thaw, enabling the advance of the People's Liberation Army (PLA). *Bridge* thus extols the worker as the embodiment of revolutionary consciousness and contributor to the ultimate success of the PLA. *Democratic Northeast*, by contrast, highlights the work of another component of "the people," the soldier. As the first CCP documentary to record the scenes of liberation of the Northeast it established a visual and textual framework through which to enact the spatial contours of liberated China. In *Democratic Northeast* and similar documentaries, the PLA becomes the agent of History, rendering spatial expansion of the PLA/CCP and the progressive movement of time intimately connected phenomena.

The large number of films in the 1945 to 1949 period that provided (socialist) realist footage of the liberation of territory by the CCP stands as testament to film's role in the redrawing of the boundaries of the nation-state. In the second half of the civil war between the CCP and Guomindang, films resonating with *Democratic Northeast* such as *The Final Battle for the Liberation of Dongbei* (Jiefang Dongbei de zuihou zhanyi), *Liberating Tianjin* (Jiefang Tianjin), *The Three Year War of Liberation of Dongbei* (Dongbei sannian jiefang zhanzheng), and *Entering Beiping* (Beiping ru chengshi) (Ding 1995: 153) functioned to document and propagate history-in-the-making. Film, in these instances, followed the extension of power by the CCP and the PLA. In the post-1949 period, these dynamics of conquering territory persisted in national narrative and practice but acquired new forms with the CCP notion that the medium of film itself acted as a means of territorial inclusion. Film projection workers took up the historical project of delimiting the boundaries of the nation through the areas they reached, while in a dialectical relationship filmmakers captured images of the historical struggles of the newly imagined Chinese people and landscape and prepared them for dissemination nationally and internationally.

The dialectic process informing filmic practice and textual communities can be seen in how localized practices of film projection units were informed by national and international filmic and extra-filmic textual communities. Chinese regional offices distributed films and promotional materials produced by the major nationalized film studios that were used to introduce and structure local understanding of films. This practice established a common textual framework within which film projectionists worked. Film projectionists did not have a uniform experience, however. Their experience depended on the area covered by the film projection unit, and its access or lack thereof to permanent buildings that housed 35mm projectors. What is important to note is that those who went to the "remote areas" and faced the greatest limitations by way of supplies and selection were the most widely celebrated in the national media. I suggest that the reason for this attention to film projectionists in remote regions arose because they consolidated politico-aesthetic control over areas and people with the most tenuous link to the nation–state community. Remoteness functioned to consolidate various levels of extra-filmic textual communities, alongside filmic texts like *Village Schoolteacher* and the Chinese film *A Nurse's Diary* (Hushi riji, 1957) that paralleled the practices of the film projectionists. This ensured a continuous cross-referencing of textual communities and communities in practice, as well as the multiple levels of local, national, and international through which the CCP remade the local. Notably, textual communities and filmic practices were deeply embedded in an understanding of film and film workers as agents of a modernization trajectory and the extension of state power.

The recollections of Chen Bo, a film worker since 1949, reflect the interplay between the levels and forms of community (Tong 2001: 38-41). Chen asserts that the China Film Company served the people by bringing to the screens of the major cities Chinese documentaries and feature films. He explicitly juxtaposed these film offerings to the American films that dominated urban theaters in the pre-1949 period. The Chinese films Chen singled out included *Bridge* (Qiao), *Zhao Yiman* (Zhao Yiman), *Iron Soldier* (Gangtie zhanshi), and *White Haired Girl* (Bai mao nu). Notably, these films focus on the anti-Japanese war of resistance and Civil War period, with visual and narrative structures that culminate in the combined liberation of individual and nation as their fates become positively linked to the fulfillment of the historic role of the CCP. Chen does not dwell on the filmic representation of the new era but makes clear that the new era is one in which the Chinese nation overthrows imperialist cultural products. For Chen, overthrowing past oppression included new Chinese-produced film as well as the success of Chinese films domestically and internationally and an ever-expanding number of film units. Here Chen used precise statistics to reinforce the new reach of film under the CCP. Film units went from less than 100 in 1950 to 12,579 in 1958, of which there were 8,384 film mobile projection teams and 1,559 film projection units dedicated to minority regions and peoples (Tong 2001: 38–41).

The narrative structure of Chen's recollection mirrors the politically ratified language of the Maoist period and provides a window into how subjectivity was articulated through movement from nationally produced texts to practices located in remote areas and relations with non-Han peoples. This returns us to the discursive importance of geographic space, and the ways in which film workers participated in the modernization practices and discourses of the People's Republic of China (PRC). In interviews in 2002 with film workers (Mao, Zhong), anecdotes circulated of humorous incidents that punctuated first exposures to film in rural China. These included audiences running away from the cars on the screen, staring in wonder at the machinery on display, or a story of villagers who prepared a large elaborate meal at the conclusion of the film screenings with the misunderstanding that the actors on screen were actually present. These anecdotes, which took the form of occupational lore given that they often were presented as second or third hand stories, reinforced the pioneering role of film on the frontiers and upheld the modern(izing) position of film projectionists. Yet the Chinese filmic landscape is more complicated in the early Maoist period than a simple assertion of the authority of film workers as modernizing agents over the local.[3] We must remember that while the networks of film projectionists were both centrifugal and centripetal, the film projectionists themselves were largely peasants from the regions they served, even if they generally were not from the most remote areas or non-Han populations. They thus operated within and between the forms and levels of communities they produced and mediated.

One film ticket salesperson from Hubei province, Ma Shijun, spoke directly about her negotiation of this transactional position (Tong 2001: 47–48). She stated that the most important work for the new film industry in the 1950s was serving the peasants. In order to do this one had to ensure that the peasants could see, understand, and benefit from film. For Ma this was an issue of access to film through an increased number of venues and decreased ticket prices; at the same time, it was about enlarging her own understanding of peasants and film so that she could ensure that audiences/Chinese citizens would be served by film. The films she recalls being particularly well received were scientific films such as *Villages Safely Use Electricity* (Nongcun anchuan yong dian) that explicitly showcased technological modernization. Other films addressed health and sanitation issues, as well as patriotism. Here we can identify a double self-positioning. On one hand, Ma saw film and film workers as people who brought modern technologies and knowledge to the peasants. In this regard she was an extrinsic modernizing agent. On the other hand, she immersed herself in the local to make her more successful as a facilitator of the transfer of technology, knowledge, and modern cultural competencies. In this manner, film workers functioned as localized cultural translators.

The transactional and transformative work of film projectionists can be seen in the ways in which they traversed discursive and physical terrain that interwove the local, national, and international. Here it is useful to consider film projectionists through Raymond Williams's structure of feeling: "the distilled residue of the organization of the lived experience of a community over and above the institutional and ideological organization of the society" (Williams 1977: 132). Moreover, film projectionists' position in and across the interstices of lived experiences of community draws our attention to the alternative structures film workers produced as they disseminated texts and practices. These texts and practices were specifically articulated to a new socialist society, with the aim of liberating human capacities of cognition, affect, and volition for socialist goals. Recognizing the spaces of the textual communities and practices of film work in Maoist China and the attendant theories of human liberation, we also come to challenge scholars' acceptance of Raymond Williams's characterization of the image of the country as an image of the past and the image of the city as an image of the future (Williams 1973). The spatio-temporal framings of rural and urban communities in Maoist China were far more complex because the processes of modernization, proletarianization, and peasant-based socialist revolution abutted each other in theory and praxis so that rural spaces and remote areas were made central to the correct unfolding of these processes.

MAPPING LEVELS OF COMMUNITY
AND THEIR INTERACTIONS

With the military victory of the CCP over the Guomindang (GMD) in 1949, and the subsequent uncontested championing on the mainland that national liberation was intrinsically linked to the history of the CCP, film history entered a new phase in which the rhetoric and praxis of liberation of space was mirrored by the restructuring of the film industry (Fu 2003; Clark 1987). The restructuring involved centralization and decentralization such that the work of the film projectionists participated in the combined centripetal and centrifugal dynamics of the national. Moreover, the filmic texts in circulation shared with Soviet cinema a politics of mapping. As Emma Widdis has argued in the context of the Soviet Union:

> cinematic images mapped a single Soviet space in which centre and periphery were interdependent, documenting the construction of socialism at the level of the region. The consolidation of the centre depended, rhetorically, on the actions of the periphery; the achievements of the "little man" were a source of national pride. (Widdis 2003: 16)

Not only did the filmic texts imagine the nation in terms of the interaction between center and periphery, so too did the extra-filmic discursive frameworks and the practices of film workers.

Extra-filmic discursive frameworks of film used tropes of the old society versus the new to signify the availability of film to rural areas and workplaces as markers of the new society that socialism delivered. Much work was done to emphasize the modernity of film and to encourage recognition by Chinese that a filmic modernity was made possible by the CCP and "the people" it invoked (Chen 2003). In this regard, the lyrics to a Sichuan projection unit song are telling: "I am a member of the People's projection unit, [I] go quickly to the remote mountains and dense forests. In order to illuminate the silver screen, [my] footprints cover a thousand villages and ten thousand homes" (Anonymous 1964: 44). The footsteps of the film projectionist bring to mind Walter Benjamin's remark on the map as a Russian iconic cult. Benjamin recalled a map of Europe hanging in a Red Army Club that marked all the cities Lenin visited. He wrote: "On it Lenin's life resemble[d] a campaign of colonial conquest" (Benjamin 1986: 118). In the Chinese context, the Sichuan projectionists' song invoked a similarly inflected visual rhetoric and praxis, particularly through its relationship to the Tibetan people and region.

Film projection units in Sichuan were tasked with providing film to Tibet and other so-called border regions accessible from Sichuan. The work of film projectionists in Sichuan, in practice and in the ways in which it was reported for national consumption, could not be disarticulated from the entrance of PLA troops into Tibet in 1950. As a result, their work was embedded in the larger textual communities that established Tibet's relationship to the PRC. Similar to other regions that came under the influence of the PLA and CCP, and as captured in films inspired by *Democratic Northeast* previously discussed, the presence of the PLA and CCP in Tibet acquired national meaning as liberation (Anonymous 1950: 5). This included the documentary film *Tibetan Liberation Troops* (Jiefang Xizang dajunxing) that recorded the work of soldiers who overcame mountain barriers to build public roads and make Tibet accessible to film directors, projectionists, and Han Chinese viewers (Xu 1952: 29; 1953: 31). Feature films similarly focused on the modernizing potential of the CCP in partnership with ethnic minorities.[4]

The rendering of Tibet as liberated territory within the PRC required, on the most fundamental level, new maps and visual material that captured the integration. The visual references in mass circulation included a full-page photographic montage in *Renmin ribao* (11 November 1950: 5) depicting the PLA entering Tibet that culminated on the bottom right-hand corner of the page with a map of Tibet. The map stood out from the page because of its black ink on white against an array of black and white photos that had predominantly dark backgrounds, giving it added authority as the result of the unfolding of a particular historical narrative. Other texts then linked the work of film projectionists in the region to the new conditions of everyday life made possible in Tibet.

As we continue to consider how maps, globes, and other practices linked to mapping are constitutive of the interplay between textual communities and communities of practice related to film in Maoist China, it is worth considering Ella Shohat and Robert Stam's analysis of the tropes of "virgin land" in the colonial imagination. They argue that an aura of scientific knowledge accompanied maps and globes to legitimate the accounts of inclusion and conquest (Shohat and Stam 1994: 145–48). We can also supplement Shohat and Stam's framework of colonial conquest by considering Doane's analysis of "statistics as rupturing classical ways of thinking the relation between the particular and the general, the individual and the mass, as a logic particularly appropriate for mass culture" (Doane 2002: 112). This allows us to interrogate the overlapping textual and practiced communities invoked by maps and the globe, approaches to cinema as modern machine, and the preoccupation of the Chinese state with the reach of film/modernity tracked through the scientific aura of national statistics. Specifically by looking at how state categories for film data collection defined the contours of the nation-state, we can analyze how these categories elucidate the centrifugal and centripetal dynamics of a nation–state community under construction. Moreover, because statistics produce discursive categories even as they record practices, this is a key place to analyze the interplay between textual communities and communities in practice.

Film distribution reports published for film workers in the main trade journal *Dianying faxing tongxun* (Film Distribution Report) reflect the categories for reporting film viewership. The reports divided the country into the major regions of Huabei (North China), Dongbei (Northeast), Xibei (Northwest), Huadong (East China), Zhongnan (South Central), and Xinan (Southwest). The geographical terms presumed a center, which coincided with the positioning of Beijing. Within these geographic categories, Tibet and Xinjiang held special status and Xinjiang regularly moved in and out of the statistical category of Xibei (Northwest).[5] For these regional categories and in the calculation of national data, the following type of information was recorded: location of screening (theater, workplace, union, rural community), type of print (16mm or 35mm), audience attendance figures (sometimes broken down in terms of age), type of film (feature, documentary, short, or scientific), and national origin of the film (Chinese, socialist country, capitalist). Data collection thereby mapped the nation through film availability in such a way that it acknowledged the specificity of the urban theater experience, while it simultaneously subsumed that specificity under a newly instituted national filmic community. The new national filmic community, by its sheer numbers was one in which rural communities enveloped urban spaces. Published statistics in *Dianying faxing tongxun* reinforced the scope and nature of this national community by providing comprehensive data in every issue. National data showcased large numbers of viewers typically in the millions or tens of millions. In so doing these statistics placed viewership of any one film within a larger historical movement and phenomenon. Moreover, publicly available data on audience numbers for specific films existed only for the most popular films. The national experience of film thereby was linked to viewership of films that had the broadest circulation. These were films that the CCP pre-determined as successful films and therefore the requisite numbers of 16mm prints were produced. The result, in practice and in the national statistics, was that the national experience was predicated upon films that circulated in the "remote areas" rather than the films that had limited runs in urban theaters. In this way, film and film data offered a decentralized national map that included but did not prioritize the major cities of Eastern China such as Shanghai, Beijing, Guangzhou, and Harbin.

The circulation of localized data to film workers generally reinforced the dialectical interaction between decentralization and centralization in film work. When *Dianying faxing tongxun* (1953: 3) published audience figures for small villages in Dongbei such as Xinteluociji, Kuaile, Hong, and Heihai—each of which had a population ranging from 130 to 400 adults and 29 to 191 children—it used statistical data to reinforce claims that film served the people of China. In this manner, the national community envisioned through film work was one that rested upon a dialectical relationship between center and periphery; one that constantly referred to the dependence of the national on the cumulative effect of millions of small villages engaged in the same activities. The national community therefore was not only directed from the center, the re-mapping of China as the PRC was also an exercise of decentering the national for the local so that national statistics were to be read as a multiplication of local experiences. This is not to suggest, however, that the PRC envisioned a multi-local and hetero-geneous nation. The historical role assumed by the CCP and PRC deemed otherwise; and film followed suit. In this respect, local experiences of film were scripted through centralized materials that sought to explain to "the people" how, why, and to what end they were members of the nation.

TEMPORAL CONSOLIDATIONS OF INTERNATIONAL AND NATIONAL HISTORY

In her exploration of the individual and social fantasies of film and the spaces in which these fantasies become available in public, Stephanie Donald draws our attention to regimes of truth. She analyzes how regimes of truth function to legitimate governing structures and map the meaning of the nation onto one version of past events, with the purpose of invoking national authenticity. Donald productively suggests that truth does not exist apart from communication and that "film can narrate the present, and the political imaginary of that present, in ways that produce forms of human association based on spectatorship" (Donald 2000: 28). Her analysis of cultural public space and the ways in which films participate in this space are organized around theorization of the spectator, on one hand, and readings of community on film and through the voice/visuality of the filmmaker, on the other. Another point of entry into films' participation in mapping national history and space would be to consider how film workers gave film social meaning through specific narratives of History. This takes us to considering how film projectionists made sense of films for the people who viewed them and the mutual implication as lived experience of History with forms and levels of community.

The duties of film projectionists included not only screening films and maintaining equipment but they were also responsible, in urban and rural areas, for educating people on conventions of viewing and the meaning of film. This work entailed giving audiences basic history lessons, illus-trated by the propaganda materials that accompanied films. Introductions to films focused on the plots and related the film content to current politi-cal campaigns and the "new era" of China. On and off the screen, this meant frequent references to key moments in the anti-imperialist struggle and national liberation, as well as the claiming of subject positions in the modern socialist nation by "the people." As war/adventure films consti-tuted one of the genres (in addition to popular scientific films) that the CCP asserted was most liked by rural viewers certain historic moments loomed larger than others. For Chinese-produced films some of the most popular films featured the stories of martyrs who died fighting either the Guomin-dang or the Japanese in the late 1940s. The fascination with the historic

Figure 5.2 Sichaun female film projection unit 814 introduce the content of the film *Bumper Harvest* (Fengshou) to commune members. 1954. (China National Photography Archive. Accession No. 218224)

struggle of the 1940s in CCP culture accompanied institutionalization of film as public text. Esther Yau refers to this as a "textual weaving of a teleology" in which individual impression and emulation merged with History and Tradition to create a hegemonic system of political culture and experience (Yau 1990: 264). But within Maoist China, the History and Tradition expressed through public texts was explicitly international and national.

In 1951, at the age of 18, Wang Baoyi began her career as a rural film projectionist. In her recollection (Tong 2001: 135–38), she writes of the first films she showed. Upon arrival in a village, the villagers asked what type of shadow play they would be seeing. She responded that it was "real film" and that if they waited until the evening they would understand what the real "electric shadows" of the theaters were, using the language of modernization and authenticity that I indicated earlier in this chapter was characteristic of film work. Wang then went on to offer the following account:

> We started the film projector, the light came on, the film appeared on the screen, it was *The Fall of Berlin* (Gongke Bolin). There were 5,000 to 6,000 people in the audience, they filled the space, the rooftops, trees.... There were no sounds except the birds and the breathing of the audience. In the end there wasn't a single person who didn't watch.

Notably, the first film that this community saw was not a Chinese film but a Soviet film. As one of the most popular films during the 1950s,[6] and a historically based film that recounts the battle for Berlin at the end of

World War II, *The Fall of Berlin* returns us to the geographies of socialism and History articulated through film and film work in Maoist China.

The international geographies within which film workers like Wang Baoyi operated linked Soviet and Chinese history in various ways, including the screening of Soviet films for Chinese audiences and the larger political interactions between the Soviet Union and China. At the textual level, films like *The Fall of Berlin* and *Village Schoolteacher* reinforced the juxtaposition evident in Chinese film culture, as well as the larger politico-aesthetics of the early Maoist period, of mapped representations of the past (that were imperialist and urban centered) versus mapped representations of the present and future. In *Village Schoolteacher*, as discussed in the opening section, the globe signified enlightenment and the success of revolutionary history. *The Fall of Berlin* utilized maps to reinforce the anti-fascist and liberatory foundations of the Soviet state. In a series of scenes culminating in Hitler's withdrawal into the inner sanctum of the Chancellery and his suicide, Hitler frantically grabs, clutches, and confronts maps but never pauses to systematically study them. As Hitler's withdrawal into the interior begins, winds blow through the Chancellery, maps fly off the table, and the camera shoots Hitler from above to show him as a man battered down by the maps behind him and unable to control space or history. The film immediately cuts to a composed Stalin sitting at his desk deliberating with magnifying glass over the details of a map. Stalin's arms remain relaxed as they encircle the edges of the map. The image expresses in strikingly simple visual terms the dual aspects of Stalinist space: Stalin brings order to space and ordered space exists only within the reach of Stalin's embrace (see Figure 5.3).

Figure 5.3 The Fall of Berlin (1949). Dir. Mikheil Chiaureli.

In China, extra-filmic textual international communities also framed Stalin as an enabler of socialist space. These extra-filmic textual references undertook a temporal consolidation of History as one of the ways in which socialist geographies came into existence. For example, the front page of *Renmin ribao* on 7 November 1950 celebrated the 33rd anniversary of the October Revolution by exemplifying new constructions of space and time made possible by the victory of the CCP and the February 1950 Sino-Soviet Treaty of Friendship. Alongside a portrait photograph of Stalin, the paper

Figure 5.4 "Irresistible Force of Victory." (Originally published *Renmin ribao*, 7 November 1950)

printed short statements by the CPSU Central Committee, the CCP Central Committee, Mao Zedong, and Zhou Enlai. The statements praised the accomplishments of the October Revolution, with Mao Zedong concluding that the establishment of socialism in the Soviet Union allowed the people of the USSR and PRC to emerge as the protectors of world peace. Other articles on the page included one entitled "The Soviet Union is the Force of World Peace and Democracy" and another entitled "Korean People's Army Successfully Advances on Anzhou."

In the lower right hand corner, filling the space from the mid-fold to the foot, a cartoon ran (see Figure 5.4). This cartoon made explicit those whom the Chinese understood to be actors within a world history linked to the October Revolution and communities of revolutionary progress. The cartoon, with the caption "Irresistible Force of Victory—In commemoration of the thirty-third anniversary of the October Revolution," was composed of three squares that clearly outline the international imaginary through which world historical revolutionary communities were enacted. Square one, dated 1918 to 1920, showed an oversized Red Army soldier holding at gunpoint representatives of Czarist Russia, as well as England, France, the United States, Japan, and Poland. Square two, dated 1945, again featured the Red Army soldier who pinned down a Nazi soldier with one hand, and with the other held a Japanese soldier by his neck. Notably, in this frame, a Chinese People's Liberation Army soldier is visible—head only—and he has finished off the Japanese by skewering him with a bayonet. As the Soviets fight on two fronts, the Red Army soldier enables the Chinese to defeat the Japanese; but the decisive act of killing falls to the Chinese soldier. Frame three, dated "1950...," placed Red Army and PLA soldiers at the center, surrounded by light, doves of peace, and the people of China, the Soviet Union, Korea, Albania, and so on. Below these large figures the defeated huddle trying to suck life from a depleted US atomic bomb. The historical trajectory depicted in this cartoon mobilized explicit anti-imperialist and anti-fascist formulations that, in turn, render the triumphant joint struggle against imperialism and fascism the only possible future. The ellipses following the date in frame three reinforced the notion of a boundless future that rested upon Sino-Soviet cooperation. This cartoon, for many Chinese viewers, would be understood through recent viewings of *The Fall of Berlin* that brought together as diachronic historic moments Soviet and Chinese struggles against German and Japanese fascism, respectively, and the Chinese struggle against American imperialism in Korea.

The explicit and implicit associations between historical struggles in the Soviet Union and China, as well as contemporary struggles and friendships with Korean and other peoples fighting for national liberation and socialism constituted the broader context and political discourse framing screenings of Soviet films like *The Fall of Berlin* in early 1950s China (Chen 2004: 92–96). What I am interested in analyzing here is the temporal consolidation of History that became part of the localized practices of film workers. To do so, it is useful to consider the December issue of *Dazhong*

Figure 5.5 Full-page advertisement for Gongke Bolin (*The Fall of Berlin*). (Published in *Dazhong dianying* December 1950)

dianying (Popular Cinema). Alongside a full-page advertisement of *The Fall of Berlin* (see Figure 5.5) ran an article written by a director from the Democratic Republic of Korea about the development of Korean film (Yin 1950: 19).

The article began by explaining that with the aid of the Soviet Union, Korean film had been able to throw off the enslavement of politics and spirit imposed by Japanese imperialism. Author Yin Jieyan (Chinese transliteration) outlined the repressive nature of film from 1910 until the liberation of Korea by Soviet troops in 1945. While the article mentioned 1948 as a turning point because of American imperialism and the subsequent division of Korea, Yin took 1945 as the year in which Korean film began to develop. The article clearly privileged Soviet "liberation" and rendered this more historically significant than American intervention. In this manner, Yin reclaimed Korean film history (and history more generally) from imperialist powers. The real significance of 1948 then became that the Korean film industry produced a documentary film entitled *Friendship Forever* that commemorated the triumphant role of the Soviet army in the liberation of Korea. Yin concluded with the following proclamation:

> In order to produce even more progressive characters, Korean film workers need to study the artistic creation methods of Soviet socialist realism and study Soviet film workers. Soviet films are excellent textbooks for us, not only for our basic education but to help us study the great socialism of the Soviet Union, and make us fully appreciate the leadership of Comrade Stalin, so that we can grow and establish a communist nation. (Yin 1950: 19)

The relationships between peoples worldwide produced through international circulation of socialist films rested upon diachronic filmic and extra-filmic textual communities in which nations such as China and Korea joined a history already in progress.

Soviet films such as *The Fall of Berlin* contributed to internationalist communities in China not only through textual communities and film viewing practices within China, but also as the materials of international cultural exchange. This international cultural exchange encompassed more than importing Soviet film, however; as the passage from *Fifty Years of China Film* quoted at the beginning of this chapter indicated, it also involved the export of Chinese film. In this regard, the Chinese press enthusiastically reported on the success of Chinese films in the Soviet Union. In the 1950s, the films exported to the Soviet Union included many of those extolled by film projectionists as the most important in establishing the new era of Chinese film and socialism, like *Zhao Yiman* and *White-Haired Girl*. These films shared with their Soviet counterparts themes of struggle and liberation, often highlighting the anti-Japanese War of Resistance. Moreover, documentaries like the joint Sino-Soviet production *The Victory of China* (Zhongguo de Shengli) and Chinese-produced documentaries such as *Liberated China* (Jiefangle de Zhongguo) depicted the triumph of the Chinese Communist Party against both the Japanese and Guomindang, and participated in the textual and practical re-mapping of China discussed above.

The spatio-temporal dimensions of international and national textual communities and praxis informed *Renmin ribao* reporting on Soviet press coverage of a screening of *Liberated China* in Moscow (Xinhuashe 1950: 5). It highlighted connections between Soviet and Chinese history, past and future. The article stated that Soviet youth and Chinese youth were the same: they received the same education; they all studied Lenin. At the same time, the article relied upon characteristic categorizations of Sino-Soviet relations that showed the importance of the center in both Chinese and Soviet national geographies. The shared history of youth from China and the Soviet Union was said to exist despite the thousands of miles separating Chinese and Soviet youth. This spatial juxtaposition, of course, can be challenged by simple reminders of the extensive shared border between the Soviet Union and China. The thousands of miles reminded Chinese youth that internationalist communities were refracted through the prisms of Moscow and Beijing. Internationalism thus simultaneously emphasized and erased decentralized forces of History so evident in the textual communities of film and filmic communities in practice.

The synchronic and diachronic relationship between Soviet and Chinese history highlights the ways in which China, on the global stage, was simultaneously part of a socialist modernity (as represented by a Soviet future), and seeking to reach it. A similar dynamic marked the relationship between remote communities served by film workers and the national center. But this is not to suggest that rural Chinese spaces were more marginal to socialist modernity than the urban centers. Rather, the very framing of film work and the location of History and Struggle in China suggested otherwise. The epistemological communities of film were embedded in modernizing frameworks and teleologies of History that insisted upon the mutual dependence of center and periphery. The declared transformation of local and global therefore was inscribed within textual national and international communities that could only be realized through decentralized and localized practices. This operation of film on the Chinese landscape during the Maoist period then made film central to the intertwined local, national, and international subjectivities of Maoist History and Modernization.

NOTES

1. Research for this chapter was funded by the Social Sciences and Humanities Research Council of Canada. Chinese names in this chapter follow the Chinese convention of family name, personal name.
2. These films were produced by what is now known as Changchun Film Studios. The studio grew out of the Manchou Film Association Co, Ltd, which became the first base for film production established by the CCP on 1 October 1946 under the name Northeast Film Studio. The studio was renamed Changchun Film Studio in 1955. This studio was responsible for the first popular science film (*Prevention of Plague*), the first cartoon (*Go After an Easy Prey*), the first feature film (*Bridge*), and the first dubbed film (*An Ordinary Soldier*, from Russian).
3. I use the term *filmic* rather than *cinematic* to indicate the larger practices related to film that in the PRC are not necessarily tied to a movie theater or urban locations.
4. The use of film to create textual communities of inclusion and cooperation between Han and non-Han Chinese is evident in a number of films produced between 1959 and 1961. Typical plots are those which feature transformation of communities by an advanced minority tied to the CCP: see *A Distant Spark* (Yuan fang xing huo, 1961*)*, *A Green Land's Victory Song* (Lu zhou kai ge, 1959), *Moyai Dai* (Mo yai dai, 1960), and *A Song for Qiangs' Whistle* (Qiang di ge, 1960); or plots that see the merging of Han and non-Han as families: see *Daji and Her Father* (Da ji he ta de fu qin, 1961) and *Two Generations* (Liang dai ren, 1960). Film synopses available in Marion (1997).

5. Prior to the establishment by the Chinese state of Tibet as the Tibetan Autonomous Region in 1950, ethnic Tibetans were divided between "political" Tibet (the area ruled by the Dalai Lama) and ethnographic Tibet (those areas inhabited by ethnic Tibetans but to the east of political Tibet and the west of Han Chinese areas). Ethnographic Tibet included Kham (in present-day Sichuan and Yunnan province) and Amdo (in present-day Qinghai and Gansu).

6. On the 33rd anniversary of the October Revolution, a short article published in *Renmin ribao* 4 November 1950 announced that *The Fall of Berlin* had opened in 14 cities including Beijing, Tianjin, Liangnan, Dalian, Harbin, Shanghai, Nanjing, Hangzhou, Hankou, Guangzhou, Xian, and Dabei. On opening day, audience numbers reached 15,000 (Xinhuashe 1950b).

REFERENCES

Anonymous (1950) "Renmin jiefangjun jinjun Xizang (People's Liberation Army Enters Tibet)," *Renmin ribao*, 11 November, p. 5.

Anonymous (1964) "Buda xianfeng buzhibu (If you don't go to the perilous peaks you will not progress)," *Dazhong dianying*, 10/11.

Benjamin, W. (1986) *Reflections*, New York: Schocken.

Chen, T.M. (2003) "Propagating the Propaganda Film: The Meaning of Film in Chinese Communist Party Writings, 1949–1965," *Modern Chinese Literature and Culture*, 15.2: 154–93.

—— (2004) "Internationalism and Cultural Experience: Soviet Films and Popular Chinese Understandings of the Future in the 1950s," *Cultural Critique*, 58: 82–114.

Clark, P. (1987) *Chinese Cinema: culture and politics since 1949*, Cambridge: Cambridge University Press.

Dianying faxing tongxun (Film Distributuion Report). (1953).

Ding, Y. (1998) *Zhongguo dianying yishu, 1945–1949*, Beijing: Wenhua yishu chubanshe.

Doane, M. (2002) *The Emergence of Cinematic Time: modernity, contingency, the archive*, Cambridge, MA: Harvard University Press.

Donald, S. (2000) *Public Secrets, Public Spaces, Cinema and Civility in China*, Lanham, MD: Rowman and Littlefield.

Fu, P. (2003) *Between Shanghai and Hong Kong: the politics of Chinese cinema*, Stanford, CA: Stanford University Press.

Marion, D.J. (1997) *The Chinese Filmography, The 2444 Feature Films Produced by Studios in the People's Republic of China from 1949 through 1995*, Jefferson, NC: McFarland.

Shohat, E. and Stam, R. (1994) *Unthinking Eurocentrism: multiculturalism and the media*, London: Routledge.

Tong, G. (2001) *Zhongying wushinian*, Beijing: Zhongguo dianying gongsibian.

Widdis, E. (2003) *Visions of a New Land: Soviet film from the revolution to the Second World War*, New Haven and London: Yale University Press.

Williams, R. (1973) *The Country and the City*, New York: Oxford University Press.

—— (1977) *Marxism and Literature*, Oxford: Oxford University Press.

Xinhuashe (1950a) "'Jiefangle de Zhongguo' zai Sulian fangying zhenlibao he xiaoxi baozhe lun zanyang (A Tribute in Pravda and News of the Soviet Screening of 'Liberated China')," *Renmin ribao*, 25 December, p. 3.

—— (1950b) "Qingzhu Sulian geming sanshisan zhounian. Sulian mingpian 'Gongke Bolin' jiangzai wo guo shisi dachengshi fangying (Celebrating the 33rd anniversary of the October Revolution: Soviet Film 'The Fall of Berlin' opens in 14 large cities)," *Renmin ribao*, 4 November, p. 3.

Xu, J. (1952) "Ba dianying songdao Xizang qu (Sending film to Tibet)," *Dazhong dianying*, 7: 29.

—— (1953) "Jin Zang budui zai yinmyshang kandaole ziji (Troops entering Tibet see themselves on the silver screen)," *Dazhong dianying*, 2: 31.

Yau, E. (1990) Filmic discourse on women in Chinese cinema (1949–1965): Art, ideology and social relations. PhD dissertation. University of California, Los Angeles.

Yin, J. (1950) "Chaoxian dianying fazhan de daolu (The road of development of Korean film)," *Dazhong dianying*, 12: 19.

Interviews

Mao, Y., *Personal Interview*, 8 July 2002.
Zhong, G., *Personal Interview*, 12 July 2002.

6 Transnational communities of affinity
Patricio Guzmán's *The Pinochet Case*

Macarena Gómez-Barris

INTRODUCTION

Exile cultural production has conventionally been thought of as temporally frozen, or, in the context of traumatic memory, as frozen memory. That is, the condition of exile is treated as if one's affective investments in longing, nostalgia, loss, and melancholy were endless encounters with "working through" the original traumatic event. Of course, these affective subject positions are but one dimension of exile, and not its totality. Some of the often repeated terms that emerge to describe the exile's aesthetic include *rupture*, *discontinuity*, and *fracture*, terms that mire the figure of the political exile and her artistic endeavors in a web of endless bereavement. Moreover, in this framework the exile's experience is marked as isolated and reduced to the space of traumatic psychic repetition. What kinds of descriptions might emerge, however, if the metonymic possibility of continuity, rather than rupture, was the point of entry into a discussion of exilic cultural production? Indeed, framing the experience of exile as continuous with what came before, rather than disjuncture in its aftermath, has certain epistemological advantages, including being able to recognize particular cultural forms, habits, preferences, tastes, and intellectual and political formations that are reconstituted in the new location and passed on to similarly positioned subjects. This kind of entrance point is important on at least two levels. First, it moves the exile from a place of relative isolation and psychic discreteness, into a landscape that recognizes social worlds; and, second, it avows the possibility of challenging hegemonic models of absorption and assimilation into dominant national culture. The explicit focus on continuity as part of exile subjectivity, practices, and cultural production, like the function of hybridity (Garcia Canclini 1995, 2001), ensures that the exile is to some degree unassimilable into the host nation.

Let me be more specific. In the period after the forced exile of tens of thousands Chileans during and after the military takeover,[1] particular aesthetic forms that were mapped onto revolutionary struggle and ideology during the Allende period continued to influence the terrain of exile, exile subjectivity, and social struggle. This was particularly so in the arenas of human rights, critiques of globalization, and critiques of US imperialism, which worked to disrupt national hegemonic memory processes, especially from the space of the transnational. In changing historical conditions, documentary film served variegated and, again I'd contend, political purposes. First, documentaries archived the counterrevolution by the political right, culminating in President Allende's death, the death of a social dream, and the installation of the military dictatorship. Second, outside of the Southern Cone, documentaries informed audiences about the violence of state terrorism, condemned its authors, and mobilized international condemnation of the military junta. From the location of dictatorship these films were tainted as subversive and were censored. By contrast, in "el exterior" they triggered human rights movements and served as visual testimony and witness for extreme rights violations. Third, documentaries worked to disrupt public debate about the past, specifically by directors who intended to rupture the political consensus of "olvido" (forgetting) in the technocratic, seamless management of the transition from authoritarianism to democracy.[2] Fourth, documentaries tackled the persistent effects of living with loss in everyday life, and its very personal and intimate manifestations, including sexual torture and the psychological effects of captivity. And fifth, documentary films imagined and reconnected communities of Chileans from Santiago to London, recording the unending encounter with loss and its productive use among exile activists.

CINEMATIC WITNESS

Many of Patricio Guzmán's documentary films (*The Battle of Chile*, 1979; *Obstinate Memory*, 1997; *The Pinochet Case*, 2001; and *Salvador Allende*, 2004) are rooted in a radical tradition of documentary filmmaking in Latin America, especially the new Latin American Cinema movement first articulated by Fernando Birri in the 1970s and characterized by the double commitment to artistic innovation and social transformation. This genre expressed the signs of the time by registering the massive mobilizations and social, economic, and political changes of the revolutionary nation that often were elaborated through aesthetic movements. In Chile, there was a massive collective effort by artists, theater performers, and musicians to engage "lo popular." These aesthetic movements, like the radical filmmaking that would follow, had connections to Brechtian theater of the oppressed, which aimed to represent collective experience and to raise consciousness about specific conditions, exercised through innovative techniques. Historically, the medium of social documentary was closely linked, in ideological and concrete ways, to these cultural efforts and to Salvador Allende's ascent to the presidency. Indeed, the *Unidad Popular* government funded the national cinema project Chile Films. Jacqueline Mouseca has discussed that with the onset of the dictatorship: "Chilean cinema suffered its share of repression" (1988: 137). Like other artistic interventions, during the authoritarian period, documentary was constituted and coded as a subversive project thus many films were destroyed and the site of Chile Films was permanently shut down by the military regime. Further, repression created a mass exodus of filmmakers to other nations, virtually stopping film production in Chile for the duration of Pinochet's reign. In stark contrast, during the first 10 years of exile outside the country some 178 films were made, the largest historical production in a single period by Chilean directors.

The majority of the film productions made in exile moved within the genre of documentaries, ranging from the denouncement of dictatorship to those that emphasized Chile's historical memory (Mouseca 1988: 144–45). The issue of exile was also a focus of many films, perhaps best represented by National Film Board (NFB) of Canada's production, director Marilú Mallet's 1982 *Journal inachevé* (Unfinished Diary). These films share common themes, a proliferation of narratives that politically worked to counter, denounce, and expose the effects of state terrorism from a transnational location. Further, after these social dreams were eradicated, especially for the context of Chile, and maybe even for Argentina, documentaries about the past worked to destabilize and renarrativize the present and force open future imaginings, especially when made in exile.

Significantly, exile produced a kind of ideological continuity in modes of production, extending the New Latin American Cinema from the earlier topic of revolution, to the later effort to illuminate and constitute a social and cultural field of memory. As Patricio Guzmán intones, "Memory matters. The historical memory of a nation shapes its expectations. It may be terribly painful to speak of terrors and tragedies of the past. But the truth inspires hope, and that inspires the will for social change" (Aufderheide 2002: 25). Like other filmmakers working in this genre, Guzmán produced a film language of social memory with the purpose of reshaping the dictatorship's historical reconstruction of events.[3]

In *The Pinochet Case*, Guzmán achieves a representation of social memory by threading two narratives together. The main narrative thread in the film provides a chronological explanation of the events leading up to Pinochet's arrest, his attempted extradition to Spain, and its legal and political aftermath. As if to contrast the voluminous false discourses propagated by Pinochet and his supporters about how those that were disappeared "must be in Miami on vacation," and "civil war," the documentary carefully mounts its evidence against Pinochet and his dictatorship at a deliberately slow and meditative pace. The second narrative thread of the film is a series of testimonials by survivors and the story of London and Santiago human rights activists and their political battles. Here, portraying the connection between Chilean communities around the world, and their identification with the Allende period, its legacies, and survival (i.e., exiles, relatives of those who were disappeared, and torture victims) becomes central to the ethical impact of the film on audiences.

TESTIFYING SURVIVAL

Patricio Guzmán has gained international recognition for documenting the complex field of social memory produced by the dictatorship and its aftermath. The first film *The Battle for Chile* (1979), provided the chronology of the steps to counterrevolution, ending with the dramatic visual footage of the September 11, 1973 military coup that included the archetypal image of the bombing of La Moneda Palace. Through conversations with different social groups within Chile, including students at a public university, students in business school, Allende's former bodyguards, and groups of now elderly former *Unidad Popular* activists, the second film *Obstinate Memory* (1997), unveiled how violence and trauma are latent themes in the social unconscious. The third film, *The Pinochet Case* (2001) uses Augusto Pinochet's 1998 London arrest as the springboard for an intimate look at private and public battles over memory and its recuperation, especially between exiles and survivors, on the one hand, and Pinochet supporters, on the other.

In the opening sequences, several relatives of "Sergio," a brother and son who was disappeared at the age of 18, sit together, and in turn comment on the exhumation of remains. Sergio's mother and brother each give a testament of his life and the impact of his death, testimonials that are punctuated by tears and gestures of sorrow. Though quick paced editing can heighten the emotional tension in to film, Guzmán leaves long sequences in the testimonies unedited, which has the effect of giving primacy survivors' stories. At the end of the sequence, a man turns intently to the camera and says:

> I'd also like to say something. What happened here was a crime. And that's what a dictatorship is. That's the government of Augusto Pino-chet: Eighteen year olds murdered and left here, torn from their family. And so many others disappeared and died horrible deaths. This is Pinochet's government, death…murder.[4]

Throughout this sequence, and notably at the end of the last testimony, the camera stays focused on the subjects for several seconds of silence. Through the visual presence of those who have experienced loss, the film produces ethical unsettlement in the viewer, forcing a confrontation with violence's effects. Moreover, silence is constituted as a prediscursive strategy that stands in for those things that are outside the boundaries of what testimonies and gestures are able to communicate, excess that remains *in view* of the camera and *out of* the audio track. The man's intent stare into the camera and the long silence begs for an emotional and perhaps political response from the viewer. This is a response that is simultaneously provoked by the parallel story, namely, the quest for accountability from legal institutions. The only audible sound on the track is the desert wind, which gives the scene an eerie quality and takes the viewer into another dimension of reality, death, and living. In this scene, Guzmán makes cinematic space for the seething presence of those who were disappeared and whose material remains continued to be preserved by the arid desert conditions.

Part of Guzmán's filmic vision, it seems, is to produce empathetic attachment. For instance, the powerful statements of denouncement from legal experts and scholars are shot in the intimate spaces of their homes and private offices. Seated comfortably in front of a table, we meet Judge Joan Garcés. Discussing a group of approximately 50 Chilean witnesses brought to Spain to testify against Pinochet's crimes, Judge Garcés explains:

> All the witnesses were moved simply by the fact that a judge had received them with dignity. The moral compensation they received, their satisfaction and emotion when a judge listened to them for the first time in their lives. They said, "It's not possible in Chile. The judges will not see us."

Rather than specularize violence, Guzmán chooses to let the content of the testimonial sink in as the camera stays on the lines and expression of the now silent subject. This stylistic device is used throughout the documentary to represent survivors; the camera, through close-ups shots of the face and medium-shots of the face and body, identifies for the audience the victims and survivors of Pinochet's regime.[5]

Guzmán presents testimonies from five women (and one man) simply titled by their first names. Through these portraits, he explores the gendered memory of emotional pain, repressed memories, loss, and witness. Gabriela is in the middle of telling her story when we encounter her. She says:

> When you've had electric shocks for a long time, you're left unable to move, as if your arms, your legs, you can't make them work. It's almost as if you're a rag and it must also be the terror you feel then. So then this guy...not to get information from me, but a case of pure rape. He started to rape me. I had the strength to say "I'm a political prisoner, not something for you to abuse." [Pause]. I don't know, maybe because I wasn't in any kind of condition for a rape...I probably didn't have the answer so he put his penis in my mouth...and he tried to force me and I tried to defend myself. I noticed something strange. This wasn't part of the interrogation. It was part of something else. The notion that we weren't people...anyone could do anything. I was a woman. It was made harder for the women. This isn't just my story. It is the story of

many. Although I feel this wasn't part of it, I think it was an attempt to break you. They would say to you: "It doesn't matter if you don't talk now, I have all the time in the world. No one knows where you are. They'll never find you. Reporters won't show up. No doctors will show up. You are in our power." That was their discourse.

During her testimony, Gabriela oscillates between weaping and silence, heightening the severity of her words. Guzmán positions this testimonial after those of pain and loss to create empathetic unsettlement in the viewer. That is, after we are given the context for these subjects' loss, Guzmán turns to hearing directly from a survivor of torture and rape. He mobilizes a range of emotions and experiences of victimhood as a dense portrayal of the terror imaginary. Gabriela's testimony relays the desire by military operatives and the dictatorship to exert total control over the prisoner, in an effort to break down the opposition. There's a sense in these testimonials by women that breaking down also means erasing women's social agency, namely reestablishing the patriarchal "order" through the control of women's bodies. Gabriela's testimony (though probably unwittingly) echoes indigenous activist Rigoberta Menchú, when she says, "This isn't just my story. It is the story of many."

Perhaps the most troubling narrative is that of Ofelia's, a testimony that breaks through silences kept between a mother and daughter. Ofelia is shown sitting next to her daughter when she says:

> Life in general in Villa Grimaldi was a torture in itself. We were blindfolded all day, weren't given any food. I think that during that month sixty people went through Villa Grimaldi and around forty disappeared. Only twenty of us went out alive. [Drawing, she says,] The street was here, and an iron gate here, where the trucks and cars came in. There was a big house here with two or three floors for offices. Then came a kind of patio, a gallery with some columns. There was a room here where the DINA guards were, and another room here...this is where I was. I had a window overlooking the yard, the pool was here...and a door here that led into another gallery.... Right in front of here was the torture room. At the torture cell there was a man at a typewriter, and a metal bed where they tortured people. There was a portrait here, a copper etching of Che Guevara. We'd see people enter through here. "There goes so and so." It was so close that you could hear, despite the loud music to cover the screams.... You could hear them....

And then, Guzmán says, "Did you ever tell your daughter?" Ofelia responds, "No never. Not to my daughter or anyone else. Not my family, no one. I pretended nothing had happened. I even tried to believe it because I was alive. That's how it had to be.... The others are dead, so you try to be happy and grateful." "Manuela, you never asked your mother?" Guzmán asks. "No, I never asked her. I didn't dare," Manuela replies. Guzmán insists, and Manuela says:

> Why? I didn't want to hurt her, because you could see she didn't want to talk about it, and I didn't want to hear about it. You just always imagine. I knew they'd done something to her, tortured her. You always imagine terrible things...and I thought...yes, of course, she'd been tortured, beaten, shocked and, more than anything the sexual aspect made me back off...I didn't want to know. Today is the first time I've heard her say it."

Ofelia reveals the sexual torture she underwent at the concentration camp Villa Grimaldi, while her daughter listens to her intense descriptions. By including this testimonial, Guzmán reinforces the widespread and differential pain that was exerted on women's captive bodies by military and secret police forces. In fact, the 2004 Valech Report (officially known as the National Commission on Political Imprisonment and Torture Report) that documented the experiences of over 30,000 survivors found that over 95 per cent of women captives were raped. When Guzmán asks Manuela if she knew about the tragic experiences her mother had undergone, she responds that she had imagined it, but never knew the details. Rather than look at her mother Ofelia keeps her eyes focused to her side, presumably where Guzmán is sitting. The lack of eye contact between mother and daughter and their fixed positions on the screen (i.e., there is no hand gesturing and little facial expression) renders the shame and stigma that sexual torture brings to survivors and the silence in its wake. As the victim of sexual torture, Ofelia was doubly silenced—by the shame put on victims of rape in society more generally, and, by the enforced silence, namely the censorship of dictatorship in most of the transition to democracy period in Chile.

On the one hand, Guzmán's powerful decision to highlight women survivors helps to shatter the official narrative that violations were necessary, exposes the patriarchal glossing of gendered effects, and suggests the power of the desire for narrative closure within neoliberal democratic Chile. On the other hand, Guzmán reproduces the problematic tying of women to the nation—that is, of figuring women as bearers of the nation's grief.[6] Even though Guzmán recycles the familiar trope "woman as victim of the nation," it is also the case that the testimonials help counter the [other film narrative which is] predominantly male, legal and elite.[7] In addition, Guzmán lets the voices of women subjects emerge, and thus we are privy to their complex subjectivities, their humor, nightmarish memories, powerful political analyses, and embodied resilience.

In the film, these experiences are also transmitted through the performative gathering of groups of survivors, who are captured as they enter the room and assemble together, and later shown as a series of still shots, echoing scenes in Gillo Pontecorvo's famous film, *Battle of Algiers* (1966) (see John Mowitt, this volume). The camera pauses on each face with the sound track in silence, moving slowly to make the next survivor visible in the scene. Silence in these shots forces the viewer to presence the suffering and loss of survivors and to imagine their daily survival. In this sense, by portraying victims as visible and powerful subjects, Guzmán creates a solution to the crisis of representation that dictatorship and democracy produce, which can never fully account for the past.

TRANSNATIONAL LOCATIONS

Patricio Guzmán's films, like other documentaries that thematicize atrocity, call upon international human rights networks, circuits, and actors to make visible their versions of history, in this case by revealing the legacies of Chile's haunted past. For instance, *The Pinochet Case* was shown on British television and screened across Europe and the United States, including at the 2002 Human Rights Watch International Film Festival in London and New York, winning numerous international prizes, such as at the Amnesty International Film Festival.[8] These public spheres gave Guzmán, human rights organizations, and Chilean activists access to sympathetic audiences who are both potential makers of collective action and likely channels of material resources.[9] To fit into the programmatic objectives of Amnesty International and Human Rights Watch, the documentary had to be imagined first by Guzmán as doing a particular kind of work; as I mentioned previously, like the Latin American Cinema movement, and Theater of the Oppressed before it, this view of cultural production subscribes that art is also a platform for education, political action, and solidarity. At the same time, in tidbits from film synopses and promotions, it becomes clear how the film's distribution relies upon liberal rights discourses, the foundation of the global organizational infrastructure of human rights.[10] The film was reviewed by Human Rights Watch as providing "powerful insight into human suffering and survival" through "harrowing accounts of how (survivors) were subjected to horrific torture and interrogation in the regime's secret prisons." In fact, the film, and human rights movements more broadly, assume a negative conception of rights, or what many have deemed as security rights, wherein the citizen surrenders "to the state the power to protect our lives and our property."[11]

Though legal efforts may reinforce subjection to the state and its legal apparatus, I'm not entirely convinced that grassroots efforts operate under the same logic with similar consequences. For instance, the film shows global networks of human rights activism (including the work of lawyers and judges) that denounce the murders, disappearances, and suffering during the Pinochet era. Portraying how Chileans come together in major cities around the world makes explicit the stakes in reproducing memories and identities that emerge from the temporality and experiences of dictatorship. The framework of 'irruptions of memory' coined by Wilde may offer another vantage point from which to understand the significance of these mobilizations. As Wilde states, these are:

> public events that break in upon Chile's national consciousness, unbidden and often suddenly, to evoke associations with symbols, figures, causes, ways of life which to an unusual degree are associated with a political past that is still present in the lived experience of a major part of the population. (1999: 473)

Even though the multiply situated mobilizations address the global dimension of the Pinochet legal case, it is also clear that this story emerges from the particular location of the nation, made explicit in the film's opening. Judge Guzmán is shown searching in the Atacama desert of Northern Chile, a region where many collective gravesites have been unearthed. He states:

> Each body that we find means another step towards social peace. The main emphasis of the case I'm presiding [over] is to ensure justice continues to be served, to find out who was responsible for the crimes as well as to find the bodies. We have travelled all over the country, and we've found many remains, the result of this violence.

Later the international judicial counterparts of Guzmán, Spanish Judge Garzón and human rights lawyer Joan Garcés, appear in the film (though Judge Garzón makes silent appearances since he was legally prohibited to comment on the case). This opening duplicates the objective of the main film narrative to showcase how the unprecedented legal human rights case emerges from an unresolved national tragedy. Ironically, and tellingly, in Chile the film has circulated minimally, perhaps because of the censorship encoded by the transition to democracy period. The film's lasting contribution, however, is that while it has yet to circulate much within the country it displays an unbounded imaginary, travelling across borders, nations, public spaces, and gendered identities to show the implications and constituencies of the Pinochet case.

In Guzmán's documentary, the viewer witnesses the deep social bonds created by exiles and the Chilean political left, extending from Chile's Pacific to Europe's Atlantic. Through street protests that use drums, banners, slogans from the Allende period, theater, and puppets one can easily imagine a community of affinity that crosses national spaces. The role of exiles in Guzmán's film is especially interesting because there has often been a perception that exiles did not bear the burden of dictatorship. While there is compassion among some Chileans for the struggles over identity that the children of exiles have confronted, sometimes there is a kind of resentment directed at those who "abandoned" the country and political struggle against dictatorship.[12] Most discussions of exile recognize the precarious positions in which exiles are put when they make the decisions to leave their homelands. As Bharati Mukherjee relates, "In the case of exile, the comparative luxury of self-removal is replaced by harsh compulsion. The spectrum of choice is gravely narrowed; the alternatives may be no more subtle than death, imprisonment, or a one-way ticket to oblivion" (1999: 73). The perception of abandoning the cause stems from the fact that at the time of the military coup few imagined its 17-year duration and the capacity of the military regime to sustain authoritarian control. Thus, the notion of abandoning a cause was heightened by what many perceived as preemptive exile, even amidst a climate of dramatic repression.

Of course, the stereotypes of exiles were and continue to be a mythology about the other, myths that Guzmán addresses in the film, although somewhat indirectly. Positive images of Chilean exiles gathering together in prominent places in London, or outside the clinic where Pinochet was arrested, collectively working together to bring justice to victims, show explicit commitment to the political project of making the dictatorship accountable for its crimes. It also illustrates an emotional connection to the historical outcome of the dictatorship that generations of exiles continue to identify with, even after almost three decades of "separation" from Chile.[13] The scenes in the film work to unpack the misconceptions of Chilean exile communities; they also connect witnesses across nations to show the persistence of activism in the aftermath of dictatorship. The camera is a register of cultural memory and agency across transnational spaces, with a potential to counter dominant forgetting about the violent past.

UNRAVELING DRAMAS

It would be difficult to argue that the drama that unfolded during Augusto Pinochet's arrest was not the prototypical "irruption of memory" which Wilde theorizes. In fact, it seems that the media event of global proportions actually came to define the postdictatorship period, even though as my informants tell me, the political impact on national human rights efforts was minimal in the short-term.[14] What Guzmán captures is both a national and global perspective, filming in London, Santiago, and Madrid to create an audiovisual narrative of a transnational irruption of memory. These affiliations provide a social network that, in the Pinochet case, began to transcend even country of origin, as it revived human rights debates and activism internationally. In some ways, the "second" narrative of street scenes and activism outplays the formal legal moves. In one pivotal scene, which connects these parallel narratives, Guzmán's camera lingers in the empty chamber of the English House of Lords as a woman "cleans up" after them. Guzmán uses the sound of the vacuum echoing in the chamber and the excessive shots of emptiness as metaphorical cues to the viewer, suggesting the empty and noisy political rhetoric and maneuvers by official government bodies.

The legal scenes are juxtaposed not only by the intimate portraits of victims and survivors, but also by vibrant street scenes where the spectacle of death and torture is invoked and performed by social activists, a move that reveals the stakes of empty legal rhetoric. Bodies march downtown in Santiago with their heads "encapuchados," covered by black cloth with rope tied around the base of the neck. The covered heads represent dictatorship torture, specialized practices that were exercised in concentration camps and torture chambers throughout the 1970s. We are startled by the emblematic choices of the protestors, who confront us with the dramatic elements of torture during Pinochet's reign. As the narrator says, "In Santiago, impatient with the slowness of the judicial process groups of young people organized to denounce in their own terms, the ex-torturers and the professionals responsible for the repression and who are still holding high positions."

At a rally we see groups of young people, and through a bullhorn one shouts:

> On this anniversary of the Police Force of Chile, we have come to salute Espartaco Salas Mercado, the institution's Director of Intelligence. Salas Mercado joined the DINA in 1974, participated in the operations of this criminal association to detain, torture, assassinate and make disappear hundreds of Chileans. He is now the Police Director of Intelligence appointed by the former president Eduardo Frei and ratified by Ricardo Lagos. We believe that [this] government that calls itself democratic cannot maintain [itself] in power.

Through scenes like these, the film works within the oppositions of "reality" versus "superficiality," which suggests that marching on the street is where the story of veracity, justice, and memory are, rather than bogged down within institutions of power and written precedents. In fact, young people take justice into their own hands, effectively outing torturers. This is work that the democratic Chilean state, and other state entities have been more reluctant to do.

Prior to Pinochet's 1998 London arrest the symbols of the dictatorship, though present, were contained by the operations of forgetting and oblivion, immense forces in the political life of Chile during the transition to democracy. As if to emphasize this point, toward the end of *The Pinochet Case* we return to Gabriela who we met earlier. She states:

> If we aren't able to take to trial those who were responsible, at least memory will make for a historical trial of them. Not just Pinochet, but of all the torturers, all the civilians who supported it and still defend it. Of those that agreed with it, those that, even today, are still in

positions of power and try to create a kind of blanket of forgetfulness "Pinochet is retiring with dignity?" Can you tell me where torturers can retire with dignity? It's shameful, it's laughing at our pain, refusing to recognize what happened here. I believe that the strength of memory...will help us heal. That's why it's so important to establish a collective memory, in order to live now and build the future.

Although Gabriela's testimony ends on a hopeful note, the focus of her comments is on the "blanket of forgetfulness" about victims' experiences during the democratic transition and in Chilean society more broadly. Gabriela argues that collective memory has the potential to reveal the past in order to shed light on the present, while also creating hope for the future. Her words attest to the complicated relationship between memory and the remaking of the nation, suggesting that the democratic project is still incomplete, both because it has not exactly recognized the perpetrators of violence as such, and because there was active denial of Pinochet's victims.

While the consequences were somewhat delayed in Chile, the impact of Pinochet's arrest accomplished at least two important outcomes: (1) The arrest was a cathartic event for thousands of victims of the dictatorship worldwide, and could have even prompted victims of other cases of political violence to begin the process of "working through" and; (2) Pinochet's captivity gave voice to victims (i.e., in Guzmán's film, the news media, and through testimonies taken worldwide), making their stories believable within the project of democracy, which was increasingly closed to these narrations. As human rights lawyer Roberto Garretón said in the documentary, "All our work was not in vain. Justice exists!" Though the justice he points to in the film is not the institutional justice that one might imagine and hope for, his exclamation underscores the importance of Pinochet's arrest for breaking through the social and political pact of silence. Of course, in subsequent years, Pinochet's reputation within Chile has been enormously discredited, with the freezing of his Swiss bank accounts, his multiple house arrests, and the public scrutiny of his family members, including his wife, Lucia Iriarte de Pinochet.

Guzmán's film shows a rich and vibrant human rights effort in London and Santiago, and the complex persisting traumatic effects. It also documents how many have not simply moved on from the past, continuing to wrestle with the ghosts and trauma produced by the dictatorship. Pinochet's arrest and Guzmán's narration illustrate how Chile's democracy was not adequately taking care of its citizens, particularly those who were the target of state terror. If the legal narrative in the film chronicles the formal aspects of the case, then the scenes on the streets of London and Santiago and the accompanying set of testimonials give palpable evidence of the afterlife of violence. Guzmán's first two films in the trilogy discuss the history of Chilean dictatorship and its effects in terms of a national imaginary, even while acknowledging that the coup that overthrew Allende's government had wider global implications for revolutionary movements, social justice, and increased US hegemony. *The Pinochet Case*, however, expands the geographical scope of the effects of state terror, reaching deeply into its gendered character, its transnational dimension, and its persistence, despite the claims of Chilean democracy that these effects have already been worked out. The film registers with human rights audiences in international, transnational locations, winning prizes, and is continually screened in prominent locations. At the same time, it has been very minimally screened in Chile, where many people involved in solidarity with survivors there mentioned to me that they have never seen the film. Thus, Guzmán's attempt to reconfigure historical memory in many ways depends on the degree to which audiences outside of Chile communicate its importance to those in the country, not only for its incriminating evidence against Pinochet, but because of the global grassroots connections the film elucidates.

NOTES

1. The military junta of four generals overthrew Salvador Allende's government on September 11, 1973. Pinochet ruled Chile from 1973 to 1989, after which the long transition to democracy began (1990 to the present).
2. On this point there is an excellent and rich bibliography, which includes Tomás Moulian's *Anatomia de un Mito* (Santiago: Arcis, 1997), and Nelly Richard's *Residuos y Metaforas* (Santiago: Lom Ediciones, 1998).
3. I'm using Paul Connerton's very useful distinction between social memory, one specific practice, and historical reconstruction, the wider activity in which social memory is embedded (1989: 13-21). This genre includes such titles as Silvio Caiozzi's *Fernando Ha Vuelto* (Fernando Returns, 1998), Guzmán's films (1997, 2001, 2004), as well as Marilú Mallet's *Journal Inachevé* (1986) and *La Cueca Sola* (2003).
4. Rather than retranslate the interviews from Spanish to English, I have used the translations that are already in the English subtitles of the film.
5. Citing some additional film credits seem appropriate, since I'm discussing editing and camera shots, including editor Claudio Martínez, cameraman Jacques Bouquín, sound, André Rigaut and assistant director, Camila Guzmán.
6. See my forthcoming book *Where Memory Dwells* (University of California Press) for a detailed discussion of the way that female subjectivity is positioned as an embodiment of the nation, especially during the Chilean dictatorship. Guzmán follows similar masculinist renditions in *The Pinochet Case*. I don't focus too much on these dimensions here, instead highlighting the ethical rendering of the film that the director hopes to produce, since by centering women's testimonials he expanded the boundaries of the conversation within public national domains.
7. One example of this male narrative is the clunky use of chess as a way to symbolically show the various legal moves (on the part of the House of Lords, Jack Straw, and the Spanish government) to extradite Pinochet to Spain.

8. Prizes included award of merit in film, Latin American Studies Association, Semaine de la Critique at 2001 Cannes Film Festival, and 2002 Amnesty International Film Festival and 2002 Seattle International Film Festival, Online. Available HTTP: <http://www.frif.com/new2002/pino.html> (accessed 2 June 2006).
9. *The Battle of Chile* (1979) was featured in the 1999 Human Rights Watch International Film Festival, as well as screened at countless solidarity venues internationally throughout the 1980s and 1990s.
10. Importantly, the same synopsis states: "the filmmaker presents a scrupulously balanced argument by including footage of pro and anti-protestors." It is impossible for the liberal rights discourse to imagine a rendering of history outside of "balance" and presumably "objectivity," which this quote seems to suggest, Human Rights' Watch synopsis of *The Pinochet Case* (2002) Online. Available HTTP: <http://www.hrw.org/iff/2002/london/pinochet.html> (accessed 26 May 2006).
11. In fact, the foundation for the social contract, as Brown states, is the collective's willingness to give up authority to the State and the police: See Wendy Brown's well-known and expansive treatment of rights, injury, and freedom (1995: 110–11).
12. I say "sometimes" rather than something more empirically founded since it is difficult to pin down sentiments that shift and are reconstituted. However, in numerous informal conversations in Chile and with Chileans in the United States, it is clear that hierarchies of victimization, guilt, and pain exist.
13. It is important to note here that I'm referring to large social tendencies and identities, and that the experience of Chileans exile is actually quite heterogeneous (Gómez-Barris, 2005).
14. Throughout fieldwork in Chile, on several trips, I asked informants repeatedly the question: "What change did the arrest of Pinochet and subsequent events produce in Chilean politics?" From all quarters the response was similar, that basically after a few months there was no substantial shift in the nation, in terms of political outcomes or in terms of positive human rights outcome. Only one informant, Mireya García, vice-president of the *Agrupación de Familares Desaparecidos-Detenidos* (AFDD) had a more nuanced response, which included a more positive judicial outcome with old cases being reopened, and the full-time assignment of five judges to the human rights cases resulting from the dictatorship. She too had many negative comments about the institutional capacity to forget such a momentous event (presentation and personal communication, Santiago, 29 May 2002). Of course, looking back now and noting the route to Pinochet's denunciation, the multiple accusations, including those by former secret police head Manuel Contreras, makes it difficult to argue that the attempted extradition did not have a long-term and lasting impact.

REFERENCES

Appadurai, A. (1996) *Modernity at Large: Cultural Dimensions of Globalization*, Minneapolis and London: University of Minnesota Press.
Aufderheide, P. (2002) "The Importance of Historical Memory: An Interview with Patricio Guzmán," *Cineaste*, 27.3: 22–25.
Brown, W. (1995) *States of Injury: Power and Freedom in Late Modernity*, Princeton, NJ: Princeton University Press.

Connerton, P. (1989) *How Societies Remember*, Cambridge: Cambridge University Press.

Garcia Canclini, N. (1995) *Hybrid Cultures: Strategies for Entering and Leaving Modernity*, Minneapolis: University of Minnesota Press.

—— (2001) *Consumers and Citizens: Globalization and Multicultural Conflicts*, Minneapolis: University of Minnesota Press.

Gómez-Barris, M. (2005) "Two 9/11s in a Lifetime: Chilean Displacement, Art, and Terror," *Latino Studies*, March 3:1, 97–112.

Guzmán, Patricio (2001) *The Pinochet Case* [VIDEO] New York: First Run Icarus Films.

—— (1979) *The Battle of Chile* [VIDEO] New York: First Run Icarus Films.

—— (1997) *Obstinate Memory* [VIDEO] New York: First Run Icarus Films.

Mallet, M. (1982) Journal Inacheve (Unfinished Diary) [VIDEO] Quebec: Films de l'Atalante and National Film Board of Canada Production.

Moulían, T. (1999) *Chile Actual: Anatomia de un Mito*, Santiago: Lom Ediciones.

Mouseca, J. (1988) *Plano Secuencia de la Memoria de Chile: Vientecinco años de cine Chileno (1960–1985)*, Madrid: Ediciones del Litoral.

Mukherjee, B. (2001) "Imagining Homelands," in A. Aciman (ed.) *Letters of Transit: Reflections on Exile, Identity, Language, and Loss*, New York: The New Press.

Richard, N. (1998) *Residuos y Metáforas: Ensayos de crítica cultural sobre el Chile de la Transición*, Santiago: Editorial Cuarto Propio.

Wilde, A. (1999) "Irruptions of Memory: Expressive Politics in Chile's Transition to Democracy," *Journal of Latin American Studies*, 31: 471–500.

Part II

Historical feeling in the sites of production

7 Moving intimacy

The betrayals of a mother called "Yesterday," a child called "Beauty," and a father called John Khumalo[1]

Neville Hoad

Darrell Roodt's 2004 film *Yesterday* bills itself as the first IsiZulu language feature film.[2] It is also something like an AIDS pastoral, a film set mostly in rural Kwa-Zulu, strangely out of time in a number of ways from the postapartheid or what Loren Kruger calls the post antiapartheid moment of its ostensible setting (Kruger 2001: 223). While the major aspiration of this chapter is to track the temporal structure of the film as fantasy, I subject its representations to anecdotal and anthropological forms of reality testing. The driving question is how to read the dynamics of affect for (1) the protagonists (and those they wish to represent), and (2) the impossible heterogeneity of viewers that the film imagines as its audience. *Yesterday* is an emotionally powerful film, inviting viewers to invest themselves in and distance themselves from scenes of suffering and alienation. I wish to understand how *Yesterday* moves us, to work a sense of the failure of feeling against feelings of failure in the face of the pandemic.[3] That formulation is both too neat and overly ambitious, but is produced by a sense that the social organization, or construction, if you like, of affect is profoundly historical and that the phenomenological experience of affect cannot hold this constraint if it is to remain in the domain of feeling.

This essay proceeds from the claim of a massive historical and geographical diversity of intimate norms and forms that the intimate forms of modernity struggle to organize.[4] It understands monogamous, companionate heterosexual marriage as the privileged normative form of sexual intimacy under modernity, with modernity understood as an extremely uneven historical periodization.[5] While there is neither the space nor the erudition in this essay to argue that general claim into being, in the part of South Africa that *Yesterday* ostensibly brings into representation, this kind of marriage cannot be held up as either the empirically prevalent form or the normative one over the course of the last 200 years. It is this institution of marriage with its legal, economic, sexual, intimate, and familial ramifications that I somewhat riskily claim as evidence of a globalizing neoliberal structure of feeling.[6] The massively heterogeneous viewership of the film feels itself as feeling at least partially through the affective recognition of this structure, and the critical acclaim of the film as "a universal story" depends on this recognition. In the Zululand that *Yesterday* brings into filmic representation, this structure of feeling is phantasmatic. Given the fact that HIV/AIDS is mostly a sexually transmitted disease, the question of normative forms of sexual intimacy acquires considerable political urgency.

In the case of *Yesterday*, John and Yesterday have an ahistorical marriage—and a viewer's cathexis of this spatially and temporally displaced companionate marriage may be what facilitates the most emotionally devastating scenes in the film. As I will demonstrate, their marriage is ahistorical in the time-space of rural Kwa-Zulu, but the kind of marriage they have in the film I read as something like a symptom of a globalizing neoliberal structure of feeling for the privatization of affect in the gendered sphere of social reproduction. *Yesterday* is paradoxically a family values film that astutely and painfully recognizes the material impossibility of being a family values family for its protagonists.

NARRATIVE

Yesterday tells the oldest South African story from a number of angles. It is a story of family destroyed by migrant labor, though the temporality of this family form is clearly a palimpsest whose history is oddly out of place. The narrative unfolds in hauntingly familiar ways with AIDS as a new wrinkle in the drama of the affective and subjective forms of colonial modernity in what could be termed the South African liberal imaginary.

A young mother called Yesterday living in a rural village called Rooihoek falls ill, discovers she is HIV positive, goes to the mines in Johannesburg to confront her husband, who beats her up. The husband soon is too sick to work and returns to the village where Yesterday nurses him until he dies. The villagers do not want such pestilence in their village, so Yesterday must build her dying husband a shack. Yesterday tells her white doctor in a neighboring village that she wants to live until her daughter Beauty can go to school. The film ends on Beauty's first day of school and with Yesterday taking a sledgehammer to the shack she had built as a private hospital for her husband.

The husband's name is John Khumalo, making the echoes of Alan Paton's 1948 classic *Cry, the Beloved Country*, at least self-conscious (even though Khumalo is a common Zulu last name—the lead actress in the film is Leleti Khumalo, this appears stronger than coincidence). In that novel, a Reverend Stephen Khumalo went to Johannesburg to rescue his sister and discovers that his son has become a murderer. Ezekiel Mphahlele called the novel Paton's sermon for its biblical language, moralizing tone, and sentimental outcome. The novel concludes with the son of the murdered man visiting the village and the promise of a new cross-racial patriarchal stewardship of the land. *Yesterday* locates its sentimentality elsewhere and is a fascinatingly secular film. Social distinctions between Christians and animists—a feature of rural life in Zululand for at least a century (Hunter 1936; Krige 1965)—get no representative space in *Yesterday*.

The reworking of the land as a central protagonist is apparent from the opening credits—the bifurcation of the land this time is not in terms of the rich green hills belonging to white farmers and the barren valleys as home to the Zulus. Here is Paton's famous description:

> Where you stand the grass is rich and matted, you cannot see the soil. But the rich green hills break down. They fall to the valley below, and falling change their nature. For they grow red and bare; they cannot hold the rain and mist, and the streams are dry in the kloofs. Too many cattle feed upon the grass, and too many fires have burned it. Stand shod upon it for it is coarse and sharp, and the stones cut under the feet. It is not kept, or guarded, or cared for, it no longer keeps men, guards men, cares for men. (Paton 1995: 33–34)

Instead, *Yesterday* opens with a long tracking shot across a broken, dry terrain with a barbed wire fence separating *dongas* with the green hills explicitly in the background. A massive storm breaks out when Yesterday first collapses from her illness, and the film cuts to a plastic bag clinging to the barbed wire fence. The natural world risks the trope of pathetic fallacy here, but the tragedy of *Yesterday* is more personal, less open to allegorizing than its literary progenitor, and inscribes the scene of national fantasy in a more privatized way as nostalgia for a purity that never was. Paton can hold the fertility of the land as a ground for a better yesterday. *Yesterday*'s yesterday was apartheid, which the film refuses to see as any kind of nostalgic grounding. I am interested in the iconic force of this plastic bag as at once a symbol of the pollution of commodified culture and its circuits of social reproduction, but also as a resource in a resource-scarce community. In 2003, the South African parliament passed legislation to require that supermarkets charge for plastic bags as part of a wider antilittering national campaign—which satirically rendered the plastic bag as the national flower of South Africa. The opening shot, however, clearly resists a sentimentalizing of an African landscape, so often the defining feature of filmic representations of Africa—think *Out of Africa* (1985) as the classic case. The landscape is desolate without grandeur, and the green rolling hills of Paton's pastoral are outside *Yesterday*'s purview.

The journey to Johannesburg no longer takes place on a train but instead in a minibus-taxi, in which, entirely implausibly, Yesterday is the only passenger, indicating perhaps unwittingly her status as a singular, if fantastic representative subject caught in a set of private relationships, only explicitly brought into the network of exchanges through city and countryside, the state and intimate life through the vector of disease coming from the city. Thomas Blom Hansen has recently written on the minibus-taxi as the agent and symbol of new social velocities in South Africa producing the township as no longer "a site of quasi-domestic stability, but a properly urban space, marked by unpredictability, difference, and the incessant movement of anonymous bodies and signs" (Hansen 2006: 186). That this might hold for not just the urban ancillary space of the township but for the ostensibly rural village depicted in *Yesterday* is apparent when watching the film and listening to the director's commentary, in which Roodt repeatedly describes the difficulty of blocking out the background noise of people and music in representing the village as a place of rural quiet and isolation.

Robert Sember points to the many omissions in *Yesterday*'s attempt to represent the pandemic in South Africa, interestingly in the mode of a counternarrative as an imagined sequel:

> Perhaps Singh/Roodt will consider making a sequel, one of the more positive possible outcomes of the success the film is now enjoying. "Tomorrow" will show *Yesterday* working with other women in Okhahlamba and members of the local hospital there to set up an anti-retroviral treatment program ahead of the scheduled government roll-out. Which is indeed happening. It will show how not all men in the community are absent, hostile, and sexually violent but actually work to educate the community about the epidemic. Which is indeed happening. And Beauty will participate in theatre productions with other children in which she will be able to voice her experience as a child affected by HIV/AIDS. Which is indeed happening. "Tomorrow' will not pay homage to the strength of South African women to deal with suffering but to the history of collective struggle and resistance that have placed South African women at the forefront of social transformation. (Sember 2004)

Sember notes many of the features of the struggle against the pandemic in Okhahlamba, the real world equivalent of a place like Rooihoek, which the film leaves out. I think the accusation of *Yesterday* as being "a narrative without a history" is a plausible one, and the political risks of presenting *Yesterday* as a kind of timeless tale of feminine endurance of suffering must mitigate against the interventionist aspirations of the film. The accusation runs roughly as follows: If the film cannot represent reality, how can it change it? However, Sember's imagining of a sequel called "Tomorrow" belies a temporal intractability in bringing the pandemic into representation. The repeated refrain of the previous quote used to highlight the aspects of the epidemic that *Yesterday* does not show is "which is indeed happening." This phrase is repeated three times, but the imagined sequel is not called "Today" but rather "Tomorrow," implying that the mode of politics that Sember sees in the present are at some level still in the future. There may be more at stake in the "untimely" or ahistorical elements of *Yesterday* than representational inaccuracy: that *Yesterday* as a postapartheid film is still in the aspirational future of the antiapartheid moment, even as it avoids a discussion of the legacy of apartheid in accounting for the current HIV/AIDS pandemic.

THE FAMILY

The family form in *Yesterday* is both anachronistic and out of place, but not anachronistic in the nostalgic form that the name of the eponymous character would imply. John, Yesterday, and Beauty constitute a version of the white bourgeois nuclear family with an absent father thanks to migrant labor, which is itself anachronistically conceived. A Zulu man working on the mines is a much less typical proposition than it would have been in the 1940s to 1960s. Migrant miners in the twenty-first century are much more likely to be from outside the borders of South Africa.

There is no evidence of an extended kinship structure in *Yesterday*—no grannies, no aunts—which makes it difficult to account for why Yesterday would stay in Rooihoek, as well as questioning any realist aspirations the film may have. As Mandisa Mbali and Mark Hunter ask: "Where are the Gogos [grandmothers]—the lifeblood of rural South Africa?" (Mbali and Hunter 2004: 24). Yesterday appears also to have no paying job, though there are scenes of her hoeing the ground and sowing seed. This is a representation of an earlier economic structure of migrant labor. Historically migrant labor allowed the mining companies to pay a less than subsistence wage because reproductive labor costs were to be carried by the rural homestead. Rural women are now much more likely to meet these reproductive labor costs through participation in informal economies, but more of that later. Mother, absent father, and child are imagined as constituting the nuclear family as the structure geared toward social reproduction and affective distribution in ways that suggest to this viewer that the time of the family in *Yesterday* is the time when Zulus will have become a kind of idealized white people.

Yesterday is undoubtedly a good housewife. We see her attending to her child, fetching water from the communal pump, washing clothes with Beauty in the river. We have a pastoralized zone of domestic privacy overlaid with a thin patina of romanticized African communalism. The film works hard to preserve this zone of privacy around the married couple. In the scene where Yesterday assumedly tells John that she is HIV positive—we never hear the disclosure—the camera moves behind a barred window and all we see through the bars of the window is John's flailing arms as he beats Yesterday. A flashback montage follows as Yesterday recalls earlier happier moments with John—a series of painfully moving and banal images of married domestic bliss—the embrace after a long absence, eagerly anticipating his return with a sleepy Beauty, John's gift of a food processor called "Le Chef." In James Ferguson's analysis of the wives of Zambian mineworkers, discussed below, the mining companies are the agents of an impossible bourgeois domesticity. In *Yesterday* that bourgeois domesticity is cathected with the power of a man's love. In broad ideological terms, in a range of public debates about libidinal economies from, for example, polygyny to homosexuality in African cultures, it is possible to argue that in the African context and perhaps also in a more generalized postcolonial one, the bourgeois nuclear family may have been seen as the proper intimate form of modernity, even as its historical existence for people in the countryside was clearly economically unfeasible. In a pointed analysis of domesticity on the Zambian copperbelt, James Ferguson writes of company-run courses for the wives of mineworkers:

> A continuation of the paternalistic social welfare policies of the colonial mining industry, these courses were intended to teach mineworkers' wives to be "good housewives" by giving them instruction in cooking, cleaning, sewing, knitting and so on—all in the name of fostering modern family life in the mine townships. (Ferguson 1999: 167)

Ferguson concludes by noting the anachronism of the figure of the 1950s US housewife as a model for African modernity: "Like the Westinghouse kitchen in Tomorrowland, 'the modern housewife,' in mid-1980s Zambia appeared preposterously archaic and somehow poignantly out of place" (Ferguson 1999: 167). The bourgeois nuclear family emerges as a phantasm of nostalgia and developmental aspiration at the same time. Yesterday's housewifery is relentlessly naturalized. She needed no instruction in these arts, beyond a loving husband to give her a food processor. The family form seems to float as an imagined point of normative identification for viewers unencumbered by any acquaintance with ideas and practices of Zulu kinship or colonial and neocolonial economics beyond *Cry, the Beloved Country,* which at least recognizes, through celebration, the imprint of Christianity.

LANGUAGE

My DVD copy of *Yesterday* allows subtitles in French, English, Spanish, and two levels of IsiZulu. In having two levels of IsiZulu subtitles it appears to have pedagogical aspirations. Granted I bought it in the United States, a place where I struggle to imagine much desire for the learning of Zulu, but maybe these subtitles imagine other South Africans—largely white, I suspect, as its learning audience, though there are no Afrikaans subtitles. Despite *Yesterday*'s self-conscious staging of itself as the first IsiZulu-language feature film, it seems it is made to speak for and about, never to and from the human subjects it brings into representation. Given the film's reluctance or inability even to gesture toward bringing any imagining of African alterity or details of contemporary South African history that might break pastoral tonalities into filmic representation, I suspect the language politics of the film are not those of the self-determination rhetoric of nationalism, or even a national or cosmopolitan desire to learn something of a language and culture not quite one's own. Instead we have the benevolent imperialist versions of the romance of authenticity, the domestication of difference so that *one feels oneself* in the ostensibly Zulu world of *Yesterday,* even though *Yesterday* understands its narrative form as mediated by earlier figurations of Zuluness, and much less self-consciously, its representation of family forms as quite literally fantastic. Roodt drafted the script for the film in English, had the script translated into IsiZulu, and started off shooting each scene twice, once in English and once in IsiZulu. Ultimately, the English version of the film is junked in favor of the "authenticity" of the IsiZulu one.

Nevertheless the film is made with the financial backing of the Nelson Mandela Foundation with the aspiration of using it in AIDS education programs—showing it in rural areas and using it to prompt discussion on HIV/AIDS.[7] I wonder how much of their social worlds these viewers will see in *Yesterday.* I have not yet been able to find out how it was used and received by the people it purports to represent. The film received massive critical acclaim in the South African press, with a few important dissenting opinions, raves from the English language media abroad, and was the first South African film ever nominated for a best foreign film Academy award.

Yesterday is in certain ways the victim of her own name. It, along with the name of Yesterday's daughter, "Beauty," are the only English words we hear repeatedly in the film. From her account of her name, it would appear that the English word *Yesterday* is her IsiZulu name. It is the name given to her by her father, sometime in the early 1970s, in the heyday of apartheid, if Yesterday is 30 at the time of the film. The name marks a nostalgia for a time when things were better, but when was that time, or what could it have been?

Yesterday is the most widely distributed representation of South Africa's AIDS pandemic. Its language is IsiZulu to keep its specificity and thus distance from its imagined polyglot and international audience. Its familial and affective structure is bourgeois, white, and putatively universal—even though nothing else in the film fits any of those designations. Sympathy, as an affect, appears to need a dialectic between proximity and distance. I think this is how sympathy gets off the ground in *Yesterday.* Yesterday is a kind of everywoman, involved in the "timeless" difficulties of raising a child and loving a man. The moral outrage and deep pathos of the film arise from the fact that these things are not possible in her situation, despite her heroic effort. The reviewer for *The New York Times* writes: "The film...focuses not on the statistics of millions but on the tragedy of one death" (Stanley 2005). In one viewer's response, albeit sanctioned by a powerful newspaper, the linguistic or cultural singularity of Zuluness becomes transparent and the singularity of John's death becomes the locus of the film's value. This singularity may mark the ethical work of a fictional representation despite the documentary failures of *Yesterday*, but it is the work of this essay to argue that feeling this singularity is dependant on an affective recognition of a floating family form.

TRADITION

Tradition is a risky analytic term in the context of a fictional feature film being generically programmed as modernity in its sites of production and consumption, but *Yesterday*'s relation to the telos of modernity needs an Other. The two narrative outcomes of the film mark the film's deep ambivalence about the entry into what for want of a better shorthand could be called modern/individualist subjectivity. The father, corrupted by his encounter with colonial forms of exploited labor and the sexual practices they have encouraged, must die. The daughter must, however, go to school.

It has been Mark Hunter's extraordinary contribution to track the inadequacy of "male migrant labor as vector of infection explanation" for the rapid spread of HIV/AIDS in rural Kwa-Zulu over the last 10 years. He argues persuasively that this explanation is a transposition of discussions of syphilis epidemics in the 1940s that takes into account neither changes in Zulu courtship practices over the last 50 years or the continuing impoverishment of rural spaces, which has meant that rural women are themselves extraordinarily mobile in the search for work (Hunter 2004: 124). The pastoral scenes of Yesterday hoeing and sowing are just that: a depiction of the countryside as if it were still a space where subsistence agricultural labor could, no matter how minimally, meet the costs of familial reproduction. Hunter notes "multiple partner relationships, underscored by gifts, are a key informal survival strategy for many women." The folk wisdom is "one man for rent, one man for food, and one man for clothes" (Hunter 2001: 1–3). The presence of "transactional sex" models of intimacy on the terrain *Yesterday* wishes to bring into representation renders Yesterday and her life trajectory in the film as the site of a reinvestment in the fantasy of the privatizing of intimacy (Hunter 2004).

In the landscape of feminine support in Rooihoek, Yesterday seeks help from two very different women—a *sangoma* ("traditional healer") and a teacher in the primary school who becomes her friend and will presumably look after Beauty when Yesterday dies. The *sangoma* is consulted after Yesterday is denied admission to the Tuesdays only clinic in Kromdraai—a two hour plus walk from Rooihoek—for the second time. The *sangoma* is clearly irritated that Yesterday has not consulted her earlier about the mysterious illness.

The *sangoma* appears in the film as a kind of mildly malevolent New Age guru—a Zulu Caroline Myss or Deepak Chopra with an attitude problem. According to her diagnosis, Yesterday is sick because, despite her protestations to the contrary, she is too angry. While on the one hand, this is an absurd psychologizing reduction, on the other hand it may contain an unwitting recognition of the growth of certain kinds of spiritual tourism to South Africa. Surgery and Safari is already a big business.[8] *Sangoma and Safari* is beginning. The *sangoma*'s office is spectacularly sanitized for western consumption: there are no lopped off vulture wings, no dried baboon heads, no brightly colored powders or piles of roots and herbs—some of the tools of the trade. There is no diagnosis of angry ancestors, no calls for ritual animal sacrifice, no accusations that Yesterday is the victim of someone's witchcraft. I suspect that this literally sanitized version is produced in the attempt to avoid criticism of exoticism and racism within the film's prevailing ideological task of producing white sympathy for these people whose humanity must depend on them being as close to some normative "us" as possible. The medicinal smoke offered to Yesterday as medicine makes her cough, alerting viewers, as if we did not know already, that the *sangoma* is a quack more likely to hurt than help. The bunch of burning herbs Yesterday is instructed to inhale looks like nothing so much as a sage smudge-stick, familiar to me from New Age appropriations of some generalized rituals of Native American societies. These have undoubtedly gone global. (A friend of a friend in Cape Town makes dream-catchers out of Guinea Fowl feathers and indigenous semiprecious stones.) Viewers are encouraged to disapprove of the *sangoma*, but not be horrified by her. Given the secular frame of the film, the ancestors cannot enter the time of modernity through her. The *sangoma* appears again as the spokesperson for the angry women who want John removed from the village—as part of the reactionary force of prejudice and fear in the face of the pandemic. That this task is undertaken by the *sangoma* and the women rather than by let's say Yesterday's landlord locates the film once again in the "no-time, no-space" of the pastoral.

The teacher appears early in the film as she walks the country road with a fellow teacher, hoping to find employment in Rooihoek. Both women carry umbrellas, one wears glamorous sunglasses, and together they offer a vision of educated, respectable, and relatively empowered single African womanhood. The teacher seems free of the perils of menfolk. She becomes Yesterday's friend and gives Yesterday the five-rand taxi-fare she needs to avoid the long walk to the clinic so she can get there before the lines get too long for the doctor to see her. She thus enables Yesterday's diagnosis, but since Yesterday gets no antiretrovirals from the clinic, the moral victory of westernized medicine over the *sangoma* is rendered pyrrhic. The film fails to mention antiretrovirals at all.

This brings us to the doctor—a young white woman who speaks fluent IsiZulu. Yesterday persists in calling her "madam," even after the doctor requests to be called "doctor," marking the persistence of racial honorifics in a national time frame when race no longer has the legal force it had under apartheid. The doctor asks Yesterday frank questions about her sex-life, establishing the cause of her illness: "Do you use a condom? Do you have sex only with your husband? Does he have other wives?" Yesterday is illiterate. How do protocols of consenting to her treatment work?

Yesterday's brushes with specific histories of the present reveal a continued attachment to the emergence of a gendered individualism as the only viable form of human subjectivity and interiority. In a conversation with the teacher, she produces what I will call "the parable of the woman of Bergville." Yesterday tells the teacher of a young woman who was very clever and that her village saved money to send her to university in Johannesburg, where she acquired HIV, and when the villagers find out, they stone her to death. This references the very public scandal of the murder of Gugu Dlamini, an activist for the Treatment Action Campaign, phrased in the timeless language of village gossip and ignorance. It is a story that shows Yesterday experiencing her helplessness, that the only point of her identification with Dlamini can happen in her death by the forces of some paradoxical "traditionalism" itself invested in the trajectories of individualized upward mobility—they pool their meager resources to send the women to university. She comes back with something else. They kill her. I agree that Beauty must go to school, but then what?

THE HUT THAT YESTERDAY BUILT OR A HOSPITAL OF HER OWN

Yesterday building a shack from scrap metal for her dying husband marks the film's strongest critique of the postapartheid state's failures to meet the needs of its citizens. There is no room at the hospital—the only time viewers see the pandemic as anything other than one family's crisis, but this moment is short-lived. The resilience of the African woman, herself HIV positive, allows her to build her own.

Yesterday and Beauty forage through the landscape, collecting bits of scrap metal to build the shack where John will die. It is clear that Yesterday needs help in this task. In another revealing moment from watching the film with the audio of the director's commentary on: as Leleti Khumalo—the actress playing Yesterday lifts an improvised window into a hole in the wall of the shack, Darrel Roodt, the director states, "of course, she [Yesterday/Leleti Khumalo] couldn't lift that by herself, the crew is outside helping her." The camera is inside the shack. Here the ruse of filmic representation encapsulates the impossibility of Yesterday's predicament and the fictiveness of the solutions it finds for the painful problems it presents. I hope my ontological confusion between what is shown and how the illusion was enabled can be pushed into an allegory here of the necessary trickery of the film's individualist and *faux* familist understanding of the pandemic.

There is another moment of help—this time on camera, rather than behind it. While attempting to extract the rusted bonnet from an abandoned car by the side of the road, Yesterday and Beauty finally receive some help from a group of women wearing the familiar orange of "a road gang," seen earlier in the film working on the repair of a bridge. None of the village "housewives" help. Why the informal volunteer labor of women who are strangers? The impersonal goodwill of strangers who do not know of Yesterday's purpose seems the closest thing the film can imagine to a collective response. No politics. No Treatment Action Campaign fighting for adequate treatment. No other civil society organizations. No claim on fellow citizens, just the kindness of passing strangers.

There are many tragedies in *Yesterday* beyond the palpable suffering of the protagonist. Let me parse, somewhat sentimentally, one that could be called a globalizing neoliberal structure of feeling, or the privatization of affect in the gendered sphere of social reproduction. John and Yesterday love each other, though this love broaches domestic violence in the undomestic setting of the corridor of the mine office. They both love Beauty. When John gets sick, his loving wife will take care of him, but she is now without his wage, formerly her only visible means of support. When he dies, she will smash the work of her fictive labor (the shack), sufficiently grief-stricken not to think that she might need it herself. What will she do when she is dying, rebuild the hut she could not even build herself when healthier without the random kindness of strangers, or the behind the scene's work of a film crew?

A reading which supplements the film's representations with accounts of the pandemic attached to historical accuracy can imagine the kinds of massive economic and political resources needed to avoid the tragic outcome—jobs, hospitals, public infrastructures of survival. But that reading still begs the question of what kind of affective resources or narratives could mobilize something more than sympathy—active like that of the "road crew," passive like the weeping viewer. Or will those affective resources continually need a recathexis of a family form that never was, that demands love and loyalty as it fails again in order for the dispersed subjects of these affective resources to feel themselves as feeling?

I conclude with this question because the mobilization of global feeling is crucial in the fight against the pandemic. *Yesterday* allows us to feel for a resilient young mother betrayed by a husband, but cannot imagine feeling for and with the many others affected by the pandemic, who stand outside the normative affective institution of companionate marriage, with those whose forms of sexual intimacy require imaginative extension rather than recognition. While much of the pathos of *Yesterday* resides in the ways in which that normative institution provided our protagonist with no protections and as much assistance, the film only allows us to feel despair at that failure. I hope that other cultural representations, which will risk representing the various local specificities of life with the pandemic and the collective struggles they have prompted, may prompt us to feel more and differently.

NOTES

1. I would like to thank the participants at the Film, History and Cultural Citizenship Workshop at the University of Manitoba in April 2006, where this work was first presented, particularly the organizers David Churchill and Tina Chen. Barbara Harlow talked to me about *Yesterday* in ways that were helpful, Hylton White shared key references, and Gabriela Redwine provided superb and speedy research assistance.
2. Darrell James Roodt is a leading South African filmmaker with a long history of collaboration with Anant Singh, arguably South Africa's leading film producer. Roodt came to prominence with the important antiapartheid film, *Place of Weeping* (1984)— the first antiapartheid film shot solely in South Africa.
3. This essay takes its inspiration from a range of discussions on the place of affect in the public and private life of the AIDS pandemic, particularly Douglas Crimp's "Mourning and Miltancy" (1987) and its subsequent re-write, Ann Cvetkovich's *An Archive of Feelings* (2004), and more broadly Lauren Berlant's *Intimacy* (2000). It struggles to set such predominantly US-based texts in dialogue with mostly anthropological and epidemiological discussions of the HIV/AIDS pandemic in Southern Africa.
4. Rudi Bleys's *The Geography of Perversion: male- to-male sexual behavior outside the West and the ethnographic imagination 1750–1918* (1995) does the work of establishing the diversity of behaviors which may now be called homosexual.
5. Increasingly, forms of sexual intimacy such as homosexuality are laying claim to the couple form as a route to legitimacy. The current gay marriage debates in a range of national contexts are a case in point. See inter alia George Chauncey, *Why Marriage? the history shaping today's debate over gay equality* (2004).
6. Here is Raymond Williams's classic definition of a structure of feeling:
    Characteristic elements of impulse, restraint, and tone; specifically affective elements of consciousness and relationships: not feeling against thought, but thought as felt and feeling as thought: practical consciousness of a present kind, in a living and interrelating continuity (Williams 1988: 132).
7. John Samuel, CEO of the Nelson Mandela Foundation stated: "what we are aiming to do is get this on the back of trucks and go from village to village to show the movie, and in the evening have discussions with the community about what we can do," Online. Available HTTP: <http://yesterdaythemovie. co.za> (accessed 18 May 2005).
8. Just because this is too painfully delicious, from a web-based magazine called *Travel Lady*: "Established to provide a personalized program of cosmetic surgery in complete privacy, Surgeon & Safari combines recuperation packages

featuring pampering health and beauty treatments with opulent surroundings. Guests have the option of embarking on an exciting safari following their treatment as well at Orient-Express' Gametrackers camps in Botswana. 'South African surgeons are among the best in the world,' said Nick Seewer, managing director for Orient-Express' Africa Collection. 'Given our favorable exchange rate, cosmetic surgery can cost less than a fifth of what it is in the U.S., making it an attractive option for our affluent guests,'" Online. Available HTTP: <www.travellady.com/ARTICLES/article-surgery.html> (accessed 12 April 2006).

REFERENCES

Berlant, L. (2000) *Intimacy*, Chicago: University of Chicago Press.

Bleys, R. (1995) *The Geography of Perversion: male- to-male sexual behavior outside the West and the ethnographic imagination 1750–1918*, New York: New York University Press.

Chauncey, G. (2004) *Why Marriage? the history shaping today's debate over gay equality*, New York: Basic Books.

Crimp, D. (1989) "Mourning and Miltancy," *October*, 51: 97–107.

Cvetkovich, A. (2004) *An Archive of Feelings*, Durham, NC: Duke University Press.

Ferguson, J. (1999) *Expectations of Modernity: myths and meanings of urban life on the Zambian copperbelt*, Berkeley and Los Angeles, CA: University of California Press.

Hansen, T.B. (2006) "Sounds of Freedom: Music, Taxis and Racial Imagination in Urban South Africa," *Public Culture*, 18.1 (Winter): 185–208.

Hunter, Mark. (2001) "The Sexual Economy: Poverty, sex and survival," *South African Labour Bulletin*, 25.6 (December): 1–3.

—— (2004) "Masculinities, Multiple-Sexual-Partners, and AIDS: The making and unmaking of Isoka in KwaZulu-Natal," *Transformation: Critical Perspectives on Southern Africa*, 54: 123–53.

Hunter, Monica. (1936) *Reaction to Conquest: effects of contact with Europeans on the Pondo of South Africa*, London: Oxford University Press.

Krige, E.J. (1965) *The Social System of the Zulus*, 2nd ed., Pietermaritzburg: Shuter & Shooter.

Kruger, L. (2001) "Theatre, Crime and the Edgy City in Post-Apartheid Johannesburg," *Theatre Journal*, 53.2 (May): 223–52.

Mbali, M. and Hunter, M. (2004) "*Yesterday*'s Stereotypes are a Thing of the Past," *Sunday Tribune*, 17 October: 24.

Mphahlele, E. (1959) *Down Second Avenue*, London: Faber and Faber.

Paton, A. (1995) *Cry, the Beloved Country*, New York: Scribner's.

Sember, R. (2004) "Is *Yesterday* History?" *HIVAN—Center for HIV/AIDS Networking*, Online. Available HTTP: <http://www.hiv911.org.za/edit_essays/October%202004.asp> (accessed 23 May 2006).

Stanley, A. (2005) "Brave Spirit Under the Unsheltering Sky," *The New York Times*, 28 November, Online. Available HTTP: <http://www.nytimes.com/2005/11/28/arts/television/28stan.html?ex=1290834000&en=0b10f8edc081a7af&ei=5088&partner=rssnyt&emc=rss> (accessed 18 May 2005).

Williams, R. (1988) *Marxism and Literature*, Oxford: Oxford University Press.

8 Queer grit
Jane West rides through the violence of the Hollywood Western

Roewan Crowe

She's been watching *Unforgiven* for days now. Replaying the violence of this Western over and over again. She tries to stretch out her body, tough and tight, legs and ankles twisted, her black boots welded together, but her body will not respond. She's been seized tight by the story, held captive by the heroic Western tale. Can't say how it happened, her being pulled down deep into the guts of the Western. How is it that a feminist artist and academic finds herself riding through mud and blood and tales of revenge? One last time, she promises herself as the first scene of the film returns, a sunset, a shack of a house, a man digging a grave beneath a lone tree silhouetted against a darkening red sky. She can't see much of anything in front of her except the wide horizon, open and endless, the line where land meets sky flickering under a hot burning sun. There in the distance is the legendary rise of John Ford's Monument Valley looming before her. The unyielding

Figure 8.1

masculinity of a towering John Wayne is shadowing the land. A stagecoach ride through the canyons and you will inevitably discover a small community living in fear. Trains pull into town at high noon, hauling in danger down the steel tracks of progress. The expansionist westward movement of empire covering the prairies. Revenge and murder, a fact of life. Vigilante justice. Guns are the law of the land. The landscape emptied out of its first residents. Cowboys and farmers. Familial succession. Lawlessness and the law. Settlers and Indians. Captivity narratives. Burning wagons. Screaming white women. The cavalry rushing in. Manifest destiny writ large.

This is how the classic Hollywood Western story goes, an enduring myth, some even say history (Walker 2001b). The collision of North American colonial history and Hollywood Western narratives created this space she has purposefully stepped into, where the popular imaginary and the real blur. The "classic Western" (Wright 1975) produced this powerful colonial myth that has layered itself upon the land, our bodies, and our collective imaginary of how the West was "won." "Indians never lost their West, so how come I walk into the supermarket to find a dozen cowboy books telling me How the West Was Won?" (Alexie 2001: 253). Violence is at the core of these narratives. As Jim Kitses writes, "The national myth rehearses a foundational violence necessary to the frontier's resolution of problems, a promise of rebirth and redemption through conquest" (Kitses 2004: 21). This foundational violence continues in the myths and reality lived throughout North America. The result of this frontier myth, historian Richard Slotkin has argued, "is a 'gunfighter nation' that has grown by destroying the Other, that demonizes adversaries and authorises a regenerative violence" (cited in Kitses 2004: 21).

Hollywood Western narratives are often about events situated in the United States, occasionally heading over into the contested borderlands of Mexico. However, these stories are powerfully evident in Canada. Borders don't contain stories and culture. Stories flow through borders because they are imaginary. This is their power. The Western Canadian landscape—forests, prairies, foothills, badlands, and mountainous regions—often stands in for the cinematic American West. *Unforgiven* and *Brokeback Mountain* were filmed primarily in Alberta, and the soon to be released *The Assassination of Jesse James* was filmed in Manitoba and Alberta. In John Ford's classic, *The Searchers*, John Wayne's character Ethan Edwards journeys from Monument Valley to the wintry landscape of Canada. The Canadian landscape is layered with these filmic tales. Certainly they are taken up and understood differently in Canada, but you would be hard pressed to find a person living in Canada who did not recognize the face of John Wayne and understand what he stood for, even if they had never watched a Western. The overt violence of colonization in the United States has long provided Canada with an alibi when it comes to Canada's own colonial and frontier history, and this has been central to a Canadian nationalist identity:

in order to maintain Canadians' self-image as a fundamentally "decent" people innocent of any wrongdoing, the historical record of how the land was acquired—the forcible and relentless dispossession of Indigenous peoples, the theft of their territories, and the implementation of legislation and policies designed to effect their total disappearance as peoples—must also be erased. (Lawrence 2002: 23–24)

The violence of colonization is seldom acknowledged in Canada. This is the Western she has stepped into, this is her history. Can she step into this frontier story and extend the horizon in a direction that might open up space for new stories?

Unforgiven is, hands down, one of her favorite Westerns. Odd to call something so violent a favorite, like a kind of pie, which, if anyone was asking, would be a slice of lemon meringue. In this particularly self-conscious and bloody tale, Will Munny, a notorious former thief and murdering outlaw played by Clint Eastwood, is called back to his guns by a young wanna-be gun-slinger, the Schofield Kid. The Kid wants Clint to help him claim the bounty set by a group of working girls on the life of a couple of cowboys who cut up the face of one of their own. Clint calls his old friend and partner, Ned Logan played by Morgan Freeman, to join them. Both men come out of outlaw retirement and domestication for one last bounty. Time reveals that the Schofield Kid can't see any further than 50 yards, and really doesn't want to kill anyone. Ned, though he once used his gun as an outlaw, can't kill a man anymore. How did he in the first place, she

Girl & Law, Still from Queer Grit by Roewan Crowe ©

Figure 8.2

wonders? All of them are packing pistols and rifles, their bodies, their guns, this particular kind of masculinity, a part of the landscape.

She wonders how things might have turned out differently. Maybe if the Schofield Kid hadn't ever dreamed of being a gun-slinger. Hadn't ever heard outlaw tales told at twilight as he fell fast asleep. "The truth about stories is that's all we are" (King 2003: 62). Maybe if he had been told different tales he wouldn't have called Clint back to his guns to claim the bounty set on those couple of cowboys, by the whores of that small town. Maybe if those randy cowboys hadn't ridden into town in the first place to claim the body of a working woman. One of the cowboys had taken a knife to Delilah's face when she laughed at his penis because it was small. He left his mark. "The film opens under the sign of the 'teensy little pecker' and the cut whore, masculinity and its discontents.... *Unforgiven* offers a Freudian account of American's past, where the gun stands in for the penis, as well as embodying the phallus" (Kitses 2004: 308). What if Delilah had held her laugh inside? Quiet, woman, hush, don't upset a naked cowboy with a knife. What if the Kid hadn't found his hero, once a famous thief and outlaw, on a dirt farm, burying dead pigs and trying to raise two kids on his own? What if Ned could still squeeze the trigger and kill a man, or if the Kid could see further than 50 yards? What if traditional masculinity and nationhood weren't premised on the protection of some women and the violation of others?

What if, she thinks, now riding atop her palomino mare, trudging on through the mud and thunder. Perhaps it is on this ride through the streets of Big Whiskey, on the back of her horse beside Clint, that she might better understand the violence of the Western, the violence that is her nation's history. She glances over to Clint who is now riding slightly ahead of her. How many sinister towns has he ridden through? How many times has he lowered his head to death? Raised his rifle in revenge? Now in *Unforgiven* they are searching through the storm for his old, dear friend. Rain-drenched, they ride toward Greely's saloon. "There he is," she calls out to Clint pointing to the lifeless body that used to be Ned, propped up in a rough wooden coffin out front of the saloon. She searches for some expression on Clint's face. Nothing. Just a cold, blank stare.

> The death of the heart, or, rather, its scarification and eventual sacrifice, is what the western genre, more than anything is about. The numbing of the capacity to feel, which allows the hero to inflict pain on others, requires the sacrifice of his own heart, a sacrifice kept hidden under his toughness, which is inseparable from his heroic character. (Tompkins 1992: 219)

He doesn't look over toward his old friend, dead and on righteous display. A steady stream of water falls from the brim of his hat. He nods toward the hitching post out front of the saloon. They ease off their horses, tie them to the post. She watches each movement with purpose, trying to see how it is all done. Clint unbuckles his saddle bag and pulls out a leather holster; held inside this steel lined case is a Colt .45, dubbed "peacemaker" on the frontier. He hands it over to her. She straps on the holster and buckles the rig snug. Her hips buzz. There is no denying the power of a gun. They walk by Ned, a sign hangs around his neck. She watches Clint's steady eyes trace the words as they flicker in lightning flash and flame, "This is what happens to assassins around here." They walk on, leaving Ned behind. Such a kind face, she notices, even though the life's been blasted out of him. She follows Clint's lead, their movements are in synch, or rather she is doing exactly what Clint is doing, simultaneously. They stalk undetected into the saloon. Her confidence grows as the looming shadow of his double-barreled rifle descends upon the room. Funny how a gun can make you feel that way. Clint motions for her to stand by the door. She tentatively pulls out the Colt and sets her sights on Little Bill, the evil lawman played by Gene Hackman. She recalls one of the most disturbing scenes in the film, Little Bill brutally whipping Ned, the history of American slavery and police brutality held firmly in his hand. "Gene Hackman was persuaded over his initial reservations to play the role of the sadistic sheriff, Little Bill, only after watching the infamous 'Rodney King video,' and he even refers to the beating of Ned Logan as '[his] Rodney King scene' (Schickel 1996: 461). Could she kill this man? She listens guardedly as Little Bill reveals Clint's murderous past. He's been to hell she thought, somewhat repelled by his transgressions, but neither surprised nor judgmental. Just oddly calm.

Then the killing starts. Clint blasts Skinny first, the owner of Greely's, the roar of the rifle booming through her heart. Clint is looking to Little Bill with a murderous fury. "You're dead for what you did to Ned," she finds herself calling out, cocking back the hammer of the Colt. She is surprised how easily she has fit into this scene. How quickly she has a gun in her hand, ready to use it. Clint fires at Little Bill, and with the dry click of his rifle her heart tightens and falters. Misfire. Hoping her aim is sure, she steadies her sight on Little Bill. She could kill him right now. A surge of frightening energy and power radiates out from her gun. This is almighty power. Her gun glistens and she feels dangerous. But she doesn't fire. She isn't ready to kill someone, not even someone like Little Bill. *What stops her? Perhaps it is the voice of Grace Kelly in High Noon, "I don't care who's right and who's wrong, there has to be some better way for people to live."* She holds Little Bill steady in her sight. Clint heaves his empty rifle at Little Bill and then reaches for the Kid's Schofield pistol that he had, earlier, tucked into his belt. Clint doesn't hesitate and she counts the bodies as they fall heavy and fast to the wooden floor; one, two, three, four, plus Skinny, that's five men down. Really that's five men dead, just like that. Five men, now five dead bodies piled on the wooden floor.

After the killing's done, Clint retreats to the bar and a bottle of whiskey, downing a shot of rye as if applying a hot poultice to an open wound.

Before joining him, she steps out of the saloon. She wonders, "*What is my place in all of this? Where will inquiry into genre take me?*" as she looks down the dusty street. The soul's been blasted out of this wicked little town and out of her too. Is this the death of her heart? This monstrous violence has crushed the thin line between fantasy and the real. Separation of the past from the present has been blasted apart. She returns inside, steps through the bodies and blood and guts and joins Clint at the bar. She lays down her gun. There is so much she wants to say, to ask him. Why do you keep coming back to the Western, an inescapably violent tale? What do you think of *Brokeback Mountain*? Do you think John Wayne is rolling in his grave at the sight of the Hollywood Western landscape marked in so visually powerful ways by Queer cowboys? What does it take for a man to lay down his guns for good?

Silence reigns. Grave silence and a bottle of whiskey. There is no redemption in this scene; what first appeared to be righteous revenge, first in protection of a woman who worked as a whore, and then of a friend, is now only one thing, cold-blooded murder. Her thoughts and their descent into the bottle are interrupted by the sound of Beauchamp, the writer, struggling out from under a dead body. "What about the writer?" she asks Clint. Beauchamp exclaims in defense and fear, "I don't have a gun. I write. I'm a writer." Clint calls the writer to retrieve Ned's Spencer rifle and the bullets from the floor, before sending him away. The writer hands over the weapon to Clint, like he was handing over all responsibility. She recalls the writer's part in the unfolding of one nasty event after another. *What responsibility does the storyteller carry?* Just then, the wounded Little Bill reaches for his gun, again. Clint is quick to knock the pistol out of his hand and positions the Spencer rifle inches from Little Bill's face, his last words echoing—"I don't deserve this. To die like this." "Yes you do deserve it," she snarls, picking up her gun again, recalling every beating and vicious act he had committed; his Sheriff's badge a license for his sadistic acts. Her gun gleams again, a chilling wind rustling the souls of the barely dead bodies around her. She knows she is on a dangerous edge. What happens when you step into the imaginary, look down the barrel of your gun and think someone deserves to die? What happens when you are tempted by vigilante justice? Clint kills Little Bill point blank, without flinching. She is blasted by this final fierce deed. There is only darkness in this town.

Unforgiven is a film that wrestles with the violence of misogyny, male violence against women, the violence of the Western itself, and racism. While it takes on these themes, it shows the ultimate failure of the Western to step outside of its violent ways and history. *Unforgiven* is unable to disrupt this unending cycle of violence, even when it attempts to do so. "Ambitious, compelling, but finally flawed, Eastwood's critique of the Western as a genre sustained by masculine codes of violence is itself all too satisfyingly sustained by that same violence" (Kitses 2004: 312). Even though Clint Eastwood is attempting to question the brutality of male vio-

Girl & Gun, Still from Queer Grit by Roewan Crowe ©

Figure 8.3

lence, and the violence of the Western, Will Munny, the character played by Eastwood, returns to the use of savage violence to avenge the death of his friend. It is as if he cannot help himself, or as Clint Eastwood puts it, "a kind of machinery was back in action" (Tibbetts 1993: 11). What is this machinery at work in the Western genre? Is this insistent return of violence something that cannot be escaped? It is this return of the repressed trauma that is interesting to me. In the epilogue of *West of Everything: The Inner Life of Westerns* (1992) Jane Tompkins reflects on the violence of the Western. Having studied and written about Westerns for many years, she writes that, "The definition of violence most of us carry around in our heads differs very little from the one the Western offers: violence is killing or beating up on other people, deliberately inflicting pain" (Tompkins 1992: 227). She goes on to write that "Working on Westerns has made me aware of the extent to which the genre exists in order to provide justification for violence" (Tompkins 1992: 227). Film scholar Janet Walker argues for a subgroup of Westerns called "traumatic westerns, in which past events of a catastrophic nature are represented so as to challenge both the realist representational strategies of a genre that often trades on historical authenticity and the ideological precepts of the myth of Manifest Destiny." Traumatic Westerns, she goes on to argue, "are counter-realistic and counter-historical" (Walker 2001a: 221).

The traumatic Western genre and its characteristic traumatic event from the past are particularly interesting. Cowboys are always returning to sites of trauma. This story is not questioned or scrutinized the way contemporary tales of sexualized violence are, for example, particularly if those

Figure 8.4

stories are about sexual abuse within the family: especially if they are stories about rape and incest told by women in literature, film, and academic prose. The Western allows for this return to trauma to recount and work through a violent past. This includes both the individual trauma experienced by the cowboy hero and his family, and perhaps more powerfully the historical context, that is, the return of the unacknowledged trauma of colonization and its continued historical legacy. The history of violence as a strategy of nation-building cannot be suppressed and this story keeps resurfacing through the Western narrative. This might also account for the changing nature of the Western over the years toward a counter-Western narrative.

"I WISH I KNEW HOW TO QUIT YOU"—JACK TWIST TO ENNIS DEL MAR IN *BROKEBACK MOUNTAIN*

To further deepen my inquiry into the Hollywood Western and make material some of my conceptual and theoretical questions, I move from the page to the moving picture. By stepping into *Unforgiven* to take a fictional ride with Clint Eastwood, I gained a better understanding of the Western genre and the foundational violence that lies at its core. The narrator comes to understand both the power and seduction of the gun and the lure of vigilante violence. It is from this place, informed by both the possibility of the genre and my deep ambivalence with it, that I created the short stop-motion animated video *Queer Grit* (2004).

Rather than an empty vehicle breathed into by the filmmaker, the genre is a vital structure through which flows a myriad of themes and concepts. As such the form can provide filmmakers with a range of possible connections and the space in which to experiment, to shape and define the kinds of effects and meanings they are working toward. (Kitses 2004: 10)

As a cultural producer I am interested in the tactical deployment of self-reflexivity, oppositional/differential politics, and transformational artistic practices. Living and working in the Canadian Prairies necessitates artistic production and creation that acknowledge the context of colonization in North America. I situate myself within the frame of the traumatic Western narrative as a feminist who is invested in wrestling with this history. I recognize that the legacy of the West is still replicating itself. I enter into this fatal environment—a violent and xenophobic narrative—to continue my investigation. I explore the possibilities that open up when I inhabit the form of the Western, a form and a story I have inherited, to subvert and play with the form to tell tales of trauma, exile, and resistance.

Queer Grit has been screened at national and international film festivals. It has also been shown in gallery settings in Winnipeg and Toronto. The work is intended to be shown as part of a larger installation that situates the video in a 1960s living room with plastic toy cowboys and Indians littering the floor. Although the work explores a broad range of themes—questions about the Western and the foundational violence that lies at its core— it is interesting to note that it has only been picked up by Queer film and video festivals. Independent video production and distribution exist in a space far outside the machinery of Hollywood film production and distribution. The creation of *Queer Grit* was supported by a community of artists in Winnipeg. It was funded and facilitated by a "First Video Fund" grant from Video Pool Media Arts Centre. Video Pool is an artist-run centre that functions like a prairie co-op, making accessible the technology (computers and software), equipment (camera, lighting, microphones, etc), and providing the support needed to make video art. Video Pool also distributes a wide range of media art. It is in this context that *Queer Grit* becomes possible, affordable, and accessible.

Following in the footsteps of the self-conscious Hollywood Western, I create a counternarrative. I seize the Western to tell a story from a Queer point of view, narrated by Jane West, a conscientious Queer cowgirl from the "Best of the West" action figure collection. In the video I explore the interconnections between the landscape, our bodies, and Western narratives that have been passed down through toys, TV, and film. *Queer Grit* is an interventionist piece, I toy with the past, and with the Western. I manipulate the tension between what is real and what is fictional, in image and in story. As I've discussed earlier, Westerns tamper with truth and facts, constructed cinematic events displace historical accounts in the popular

Figure 8.5

imaginary. I mimic this powerful practice. Utilizing artful inquiry into the prairie and its past, I open a space for the viewer to step into the imaginary with me to question the Western and the West, asking who can freely roam the prairie landscape? I use photography, video, feminist theory, autobiography, and the "Best of the West" action figures to acknowledge the history of colonization, insert the missing Queer, and to expose the brutal violence of the Western and of the West.

The video tells the best story and I am reluctant to flatten it into a silent, static text, yet it is necessary. Jane West is a child of the rural landscape. As a white girl-child growing up in a working class family there were several opportunities for her to view working class culture such as Hollywood Westerns. She could watch *Gunsmoke* and *Bonanza* on television. She could head out to the drive-in to watch a duster projected onto the prairie night sky. Or, in some small towns, she could see a movie at the local community centre (such as the Elk's Hall) or at the school gymnasium. Jane reflects on the Westerns she watched as a girl and their impact on her:

> On bright summer days when my dad wasn't busy pumping gas or fixing cars, we'd head over to the drive-in, across the highway. Anything was possible. Horses thundering, dust kicking up, a gun fight, the West being "won." Not "stolen." Those Western stories laid down the law on my white girl skin, down deep into my bones, who I should love, what I could do, who I could be. My dad believed those stories and I suppose I did too. Cowboy justice and revenge, the law of the land, but

I knew there were other stories that weren't being told and I was drawn to the blank screen.

Drawn to the horizon, Jane leaves the country for the city landscape, "In the city, I found all kinds of love, love I hadn't even imagined. And I found my Queer love, handsome trans stole my heart." Jane must come to terms with her Queer desire, and the narrative continues with Jane confronting her deepest fears to untangle herself from the violence of the Western, and of the West, to disobey the law and take her rightful place on the prairies. Rather than resort to violence herself, as the classic Western goes, Jane West rides through her internal landscape to undo the violence of the Western narrative that has staked its claim inside of her.

I was tied up by those western tales and I had to work hard to undo them, to free my love from shame and fear. It's not easy being a Queer from the prairies when your dad is John Wayne. How did my dad get to be the law? The violence of the West had taken its place inside of me. I had to fight to win myself back—there would be a showdown.

There is a violent showdown. Through image and narrative I work to lay bare the violence so we might see it more clearly. The West was founded on a practice of dispossession and violence, and was established through the use of force. Part of this has been the use of sexualized, racialized, and gendered violence, and also a violence against Queer bodies. Jane confronts

Tied-Up, Still from Queer Grit by Roewan Crowe ©

Figure 8.6

Figure 8.7

the history of this violence in a graphically animated scene. It is a slow and drawn out stop-motion scene where the Law, the father, rapes Jane with his rifle. Even though I am working with plastic toys this representation of sexualized violence was remarkably difficult to shoot and it is (for some) difficult to watch.

With this historical and internal reckoning, Jane steps outside of the traditional narrative to confront the Law. This is her resolution, both visually and emotionally.

> What appears to personal imagination is social imaginary: for...history is a process of humanity's self-fashioning, through creating institutions, languages, structures, and relations. Trauma is a product of history precisely because it is manmade and self-inflicted, and hence can be understood and altered by self-conscious human acts. These acts for making change, for working through traumas, are imaginary, because given the depleted and exhausted cultural resources, little but the imagination is readily available for the reinvention of new narratives, new social forms. (Kaplan and Wang 2004: 13)

Jane comes face to face with the Law in the prairie landscape and speaks directly to him. Jane says, "When I told him, he didn't say a thing, he just shook his head and walked away." The Law, the father, leaves Jane standing alone. Her narration here is intentionally vague. She could be telling him the violent history of the West including the rape of women and children; of colonization and the harm it has done; she could be telling him that she and others are violated by these laws, such as enforced compulsory heterosexuality or strict gender prescriptions. Or she could be telling him that she is Queer. Those who transgress laws about gender, sexuality, and race are attacked, condemned, exiled, or erased. "Belonging" is provisional and tentative, the threat of violence a reality. This is grounded in the experiences of those who live in exile on the prairies because they are Queer, or Aboriginal, or in some way "other." We who are exiled cannot travel freely to western spaces, nor can we return with simple nostalgia to places from our past. These are dangerous places for those who live outside of the law of the West.

Unfortunately, there are many examples from the contemporary west. In a farmhouse outside Humboldt, Nebraska, in December, 1994, two men killed transgendered (FTM) Brandon Teena (who self-identified as simply Brandon), along with Lisa Lambert, a young white woman, and Philip DeVine, a disabled black man. One week earlier, the killers had raped Brandon after discovering that he was female-bodied. Although Brandon reported the crime to the local sheriff, the sheriff dismissed the complaint despite abundant physical evidence. The men who raped and killed Brandon and murdered his friends were members of a white supremacist organization, suggesting the intertwining of misogyny, racism, homophobia, transphobia, and the regulation of white femininity. In October, 1998, in Laramie, Wyoming (the state where *Brokeback Mountain* is set), 21-year-old gay man Matthew Shepard was severely beaten and left to die by two men. Although the judge in the killers' trial recognized that the murder was a hate crime, no law existed at the time to allow it to be prosecuted as such.

On the Canadian prairies, there are frequent and unaddressed murders and disappearances of Aboriginal women. In 2004, the Native Women's Association of Canada (NWAC) launched the "Sisters in Spirit" campaign to call attention to racialized and sexualized violence against Aboriginal women in Canada. NWAC estimates that approximately 500 Aboriginal women have disappeared or been murdered in the past 20 years, while emphasizing that the actual number is unknown (http://www.sistersin-spirit.ca). Their murders and disappearances frequently are not investigated by police, particularly when the missing women were involved in the sex trade, an occupation that places them outside the law and police protection. Police have also been known to take Aboriginal men on "starlight tours," a one-way ride in a police car to the edge of town. This practice sometimes includes the removal of shoes or coats in freezing weather. An unknown number of these men have frozen to death, including 17-year-old Neil Stonechild in Saskatoon, Saskatchewan, in November, 1990. Thirteen years later, he was the subject of the largest RCMP investigation in Saskatchewan's history. The resulting "Commission of Inquiry into Matters Relating to the Death of Neil Stonechild" (Government of Saskatchewan 2004) exposed considerable evidence and forced the Saskatoon

Love & Girl Dance, Still from Queer Grit by Roewan Crowe ©

Figure 8.8

police to admit that some of their members had repeatedly transported Aboriginal persons to remote locations in and outside of Saskatoon. Similarly, Aboriginal men are still being shot disproportionately by the police. For example, in February, 2005, 18-year-old Matthew Dumas was shot by Winnipeg police. Winnipeg police initially claimed Dumas was being chased by armed policemen because he was a suspect in a robbery. While a police inquiry is pending, reports show that Dumas was not involved in a robbery. This was the second police murder of an Aboriginal man by police in Manitoba within a month. Dennis St. Paul of Norway House, Manitoba was shot by police in January 2005. These stories, this recent history of the West, illustrate a kind of vigilante justice on behalf of gender regulation, heteronormativity, and white supremacy. These incidents, particularly those illustrating police violence against Aboriginal people, pose troubling questions about the role of vigilante police actions and extralegal practices to maintain the unwritten Laws of the West.

What does it mean to belong to a landscape so powerfully marked by these stories? The song "Tumbling Tumbleweeds," performed in two different versions by Toronto singer Karyn Ellis, runs throughout *Queer Grit*. The lyrics "here on the range I belong, drifting along with the tumbling tumbleweeds, lonely but free I'll be found, drifting along with the tumbling tumbleweeds" are invoked intentionally. I do not wish to evoke these lyrics as they were first employed—that is, as an assertion of a rightful ownership of the range, against the claim of Aboriginal people. My intent is to complicate a sense of rightful belonging. Jane West is a white cowgirl and she is choosing to address the past and the privileges that come to her because of her whiteness. Jane West benefits from colonization, from her whiteness and her place in the Western, especially if she chooses to play the part scripted for her; this part ensures that she benefits from the colonization of this land and that she continues to perpetuate it. *Queer Grit* shows the possibility of staking a different claim. I join a tradition of Aboriginal and non-Aboriginal artists and writers living in Canada who tamper with the tropes of the Hollywood Western. These include: Thomas King's novel *Green Grass, Running Water;* Shawna Dempsey and Lorri Millan's video, "Calamity" (2001) and performance piece "Lesbian Love Story of the Lone Ranger and Tonto" (1997); Lori Blondeau's performance piece, "A Moment in the Life of the Belle Sauvagel: (2002); and Gerald McMaster's body of work entitled *The Cowboy/Indian Show: Recent Works by Gerald McMaster* (1991), which includes the diptych (acrylic and oil on matt board) "Shaman Explaining the Theory of Transformation to Cowboys" (1990), to name a few.

What kind of justice does a politically conscious and reflective outlaw subject like Jane West seek? Jane West steps through and beyond the real and symbolic violence surrounding her to claim her Queer desire and her desire for justice. This is made possible by addressing the violence and colonization of this land. Jane West breaks out of the classic Western form, with its focus on the heroic individual, its retaliatory and vigilante justice, and its regulation of the expression of feelings. Jane is motivated by love and desire to undo the violence laid down inside of her. By doing so she disrupts the familial succession story of heteronormativity prescribed by the

Girl & Love, Still from Queer Grit by Roewan Crowe ©

Figure 8.9

Law/the father, and turns away from a traditional masculinity. Instead Jane chooses a transmasculinity, one that refuses the scripted role of violence.

Jane rides on, into a frontier of love and desire. Surprising to me, in the making and showing of *Queer Grit*, was my reaction to a scene near the end of the video between Jane and her handsome trans lover. They share a romantic swirling embrace. I was surprised by the tenderness and seduction of the scene that was created. I found myself remarkably shy about it, but, more troubling to me, I was apologetic. I used words like *mushy* and *sentimental*, with heavy judgment behind them. This led to a breakthrough in my understanding of the work. Through this awareness I discovered my Dolly Parton twang, my western voice that narrates this particular story. I tapped into the honesty and passion of those Country & Western hurtin' songs about love and pain. This voice gave me permission to express pain, violence, playfulness, tenderness, terror, and love. It became a challenge for me to see if I could show the action figures, those hard plastic dolls, actually feeling. Remember the face of Clint Eastwood and his steely grimace? Feelings are rarely evident in the Western. By the end of *Queer Grit* the toy dolls appear to be feeling, and I find myself thinking that if plastic dolls can be transformed by an experience of resistance and love, then maybe there is hope for humanity. By choosing love and connection, Jane West rides out of the Hollywood Western and its discursive limits into a potentially liberating and decolonizing space, a "differential consciousness." This potential space can be seen as a frontier of love, or as theorized by Chela Sandoval, a "political technology of love." In her book *Methodology of the Oppressed*, Chela Sandoval writes about the hermeneutics of love: "Here love is reinvented as a political technology, as a body of knowledges, arts, practices and procedures for reforming the self and the world" (Sandoval 2000: 4). She extends the theories of Foucault who has written about a social movement infused with the revolutionary possibility of love and desire.

> What is required, then, is to reinforce an experience and technology of desire-in-resistance that can permit oppositional actors to move—as Audre Lorde puts it—"erotically" though power...Foucault asks "How can and must desire employ its forces within the political domain, and grow more intense in the process of overturning the established order?" (2000: 165)

The artistic and scholarly process of traveling deep into the violence of *Unforgiven*, animating my own counterwestern *Queer Grit*, and engaging with various theorists along the way has brought me to the edge of a potentially liberatory and revolutionary horizon. Upon reflection I see that this liminal space was opened up as I confronted the Laws of the West, named the violence of the history of colonization, and explored the notion of love as a social movement. For Chela Sandoval, "love as a social movement is enacted by revolutionary, mobile, and global coalitions of citizen-activists who are allied through the apparatus of emancipation" (184). These are the possibilities offered to a Queer cultural citizen with transnational consciousness who wishes to discover ways to move outside of the seemingly unending cycle of violence. She has stepped into the wide open horizon of the frontier of love.

REFERENCES

Alexie, S. (1998) "My Heroes Have Never Been Cowboys & Reservation Drive-in," in J. Kitses and G. Rickman (eds.) *The Western Reader*, New York: Limelight Editions.

Blondeau, L. (2002) *A Moment in the Life of the Belle Sauvage* (performance piece), Saskatoon.

Coyne, M. (1998) *The Crowded Prairie: American national identity in the Hollywood western*, New York: I.B. Tauris.

Dempsey, S and Millan, L. (1997) *Lesbian Love Story of the Lone Ranger and Tonto* (performance piece), Winnipeg: Finger in the Dyke Productions.

—— (2001) *Calamity* (video), Winnipeg: Finger in the Dyke Productions.

Government of Saskatchewan (2004) *Commission of Inquiry into Matters Relating to the Death of Neil Stonechild, Honourable Mr. Justice D.H. Wright Commissioner*, Regina: Queen's Printer.

Kaplan, E.A. and Wang, B. (2004) "From Traumatic Paralysis to the Force Field of Modernity" in E.A. Kaplan and B. Wang (eds.) *Trauma and Cinema: cross cultural explorations*, Hong Kong: Hong Kong University Press.

King, T. (1993) *Green Grass, Running Water*, New York: Bantam Books.

—— (2003) *The Truth About Stories: a Native narrative*, Toronto: Anansi.

Kitses, J. (2004) *Horizons West: directing the western from John Ford to Clint Eastwood*, New ed., London: BFI.

Lawrence, B. (2002) "Rewriting Histories of the Land: Colonization and Indigenous Resistance in Eastern Canada," in S. Razack (ed.) *Race, Space, and the Law: unmapping a white settler society,* Toronto: Between the Lines.

McMaster, G. (1991) *The Cowboy/Indian Show: recent works by Gerald McMaster*, McMichael Canadian Art Collection, Kleinburg, Ontario.

Rich, B. R. (1998) *Chick Flicks: theories and memories of the feminist film movement*, London: Duke University Press.

Sandoval, C. (2000) *Methodology of the Oppressed*, Minneapolis, MN: University of Minnesota Press.

Schickel, R. (1996) *Clint Eastwood: a biography*, New York: Vintage Books.

Simmon, S. (2003) *The Invention of the Western Film: a cultural history of the genre's first half century*, Cambridge: Cambridge University Press.

Szaloky, M. (2001) "A Tale N/nobody Can Tell: The Return of a Repressed Western History in Jim Jarmusch's *Dead Man*," in J. Walker (ed.) *Westerns: films through history*, New York: Routledge.

Talpade Mohanty, C. (2003) *Feminism without Borders: decolonizing theory, practicing solidarity*, Durham, NC: Duke University Press.

Tibbetts, J.C. (1993) "Clint Eastwood and the Machinery of Violence," *Literature/Film Quarterly*, 21: 11–17.

Tompkins, J. (1992) *West of Everything: the inner life of westerns*, New York: Oxford University Press.

Walker, J. (2001a) "Captive Images in the Traumatic Western: The Searchers, Pursued, Once Upon a Time in the West, and Lone Star," in J. Walker (ed.) *Westerns: films through history*, New York: Routledge.

—— (2001b) "'Introduction: Westerns through History," in J. Walker (ed.) *Westerns: films through history*, New York: Routledge.

—— (2005) *Trauma Cinema: documenting incest and the holocaust*, Berkeley: University of California Press.

Wright, W. (1975) *Six Guns and Society: a structural study of the western*, Berkeley: University of California Press.

9   Violence, gender, and community in *Atanarjuat*

Peter Kulchyski

By now the Zacharias Kunuk film *Atanarjuat* (The Fast Runner) has been widely recognized for the milestone in film production that it is. *Atanarjuat* tells the intergenerational story of how a dangerous spirit enters a small Inuit hunting camp, slowly spreading a web of jealousy and murderous hatred, until on the plane of everyday conflict and on the plane of spiritual conflict the miscreants are put in their place and the evil spirits driven out. Shot entirely in the arctic, near the small community of Iglulik in Nunavut, where the production company, Isuma Productions, is based, the relatively low budget film was a triumph of creativity and ingenuity. While the film established new standards for "ethnographic authenticity" (a somewhat dubious category) in narrative film, its real contribution lies in both its narrative and visual power.

This chapter will address the theme of community as it is represented, reflected upon, and built through *Atanarjuat*. In a world increasingly falling prey to the interlinked logics of possessive individualism and the rule of commodity forms, the word *community* is used increasingly while its meaningful referents recede over the horizon. Jean-Luc Nancy began his well known philosophical reflection on community by stating that "the gravest and most painful testimony of the modern world...is the testimony of the dissolution, the dislocation, or the conflagration of community" (1991: 1). Although Nancy wants to problematise this "testimony,' and although his view of community sharply diverges from my own around the question of the role of production in community building and intergenerational community, his relfection remains a fertile entry to discussion.

It is possible to identify at least two kinds of communities in contemporary social forms: the collective of serialized individuals in accidental relation to each other (what Sartre called the "serial collective" in his *Critique of Dialectical Reason*), and groupings of people united in, by, and through some project (what Sartre called the "fused group"). A close look at the forms of non-alienated community that persist serves critical thought in reminding those of us enmeshed in dominant culture of what it does not "deliver" while at the same time providing a stronger appreciation for the importance of the struggle of these alternative, resistant, communities that deserve the name.

There are at least three such communities at play in the film *Atanarjuat*: the community of Inuit represented in the filmic narrative structure, the philosophical idea of community that the film works through, and the community of film workers—themselves embedded in the Inuit community of Iglulik—which the production of the film established and also represented. *Atanarjuat* stages a notion of community ultimately built upon the end of cycles of revenge violence, distinguishing its notion of community from those constructed by directors the caliber of Martin Scorsese in the *Gangs of New York* or Lars von Trier in *Dogville*, to take some relatively recent and widely seen examples. The oscillation of female characters in *Atanarjuat* as marginal and central to the project of community supplements at the same time as it displaces this discourse on violence and community. The three communities—textual, imagined/reflected upon, and produced/embodied—intersect and overlay each other, positioning the film at one and the same time as that which "destroys the gesture" it represents (Agamben, 2000) and responds to Jean-Luc Nancy's reflection regarding the story and the community: "we know the scene..." A few words regarding the history of filmic representations of Inuit and of Kunuk's previous work are in order as a way of situating the broader discussion I would like to initiate.

It is curious that with every major advance in filmic technology, a new "Inuit" film of some significance has been produced. Perhaps this is in part because of the success of the first "great" film on Inuit, that famous product of the silent era, Robert Flaherty's *Nanook of the North*, which surely must have tempted every arctic filmmaker who followed. Like *Atanarjuat*, *Nanook of the North* is complex and appeals on many levels. It has extraordinary visual power, product both of Flaherty's gaze and of his subject's acting abilities (see Nanook's struggle at the seal hole, a scene wildly out of touch with "the real thing" but worthy of Chaplin as a comic set piece). While the film is saturated with colonial tropes—an omniscient narrator who comments with condescending affection about Nanook's struggles; the exoticization that saturates the film-text; the vanishing race thematic—its heroic motif, visual drama, Nanook's uncanny expressive abilities are among the features that give the film an emancipatory moment/movement. The representation of women's bodies in *Nanook of the North* should not go unnoticed: the film participates in and constructs what I would call "ethno porn" in the display of women's bodies: as much a bow to purience as to realism. It surely must have been one of the earliest mainstream films to display women's bodies, a display sanctioned by the categories "exotic," "primitive," "other." No doubt this played some small, never acknowledged, role in its success.

The films that followed have a self-conscious relation to *Nanook of the North*. They attempt to undo some of the colonial condescension, though they also reconstruct elements of the colonial relation. In the 1950s Douglas Wilkinson made a widely seen documentary called *Land of the Long Day*, featuring Inuit leader Joseph Idlout. *Land of the Long Day*, in black and white but with sound, used a new era of filmic technology to tell an updated version of the *Nanook of the North* story: Inuit impressed and in awe of "western" technology, at home on the land. Strikingly, *Land of the Long Day* replaced the omniscient narrator of *Nanook of the North* with a first person narrative that purported to be Idlout. The film begins with an English accented male voice intoning, "I am Idlout," though, of course, neither the voice nor the script belong to Idlout at all. In *Land of the Long Day*, Idlout says all the things about himself that Nanook's narrator had to say about him in his time. The film has much more of a dated feel and is not much watched these days (though the book of the same name exhibits both an extraordinary sympathy and understanding on Wilkinson's part as well as the occasionally painful moment of condescension). Very little attention is paid to Inuit women.

In the 1960s, *The People of the Seal* series, filmed with Netsilik with the guidance of anthropologist Asen Balicki, was made. The films used color and a degree of simultaneous sound recording, though technically the size of the equipment and the amount of sound and film recording that could be done synchronically was limited to short segments. This film, or set of films, used no narrator: the strategy involves allowing the subjects to speak for themselves as they conduct their daily activities, with as many environmental sounds as backdrop as could be used. The radicality of the (non) narrative structure marks it as a particularly disruptive viewing experience that in many ways has not been surpassed in arctic film. Few signposts are placed for the viewer to orient themselves around. The film had an extraordinary and lasting impact through its use in North American classrooms. Arguably, the filmic language of *Atanarjuat* owes more to *The People of the Seal* than it does to *Nanook of the North*. The casual, camp life scenes in *The People of the Seal* could easily be situated within the narrative of *Atanarjuat*. While both *Nanook of the North* and *Land of the Long Day* are organized around a heroic male figure, *The People of the Seal* attempted to show the gender balance that prevails in Inuit culture, giving equal time to women's activities as to men's, and no singular, individuated characters emerge.

In the 1970s, Hugh Brody's *The People's Land* took advantage of technology that allowed for color film and sound synchronous recording for extended periods. The film had something of a more direct political aim, and was self-conscious about the colonial relations being imposed, and self-conscious as well about giving Inuit opportunities to "speak for themselves." Again, there is a male Inuk who is the centre of the cast and, in my view, something of a retreat from the gender egalitarianism represented by *The People of the Seal*. Each of the filmmakers was attempting to represent Inuit in a way that might be of help to Inuit (less so in Flaherty's time), and from Wilkinson to Balicki to Brody one senses a growing awareness of colonial relations and of the degree to which film itself is implied in those relations. It is *The People's Land* that takes this about as far as *Qallunaat* can take such a representational politics, in particular by attempting to undo the "vanishing race" ideology.

Near the time that *The People's Land* was made, Inuit started getting themselves behind the camera. In the 1970s Inuit voted against receiving television transmissions from satellite until there was programming available in their own language. This eventually led to the creation of the Inuit Broadcasting Corporation (IBC) in 1982. The Inuit Broadcasting Corporation started producing community based film of widely varying quality. Among the apocryphal stories told is the one about how at an early stage "community production locations" were established by sending cameras to some of the small arctic communities, including Iglulik. Whoever picked them up from the post offices when they arrived became the local IBC contact. In Iglulik, this was not a young man named Zacharias Kunuk. Kunuk, recalling the period, says that "in 1981 I sold some carvings and bought a video camera" (quoted in Geller 2004: 10). Eventually he worked in the IBC system, but for a relatively short period.

In 1985 I met Kunuk in Iqaluit for a training session at the collection of trailers that comprised their offices and production facilities. The expert who had been called in to run the session was named Norman Cohn, originally from New York but living in Montreal, and an excellent filmmaker in his own right. Kunuk showed a startling film he had made, about hunting a seal, which I wrote about in an article called "The Postmodern and the Paleolithic" (1989). That film inspired Cohn to work with Kunuk, and with the addition of Paul Apak Angilirq and Pauloosie Qulitalik, the partnership that led to Igloolik Isuma Productions and eventually *Atanarjuat* was established. By the late 1980s, Kunuk had left the IBC to make films independently through Isuma. The first film they produced was called *Qaggiq*, about the making of a large, social-gathering iglu, woven together with a narrative of a young man fending off rivals for the partnership of a young woman. The themes of community and male rivalry carry over to *Atanarjuat*. The next film made by Kunuk and Cohn through Isuma was called *Nunaqpa* (Going Inland), and involves the reconstruction of a historical-period hunting trip; the visual language of that film more closely approximates the extensive outdoor action in *Atanarjuat*. Through the first half of the 1990s, Kunuk, Cohn, and the Iglulik collective helped make the Nunavut series, a sequence of half-hour films that show the slow but steady establishment of the community of Iglulik, beginning strikingly with *The Stone House*, which like *Qaggiq* uses the motif of building a dwelling structure to represent community itself. With the experience of these films the production company was finally prepared to move on to realize Kunuk's dream of a feature length, narrative driven, film by and for Inuit.

In 1998 I traveled to Iglulik to engage in oral history research. While there I visited Isuma Productions, and chatted with Kunuk. He was then in the midst of filming *Atanarjuat*. Igloolik Isuma Productions is in an old warehouse building on the "beach" facing out from Iglulik. Since it was the month of May, the ocean was frozen and the "beach" made no impression: discerning land from water under snow took a rough guess. The building was white, tar paper style, but quite large. As soon as I entered, I felt a sense of dislocation: I was suddenly for all intents and purposes in Montreal, surrounded by black wallpaper, pieces of equipment everywhere, and Japanese art on the walls. While Kunuk didn't remember me, he was still gracious with his time, excited about the new film he was making. He showed me some of the outtakes from the beginning of the film, and described the key sequence of the character Atanarjuat running naked across the ice (I remember thinking, "I don't know, Zach, if this'll fly..."). And then, a few years later, the film became all the rage, so much so I need not here repeat the extensive list of honors it has received.

As well as the filmic technology, which changed with each of the films mentioned above and lent some elements to how each was constructed, the social technology (cf De Lauretis 1987) that circulated around these film productions changed. Flaherty and Wilkinson themselves operated in the male-heroic mode, working largely on their own: filmmaking cast as the product of the individual genius. *People of the Seal* marks a rupture, presenting itself as the product of the community itself, with guidance provided by Balicki. Brody's work is steeped in an attempt to be anticolonial, albeit still to some extent riding on an auteurish notion of film production; it perhaps marks the liminal point of attempts by *Qallunaat* filmmakers to produce a politically effective and appreciative approach to Inuit. With Kunuk's work, the social technology behind these films is displaced and reconstructed: Inuit pervade the film production, which is certainly a deliberately collaborative effort.

The film uses digital technology and obviously involves a whole new kind of social relation in its production. In these ways it marks a distinct break with the past. Kunuk is film-literate, and quite self-conscious of his relation to *Nanook of the North*, at least, as well as other Hollywood and foreign films he is attracted to. The heroic male narrative is undercut, somewhat, by the weaknesses and uncertainties of the central character: unlike Nanook or Idlout, Atanarjuat is not wholly self-confident and in charge of his world, while at the mercy of broader forces. Atanarjuat is the weaker, younger brother, who through his misadventure becomes heroic, rather than positioned through and through from the beginning as an infallible, heroic figure. Furthermore, women play a remarkable role in *Atanarjuat*, further limiting the typically male dominant tropes that circulate in much of the earlier film work (we will turn to this issue in more detail below).

With this as backdrop I would like to turn to a thematic analysis of *Atanarjuat*, focusing in particular on the theme of community. Beginning with the end, I want to emphasize the community in which the film is embedded, which has a dual aspect: the film production crew itself, and the community of Iglulik itself. In the film, the first of these is represented in the final credits, as moments of the film production are displayed. Some critics were disappointed by this moment and thought that it "broke the spell" of the film. My own view is that the moment is very important in terms of the political reception of the film. One element of the earlier films that had to be undone was the stress on Inuit living on the land, in iglus or tents. Kunuk's film narrative is set in a period when Inuit lived their traditional lifestyle, hence he had the structural and ideological problem of potentially allowing the film to buttress continuing framings of Inuit as exotic primitives. The final sequence of the film deliberately undoes such a coding by revealing the actors in their jeans and leather jackets, joking around and having smokes, revealing the technology of film production, and emphasizing the "modernity" of contemporary Inuit. The spell is deliberately broken in order to send a very important political message: Inuit are not only "then," they are "now."

The film displays or represents the particular group of people who made the film: the filmmaking "community." Of course, such ephemeral, so called communities, are commonplace. Witness, *the university community* where the term is embraced by individualized, competitive, institutional, and socially vacuous collectives such as the ones we scholars work for. The *Atanarjuat* production group is marked by two elements—apart from the representational logic—that are noteworthy. First, a large proportion of the group members come from the community of Iglulik and have an ongoing, intergenerational relationship with each other. Hence to some extent they are a subset of an established community, those from Iglulik who work for Isuma Productions. In a way the community of Iglulik is itself the final direction and almost hidden subtext of the film. We know from a very few utterances that the main camp (Sauri's camp) is the precursor of Iglulik. Doubtless the stone dwelling that appears in a few scenes is the same one whose construction was celebrated in the Nunavut series. Iglulik is also the contemporary embodiment of the represented community the film portrays, inasmuch as it is a film about the mythic establishment of an ordered community whose descendents would eventually occupy Iglulik (note that this is also the unstated theme of the Nunavut series). Iglulik is the telos, as it were, of *Atanarjuat*. This particular community, the production crew, is established through a project and a creative effort. A second element of note about the production community is that for much of the project, they lived in camps near but not in Iglulik. As a result, the film crew needed hunters and seamstresses. Life in the *Atanarjuat* camp reproduced some elements of "on the land" life which the film represents and tries to undo. In fact, no doubt many of the actors and local technicians joined in the hunt required to support camp life. In a way, the community represented by *Atanarjuat* is haunted by an uncanny double: camp life from precontact times is best filmed by setting up a contemporary camp. Fifty years from now a film on the making of *Atanarjuat* will no doubt emphasize this point.

The second community I would like to comment on is that represented in the film, the community of the character Atanarjuat. There is a good deal of deliberate confusion about this community on the part of viewers. Some think of the first section of the film as set in a mythic time, with the characters represented being gods or spirits. Some think of the whole narrative as set in mythic time, and all of the characters as mythic figures. My own view is that the question is relevant only inasmuch as there is an ambiguity that allows us to think such deeply human characters as larger than life or more than human: the founding ancestors. In my own view, what the film clearly represents is an intergenerational community, with the first sequence showing an older generation that allows an evil spirit to enter camp. Though the spirit is coded in Inuit cultural forms, ultimately it is a certain corrosive jealousy. It is jealousy that motivates Oki and his sister Puja, turning them into malign characters. For my part, it is a story steeped in history rather than myth.

Nancy writes that "myth, as Lévi-Strauss would have it, is primarily defined as that with which or in which time turns into space. With myth, the passing of time takes shape, its ceaseless passing is fixed in an exemplary place of show and revealing" (1991: 45). Surely history accomplishes some of the same ends, giving shape and thereby spacializing temporality, finding and fixing "exemplary place(s) of show and revealing." Perhaps we are better off distinguishing the two in the more mundane, culturally embedded explanatory mechanism in which we suggest myth is the narrative of the time of more-than-humans and history is the narrative of the time of humans. Foregrounding the historical emphasizes the degree to which the communities represented in *Atanarjuat* are represented as having an immanent, human origin, even though within the narrative spirit-forces clearly play a significant role.

The represented community is not idealized. It consists of scattered family camps that intersect with each other in different times and places. While the represented community goes through difficulties, it is worth noting that all of these are created socially, by the jealousy (cf Taussig 1987) that circulates rather than by, as is common in the ideological representations of Inuit, the struggle with nature (stressed in both Flaherty's and Wilkinson's work). Critically, the crisis this represented community undergoes is an intergenerational crisis: the seeds sown in an early generation come to their (evil) fruition in the generation that follows. Intergenerational communities imply and embody a whole distinct temporality of justice: the wounds created in one generation can be exacerbated or sutured in the generation that follows. For the community to continue functioning, it must find a way to ban both the malign characters and the evil spirits, and the ban becomes central to the reestablishment of justice.

The last level of community I wish to interrogate could be called the idea of community, or the philosophy of community, staged by the film and primarily embodied in the represented community. Here, the film marks in my view its most radical break with dominant narrative tropes. This is because the film founds community precisely on the ending of a violent revenge scenario. Kunuk himself, while in Winnipeg in late 2004, noted that this was one critical change he and his writer, Paul Apak Angilirq, made to the traditional legend that *Atanarjuat* dramatizes. He said they didn't feel the revenge violence theme was "appropriate" in the context of contemporary global political events. In the source-story, the character Atanarjuat kills his enemies. In the film's most striking narrative moment, Atanarjuat says "the killing stops here" and refuses to take the full revenge he is positioned for. It would be as if at the end of *Gangs of New York* the young hero refused to kill his father's murderer, or at the end of *Dogville* the divine violence were somehow halted. But this could only happen if the films exhibited a concern with what happens after the film's end. Instead, both films happily or unreflectively allow the cycle of revenge violence to continue. Of course, this theme is so dominant in mainstream films that the notion that justice demands revenge is steeped in contemporary culture. This not-accidental dominant cultural motif is what allows an attack on Iraq as a commonsensical response to the 9/11 events.

Here, then, is an idea of community that founds sociality not on a call to justice as the perpetuation of revenge violence, but as a refusal of that perpetuation, as an interruption and, perhaps, as a ban. In this notion of community, justice is not equated with the divine, cleansing violence (à la moments in Benjamin, Sorel, and Fanon) but rather with, if not forgiveness, a deliberate and calculated "rising above" the cycle and role that are prescribed. That this lesson or thought comes from contemporary Inuit, not a lesson that can be drawn from the ancient myths and knowledge of Inuit but rather from a decision made by individual Inuit creative artists in the contemporary moment as a response to that moment, does not in my mind vitiate or in any way undercut the power of the idea, though it does continue unraveling ideology (in this case the notion that primarily what Inuit have to offer contemporary times all comes from their past).

Interestingly each of the three communities has its own historicity. The production crew community has its more ephemeral but intense history around the making of the film (in part documented by Ginsburg). The represented community's history unfolds through the dramatic narrative of the film. Most interestingly, the idea of community centers around what unmakes social bonds and what is needed in order to remake social bonds. Inasmuch as this is a perpetual work that extends intergenerationally, the idea of community in *Atanarjuat* is deeply historical in orientation.

All three communities involve intensely absorbing material pertaining to gender. While the Atanarjuat–Oki rivalry is positioned as the critical narrative device, the rivalry between Puja and Atuat acts as a mirror conflict. Interestingly, Puja initially appears as a sympathetic character, the one person in the "bad" camp whose "girlish" attraction to the hero makes her appealing. Her oscillation from a sympathetic character to a malign character is one of the stronger narrative threads. Strikingly, hers is the only female body that appears, twice, in the film. In the first instance, she is displayed briefly in the erotic encounter that takes place during Atanarjuat's inland hunting trip. In the second, she is "exposed" as a gesture of renunciation on Atanarjuat's part when he cuts up her amouti. Some of the positioning of these scenes involves an intersection of the first community—of crew and Iglulik itself—and the represented community. For an individual who lives in a small northern community to expose her body in both ways is a much more risky undertaking than it is in the atomized south.

It should be noted, though, that Atanarjuat's (or actor Natar Ungalaaq's) male body is also exposed for an extended portion of the film: woman's body as narrative focus is somewhat undone in a narrative where a man's nude, running body is the centrepiece of the film. The semiotics of male body positioning in the film deserve a whole distinct analysis. For our purposes it is enough to point out that both characters, Atanarjuat and Oki, are shown in their weaknesses, with Atanarjuat's naked running body the emblem of this, as much as the scene in which Oki unknowingly urinates on him. It is the point at which Atanarjuat and his brother are seemingly dead that Oki's most malignant characteristics and the actions they lead to come to the fore (the murder of his father and rape of Atuat); prior to then he is held in check, presumably by fear, especially of Atanarjuat's brother.

There is also a gender oscillation in terms of the overall narrative. A woman elder becomes positioned as the key filmic "witness" to the events. She sees and feels the evil spirit kill her husband, is prescient about the dangers faced by Atanarjuat's camp, and provides sympathy to Atuat when Atuat is traumatized by the rape (in which her body is not shown). She also is the one who pronounces the ban near the close of the filmic narrative. At a minimum, it can be said that there are many representations of Inuit women that circulate in the film. They are not positioned as male fantasy projections (some of which we find in *Nanook of the North*, at least) and exotic others, but complex characters with varying degrees of agency. That may in part be because, as Nancy Wachowich points out, "in 1991 Isuma also established a non profit sister organization, a video co-operative called the Tariagsuk Video Centre (also known as the Women's Video Workshop)" (2006: 133). Clearly on the production side there is a strong, organized, distinct place and attention being devoted to women's image production, which no doubt has an impact on films like *Atanarjuat*.

Atanarjuat reminds us that the mainstream glorification of violence is not necessary to achieve dramatic effects. Within the dominant film world, increasing the degree and amount of represented violence has become almost a litmus test: how many shootouts can be fitted into a 90-minute entertainment? This ultimately involves a narrative refusal: rather than working with character or event, more dynamite will create all the drama required. *Atanarjuat* illustrates how a few people running over the ice can create as much tension and narrative excitement as a multimillion dollar, pyrotechnically enhanced, car chase. It also illustrates something of the violence that violence begets and poses a challenge to the culture that equates revenge with justice.

Giorgio Agamben has written, in his evocative essay "Notes on Gesture" in *Means Without End*, that film has a complex relation to gestures: "in the cinema a society that has lost its gestures tries at once to reclaim what it has lost and to record its loss" (2000: 52–53). There is a manner in which such reclamations and records can destroy the object of such veneration. For example, James Dean, because of his life circumstances, or because of the life circumstances of those he mimed, walked with a certain kind of shoulder slouch. At one time, for some people, this slouch emerges in their bodies: a challenge to authority, a demand from within a working body that it simulate the ease it longs for, or hundreds of other combinatory lines of force. It is filmed in the famous body of James Dean. By the time Martin Sheen borrows the slouch, it is no longer coming from these embodied forces. It cannot come from experience. It comes from filmic representation, an image of an image as it were (simulacrum). We can no longer slouch in just that way without it being a homage to the James Dean image: the gesture has been destroyed. The gesture is ever destroyed where the logic of the spectacle comes to rule the logic of the body.

If this is true, it is cause for concern. A film like *Atanarjuat* may be implicated in destroying all that it holds dear. When young people "learn to be Inuk" by miming the characters in *Atanarjuat*, we move to a whole different kind of intergenerational cultural transmission. The filmic construction of community at least coincides with and may actually undo community itself. Can a barn be raised or an urban garden built with the same unselfreflective ease after Peter Weir's *Witness* and *Green Card*? There may be no way around this problem, though for my part I am convinced there is no other path that Inuit film can go down. The most compelling part of Faye Ginsburg's interesting analysis of the complex interplay between funding and regulatory issues in the making of the film, published in the trilogy of articles devoted to the film in *American Anthropologist*, is her suggestion that "the kinds of benefits that *Atanarjuat* brought to Inuit living in Igloolik and elsewhere—economic, imaginative, cultural and psychological—are exemplary of what steady funding might help produce beyond the film itself" (2003: 830). In her analysis, the film embodies the possibility that new media offers as a structure for passing on and perpetuating ancient culturally based values and for embodying those values in the process of filmmaking itself. Shari Huhndorf makes the former point central to her analysis, arguing that the scenes that end the film, of the filmmakers in contemporary clothing, "show Inuit mastery of Western technologies used to accomplish their own goal of self representation, another aspect of self determination" (2003: 825). In fact, one of the points of my own "The Postmodern and the Paleolithic" was to challenge notions of technological determinism in the domain of cultural change.

The celebrations of *Atanarjuat* among critical cultural studies scholars are largely deserved, but should not cover over the problems raised by the form of film-as-media. The formulation that film destroys gesture may itself need qualification: in certain community contexts where the spectacle remains enfolded within an embodied community, social relations may trump technological determinants. This, in part, is how I read Kunuk's reaction to the enthusiastic reception of *Atanarjuat* at its opening in Iglulik: "that day I knew we did our job right" (quoted by Ginsburg 2003: 829). The film is rather a moment in the oscillation of spectacle logic and embodied social relations, not pounded into a hierarchical relation where the former comes to determine the latter: in a certain place, Iglulik, at a certain time, December 2000, a film is shown to the very people out of whom that film emerged, "and when the credits rolled people were laughing and crying and shaking our hands" (Ginsburg 2003: 829). In those smiles, in those tears, and in those touches the work of the film is absorbed through the pores of those bodies; a new kind of ancient socious creates and imagines itself.

A community is built out of a struggle with dark forces. The community itself is both flexible and precarious. It asks its members to draw on their highest selves and forgo vengeance in order to reconstruct itself "in a good way." The community draws on its duration, on an intergenerational temporality, to achieve the measure of justice required for its continuance. In its spacings and temporalities, in the activities that ground it, the community creates something: a socious, children, meat, clothing, a script, and a film.

In these ways, as well as those enumerated by Huhndorf, *Atanarjuat* is a filmic narrative of nation. It is the film of Nunavut, the story of Inuit as social beings becoming social beings. That such a narrative might undercut the very gestures out of which it emerged is cause for reflection and concern: what if the moment of imaginatively projecting the community to itself is inextricably bound to the moment of erasing the most meaningful aspects of that very community? This is the challenge that Agamben's line of thought—following straight on the heels of Benjamin's notion of the destruction of experience—leads us down. But this story is too neat, forecloses too much. Perhaps what *Atanarjuat* has to teach critical thought is that old ways can infect new media at least as much as new media can disrupt old ways. The embedded setting of filmic production and consumption can dramatically alter the mode of reception, including elements that seem intrinsic to spectacle logic: such is the subversive power of a community that deserves the name.

The latest work, called *The Journals of Knut Rasmussen*, deals with the conversion to christianity as seen from the perspective of the last shaman. Kunuk and Norman Cohn, who co-directed, comment more directly on colonial relations. Though the film does not have the same degree of narrative coherence or visual power as the earlier work, and has been less favourably received, it nevertheless is an outstanding piece of work that in some senses stages the issue of forced reconstruction of community.

While it is a fertile time for Canadian film, the sterility of debates about whether or which of Cronenberg or Egoyan is to be seen as the leading figure (leaving aside Arcand, Masden, Ballard, Wheeler, and many others) points to the unstated agreement that "great" Canadians are white males. But somewhere, far off the map of Canadian cultural sensibilities, the incomparable is quietly turning remoteness and the intense social life of small northern communities to its advantage, running an end game around the ideological constraints of colonial culture.

REFERENCES

Agamben, G. (2000) *Means without End*, Trans. V. Binetti and C. Casarino, Minneapolis: University of Minnesota Press.

Balikci, A. (1970) *The Netsilik Eskimo*, Garden City, NY: The Natural History Press.

Benjamin, W. (1971) *Illuminations*, Trans. H. Zohn, New York: Schocken Books.

Bessire, L. (2003) "Talking Back to Primitivism: divided audiences, collective desires," *American Anthropologist*, 105.4 (December).

Brody, H. (1977) *The People's Land*, Harmondsworth, UK: Penguin Books.

De Lauretis, T. (1987) *Technologies of Gender*, Bloomington: Indiana University Press.

Geller, P. (2004) *Northern Exposures*, Vancouver: University of British Columbia Press.

Ginsburg, F. (2003) "Atanarjuat Off-Screen: From 'Media reservations' to the world stage," *American Anthropologist*, 105.4 (December).

Huhndorf, S. (2003) "*Atanarjuat, the Fast Runner*: Culture, History and Politics in Inuit Media," *American Anthropologist*, 105.4 (December).

Kulchyski, P. (1989) "The Postmodern and the Paleolithic," *The Canadian Journal of Political and Social Theory*, 13.3.

——— (2006) "Six Gestures," in P. Stern and L. Stevenson (eds.) *Critical Inuit Studies*, Lincoln: University of Nebraska Press.

Nancy, J. (1991) *The Inoperative Community*, Trans. P. Connor et al., Minneapolis: University of Minnesota Press.

Sartre, J. (1978) *The Critique of Dialectical Reason, Volume One*, Trans. A. Sheridan-Smith, London: New Left Books.

Taussig, M. (1987) *Shamanism, Colonialism and the Wild Man*, Chicago: University of Chicago Press.

Wachowich, N. (2006) "Cultural Survival and the Trade in Iglulingmiut Traditions," in P. Stern and L. Stevenson (eds.) *Critical Inuit Studies*, Lincoln: University of Nebraska Press.

10 Memory, affect, and personal modernity
Now, Voyager and the Second World War

Brenda Austin-Smith

On 7 December 1941, Jack Warner, of Warner Brothers studio, was playing golf with Harpo Marx, Al Jolson, and Louis B. Mayer. Suddenly, two men ran out of the pro shop and across the green, shouting news of an attack on Pearl Harbor. Harpo, Jolson, and Mayer turned to hear, and then started walking toward the men, leaving Warner to complete his swing alone. "I sank it!" screamed Jack, "A hole-in-one!" He turned around to find himself talking to the air: "My greatest shot of the year, and no one saw it!... Pearl Harbor. Where the hell is that?" (Sperling and Millner 1998: 239–40).

Jack Warner may not have known exactly where Pearl Harbor was, but the studio he and his brother Harry oversaw was already involved in patriotic image production, having released several short films between 1940 and 1941 about the US military, with titles such as *Here Comes the*

Figure. 10.1 "Now, Voyager" © *Turner Entertainment Co. A Warner Bros. Entertainment Company. All rights reserved.*

Cavalry, Service with the Colors, March On, Wings of Steel, The Tanks are Coming, and *Meet the Fleet*. Harry Warner, head of the studio, was a staunch Roosevelt supporter, and had been urging US intervention in the European conflict for quite some time. After US entry into World War II, Warner Brothers, known as the "Roosevelt Studio" (Bennett 2001: paragraph 13), became even more embroiled in wartime politics, producing, among other titles, *Mission to Moscow*, a film that portrayed Stalin and the USSR in a positive light, and that later brought the film and its writer to the attention of the House Committee on Un-American Activities (Bennett 2001: paragraph 3).

By the early 1940s, Warner Brothers had perfected the Fordist techniques of film production practiced by all the major studios of the Golden Age of Hollywood (1930–49). It was best known for its realist and social-themed films, earning it a reputation as the "working man's studio" (Belton 2005: 79), and was one of the Big Five, the fully integrated studios that controlled all aspects of film production, distribution, and exhibition in this period. During the early years of the Great Depression, Warner's profits had vanished, but as the decade of deprivation ended, the studio was poised to retire all of its accumulated debt, and to begin enjoying the considerable revenue that World War II brought to the entire film industry (Gomery 1986: 110).

Serious films about the military and the war effort were not of course the only ones produced by Warner during these years, nor the only film genre with emotional or expressive connections to the overseas conflict. Gangster films were a studio specialty, and Sheri Chinen Biesen has recently argued that film noir, another generic staple of the Big Five studios, has its origins in the shock and horror of the attack on Pearl Harbor (Biesen 2005). In the view of another Warner studio historian, Charles Higham, the war also informed the studio's deliberate concentration on another kind of film as a part of its production strategy. In a chapter entitled "The Home Front" in his own book on Warner Brothers, Higham writes that "Jack Warner, Hal Wallis and Steve Trilling also recognized the necessity for providing films which would act as opiates for the women at home" (1975: 172). These "opiates" were "women's films": stories of romantic tribulation and heartache, set largely in the domestic sphere, and starring a bankable female star. Curiously, given Higham's glibly expressed view of the salutary effect these films were supposed to have on their target audience, women's films often substituted female suffering and disappointment for the happy ending found in most conventional romances. Undaunted by this seeming paradox, Higham moves to incorporate this odd generic fact into his psychological portrait of wartime female movie viewers, connecting their thirst for represented suffering to the explosion in studio profits:

> Deprived of their husbands, brothers and sons, millions of American
> women patronized the movies with an intensity that was unprecedented

even during the earliest years of the talkies. In supplying them with escapist fantasies, or stories of female suffering so intense that they could forget their own misery by living vicariously through the heroine on the screen, the studio obtained the most substantial box office returns in its history. (Higham 1975: 172)

Female viewers of the woman's film "felt an intoxication, a sense of being hypnotized," writes Higham, as they walked into the theatre and saw the Warner studio shield appear onscreen, and one or another famous leading lady step into the frame (Higham 1975: 173).

Though the terms in which Higham casts women's viewing experiences are bothersome for the way in which they suggest that losing oneself in a cinematic experience is a kind of minor pathology peculiar to women, I want nevertheless in what follows to examine a specific response of one woman viewer to a particular film produced by the Warner Brothers studio during World War II. Like everyone else during the war, women used the cinema as a means of escape, or more precisely, of diversion and distraction. It is possible, though, to trace the complexities of a spectator's relations with a cinematic text in ways that make clearer to us how viewers use the global products of Hollywood not only to escape, even temporarily, their immediate material distresses, but also to negotiate and make sense of their local identities. In the circulation of both people and films in the mid-twentieth century, there are charged moments of contact between the two in which the affective engagement of spectators with films is deepened and intensified by historical circumstance. The intimacy of these moments belies the distance between the site of the film's commercial production, and the site of its reception. This is modernity made personal. The hegemony of the Hollywood studio system coincided with the Great Depression, World War II, and the beginnings of postwar reconstruction in Europe and North America, providing these epochal events and phenomena with their own image and sound tracks. The sweep and energy of images offered viewers the excitement of belonging to a larger, somehow more plentiful horizon of choices, an especially freighted opportunity in times of material privation. Though meaningful interactions between viewers and film texts take place all the time, it is in the connection discussed in this essay between a British woman and an American film during this period that we can see the relationship between viewer and screen image as a willed and durable enterprise of self-fashioning. The various situations of film viewing for this spectator—including wartime theater showings in Britain, and then postwar television broadcasts and video screenings in Canada—become "sites of travel encounters" (Clifford 1992: 101), between Hollywood and the transnational experiences and memories of an immigrant woman.

Warner Brothers released *Now, Voyager*, directed by Irving Rapper and starring Bette Davis, Paul Henreid, and Claude Rains, in 1942. It was

Davis's first film of the war. Adapted from the novel of the same name published in 1941 by Olive Higgins Prouty, the film became one of the most well-known Bette Davis vehicles, and was immensely popular with audiences in North America and in Britain upon its release. Bette Davis played Charlotte Vale, a neurotic, overweight, and unattractive spinster living under the roof and rule of a tyrannical mother. Sent away into the care of a sympathetic psychiatrist after a nervous breakdown, Charlotte is urged to begin a new life by taking a cruise to South America, where she meets and falls in love with a married man named Jerry, played by Paul Henreid. The ministrations of the good doctor result in considerable weight loss, plucked eyebrows, and a wardrobe designed by Orry-Kelly, a Cinderella-like transformation of the previously dumpy heroine upon which the camera lavishes much attention. Jerry is unable or unwilling to leave his wife, and becomes worried about the emotional stability of his youngest daughter. At Charlotte's request, Jerry finally agrees to let Charlotte, now mistress of her own home and fortune, care for this daughter. The film concludes with Charlotte and Jerry agreeing to put their shared love of Tina, the girl, above their impossible passion for each other. In an originally improvised bit of business that became the film's romantic trademark (and is still imitated from time to time), Jerry takes two cigarettes, lights them both, and hands one to Charlotte as they stand on a balcony and ponder their situation. "Oh Jerry, don't let's ask for the moon," says Charlotte in the film's last line of dialogue, "We have the stars."

At the time she made *Now, Voyager*—the title is taken from a line in Walt Whitman's poem *Leaves of Grass* (1855), quoted at one point in the film itself—Bette Davis was "one of the ten top-grossing stars in Hollywood, and the most critically acclaimed female star" (LaPlace 1987: 146). She had become Warner's "chief portrayer of vicious or wronged women" (Higham 1975: 133) in films such as *Of Human Bondage* (1934), *Dangerous* (1935), *Jezebel* (1938), and *The Little Foxes* (1939). Just before *Now, Voyager*, she had also portrayed more sympathetic characters in *The Sisters* (1939), *Dark Victory* (1939), and *All This and Heaven Too* (1941). Maria LaPlace notes that what links these films for viewers and film scholars is "the Davis style," a distinct form of performance characterized by "clipped vocal inflection; darting eye movements and penetrating stares; a swinging striding walk;...and quick shifts in mood and register" (1987: 147). These features of the Davis style, writes LaPlace, "connote assertiveness, intelligence, internal emotional conflict and strength" (1987: 147). In his study of star acting, Charles Affron considers the success of Bette Davis as a marvelous aberration, given the unattractiveness of her bulging eyes and the uncontrolled rhythms of her speech (Affron 1995: 208–9). He too makes reference to the "Davis manner," mentioning its apparent source in "the angularity of her gesticulation," but credits her eventual screen triumphs to her ability, after years of toiling in "the Warner Brothers' salt mines," to restrain herself: "Her rise in films and the power of her response to the medium are directly related to an ever increasing refinement of her identity" (Affron 1995: 209). And it is in her performance as Charlotte Vale in *Now, Voyager* that Affron sees Davis as most in tune with her director, her own acting gifts, and her star persona.

Adding to the effect of Bette Davis as an on-screen presence was her off-screen history as a rebellious career-minded woman whose achievement of stardom enabled her to challenge her bosses. Sperling and Millner refer to her as "Jack Warner's most difficult problem child" (1998: 219) as they recount the confrontation Davis had with the head of the studio over the bad scripts she was handed after the release of *Dangerous* in 1935. Furious, Davis left the studio, signed with an agent who worked for British studios, and flounced across the ocean in high dudgeon. Jack Warner took her to court for breach of contract in 1936. Davis lost the case, but won the war against Warner. Her roles improved significantly afterwards. The sympathetic accounts of the court trial in publications such as *Life*, which did a cover story on Davis in 1939, three years after the case, consolidate a star image that signified, in LaPlace's terms "rebellion against authority and a willingness to fight for herself and her autonomy as an artist" (LaPlace 1987: 149). Other important elements in this portrait of Davis were her relationships: the *Life* article mentioned above refers to her divorce and remarriage after 1936:

> Another indication of how satisfactory Bette Davis finds her professional life was [her] opinion of marriage… "Domesticity is all right if it's not carried too far."… Characteristic also was the reason Harman Nelson divorced the screen's most celebrated impersonator of vixens… she studied her parts in bed. ("Bette Davis," Life, 8 January 1939, 58)

A certain degree of romantic indifference, born of her independence of mind and concentration on her art, shades the picture of Bette Davis that emerges from these accounts.

Though there is no evidence that all of this material about the off-screen Bette Davis circulated widely in Britain in 1942, publications such as *Picturegoer*, *Film Post*, and *Screen Stories*, fan magazines of the period that supplied many of the stories and biographical tidbits that made up the nimbus of fantasy and fact surrounding stars, certainly did. And Davis's many films were screened all over Britain in movie palaces like the Carleton, a cinema in Nottingham, where a fourteen-year-old woman I shall call "Harriet" worked as an usher. Harriet was 72 years old when I talked to her about her experiences during the late 1930s and early 1940s as a film fan. As a young woman who maintained her film fandom as she lived and worked through the blitz, and who made a home in Canada after the war, Harriet animates the imbricated elements of media and migration discussed by Arjun Appadurai in *Modernity at Large* (1997: 3). Her recounting of cinema memories also provides a glimpse of the underdetermined nature of film spectatorship and the positioning of the self in relation to popular culture.

When Britain was bombed, shortly after declaring war on Germany in 1939, some movie theatres closed, but as people adjusted somewhat to their situation, Hollywood revenues "soared to twice pre-war levels" (Gomery 1986: 23). According to Annette Kuhn's book on cinema culture in Britain, the thirties had seen a rise in movie admissions from 903,000,000 in 1934 to 1,027,000,000 by 1940 (Kuhn 2002: 1). By 1942, the year of *Now, Voyager*'s release, Harriet was thus one of the 40 per cent of the British population that Kuhn estimates was going to the movies at least once a week. The upward trend in movie going continued for the next few years: Jackie Stacey reports in her book *Star Gazing* that box office returns for 1945 in Britain totaled £114,200,000, almost three times the equivalent figure for 1940 (Stacey 1994: 83). According to Jeffrey Richards's study of film-going in Britain in the 1930s, the audience for cinema was "young, working class, urban and more often female than male" (1984: 15), a description that captures most of the markers of Harriet's sociological identity as a miner's daughter in a northern British military centre. Richards, Kuhn, and Stacey all stress the enormous importance of cinema to the British public in the middle decades of the twentieth century. And from an analysis of 350 written responses to her request for women's memories of female stars, Stacey draws the general conclusion that "the significance of the cinema in women's lives in the 1940s and 1950s cannot be overestimated" (1994: 81).

For Harriet, working part-time in a Nottingham theatre in 1942, *Now, Voyager* was a revelation. In the first week of the film's release, Harriet and her sister went to see the film eight times. This indulgence was rendered affordable by one sister's buying the ticket, going into the bathroom, and handing the ticket out the window to the other sister. Recalled Harriett: "The war was on and there wasn't, you know, no money, and it was blackout, so she'd go to the washroom and pass me the ticket out." Always a Bette Davis fan, Harriet was captivated by *Now, Voyager*, and by its specific enunciation of the Davis star persona. By the time the film finished its run in Nottingham, Harriet had formed a very personal relationship with the film and its star. She resembles, in her life-long devotion to Bette Davis and to this film, the "enduring fans" studied by Annette Kuhn. Kuhn writes of enduring fans: "The very intensity of their engagements with their chosen stars and films means that their testimonies yield illuminating insights into the interrelations between cultural memory, cinema memory and films" (2002: 197). Enduring fandom is signaled not only by the fan's ability to recount, often to the very day, the moment when the passionate relationship with the film or star began, but also by the fan's maintenance of devotion to the star or film through relationships in the present. For Harriet, the most significant of these relationships is with her daughter-in-law, a woman with whom she now rents *Now, Voyager* for home viewing, and in whose company she can experience the complex set of emotions the film triggers for her without self-consciousness. At the screening of the film I held on campus in the fall of 2000, for example, Harriet and her daughter-in-law sat in the dimly-lit room together, and reached out to hold each other's hands at one very emotional point in the film, when Jerry, walking up a flight of stairs to embrace his daughter, says "I love you" to Tina, all the while looking up and over her shoulder to Charlotte, who stands on the stairs above them both.

Harriet's embodiment of enduring fandom took shape in those first few days of sneaking into the theatre to see *Now, Voyager*. The blitz was underway, and though Harriet remembers most of the bombs falling on Nottingham as incendiary, fires and fatalities were still common. Her father, whom she described as a good man, though very strict, eventually made her quit her job at the theatre, because it had been set ablaze by an incendiary, though she reports being unconcerned by the danger. Harriet was a fan of films generally, and she and her sister took turns purchasing *Picturegoer*, which they hid under the mattress of the bed. But it was Bette Davis, and especially Bette Davis in this film, who affected Harriet most powerfully. Harriet loved the Davis style, and defended the actress vehemently against the criticisms of her own older sister:

> She was such a fantastic actress that you could hate her, and you could love her, you know, and my sister and I used to argue about it. She'd say, "Oh, she's awful. I hate her for this." Why? And I says, "Look at, look at. Woo," you know, because the way she was, but that was the way, she was such a good actress, and the way she would strut along with that cigarette, you know, the way she'd walk and strut along. Just the way she was.

Harriet's repetitions and hesitancies here suggest a degree of satisfied wonder at the sight of Davis onscreen that cannot fully express itself except by reference to the fact of the actress's sheer presence, as well as her dramatic range. Harriet is exasperated by those who cannot, as she can, see and appreciate the plenitude of signification in the star's image, a fullness that demands some sort of witness even as it defies explication. Like many fans, Harriet eventually extended her adoration of the star into imitation, a fan practice Jackie Stacey describes as a taking on of star gestures, postures, or mannerisms (Stacey 1994: 162-67). Stacey also noted that in her study of female fans of movie stars, the ones most likely to be imitated "tended to be those associated with the more 'confident,' 'powerful' feminine identities, such as Bette Davis and Joan Crawford" (Stacey 1994: 167). Harriet imitated Bette Davis's look, and continued to make use of this imitative gesture for years after she immigrated to Canada as a war bride and started a family.

Harriet's interest in Davis was also rooted in the actress's emotional vehemence, bravery, and stubbornness, which Harriet admired:

> She could be nice, and she could be, she had the look. In fact, my daughter will say, "You've got the look." "What do you mean?" She says, "You've got that look." And I don't know what it is. Kelly's dad says the same thing, "You've got that look." And, I'll say, "Well, the Bette Davis look?"

Long after her youthful connection with Davis as someone whose personal dress or hairstyle was worth copying had passed, Harriet used "the Bette Davis look" to signal her displeasure at family members who crossed her, borrowing from the star's feisty image to make herself, like Davis, a woman to reckon with. Harriet's citation of Davis as the source of this look also kept alive an aspect of Davis' star power years after the actress's death, a form of fan worship more vivid and corporeal for Harriet than preserving newspaper clippings and photographs.

But the power of the Bette Davis cultural formation, which was fed by fan press and advertising tie-ins that featured makeup tips and fashion advice from the star herself, does not account fully for Harriet's persistent attachment to this one film over several decades of her life. Rather, the practice of wartime cinema going itself, combined with *Now, Voyager*'s story arc and thematic content, enabled Harriet to ally herself through fantasy with elements of Bette Davis's star persona as channeled through the character of Charlotte Vale. Harriet's self-construction, made possible through the vehicle of mass culture, is an illustration of Appadurai's contention that imagination "is a form of work...and a form of negotiation between sites of agency (individuals) and globally defined fields of possibility" (Appadurai 1997: 31). In this pleasurable alliance, Harriet experienced a temporary escape not only from the stress of wartime and the blitz, but also from a patriarchal working class household, whose restrictions intensified her experience of wartime privations such as rationing:

> I was working in a lace factory, making lace. And I was in a clerical position and then I went to work in guns and ammunition. You went to work and you brought your pay packet home and opened it and you gave it to your parents. And if they wanted to give you something, I used to get sixpence on a Friday night; we could go to the show, and get a chocolate bar. No, I couldn't get a chocolate bar because they were rationed. An ice cream bar, maybe. That was your allowance.

As a young unmarried working woman, Harriet was technically "mobile," the term given by the British Ministry of Labour to women conscripted and moved anywhere for work during the war effort after the 1941 National Service Act (No. 2), though her parents' reliance on her pay packet rendered her somewhat "immobile," confined to a local work region because of family responsibilities (Lant 1996: 15). The shift in her employment from lace making to gun manufacture as the labor shortage in Britain became more acute is an occupational reflection of the "complicated and contradictory interaction of femininity and nationhood" during World War II (Lant 1996: 14). Throughout these work experiences, Harriet recalled Bette Davis as a woman able to combine glamour successfully with emotional toughness, something British women were also encouraged to do by the often conflicting discourses of film, radio, and print media during the war, which stressed the necessity for them to both retain their femininity and to become skilled and efficient contributors to the war effort (Lant 1996: 24–28). Glamour was in short supply on the ground in wartime Britain, but on conspicuous display in films like *Now,Voyager*, with its depiction of extravagant clothes, richly appointed homes, dinner parties, concerts, and international leisure travel. In contrast to the scarcity and class stratification of Nottingham, Hollywood film offered Harriet the abundance and social possibility associated with the United States. Indeed, the role of the United States as a site of modernity in the cultural imaginary of Britain increased in influence as the war came to its end, as the editors of *Moments of Modernity* stress in their introduction, writing that "modern life in Britain after the war was inextricably bound up with the material provision and cultural symbolism of the United States" (Conekin et al. 1999: 19). Appadurai also testifies to the transnational reach of America's glamorous image, and the air of cosmopolitanism transmitted on the waves of its electronic media (Appadurai 1997: 1–3). The lure of America is evident even in *Now, Voyager*'s storyline, with the Austrian-Hungarian Paul Henreid cast as a South American architect who eventually takes up residence in Boston as his career blossoms.

Growing up in Nottingham, Harriet remembered being scapegoated at school, punished for infractions of which she was innocent, all because her father was a miner. Her family lived in a blue-collar neighborhood, but Harriet recalled being looked down upon by neighbors who believed that they should rightly have made their home in the area of town known as "the Bottoms." Throughout her adult life, Harriet remained acutely conscious of the class prejudice she suffered as a girl and then as a young woman. Her experience of class prejudice and social mockery also informed her affection for Davis's portrayal of Charlotte Vale in *Now, Voyager*. Charlotte, the daughter of Back Bay wealth, was similarly teased and humiliated in the film, and shared familial difficulties with Harriet: regardless of Charlotte's riches, she was downtrodden and oppressed. Far from being the intoxicated, hypnotized spectator of Charles Higham's creation, then, Harriet, and presumably thousands of others like her, used the images before them in the cultivation of what Richard Dyer calls a "utopian sensibility." Entertainment, argues Dyer, offers us "[a]lternatives, hopes, wishes…the sense that things could be better, that something other than what is can be imagined and maybe realized" (Dyer 1993: 273). In the story of Charlotte Vale, a woman who is ordered by her doctor to go on a cruise, who asserts herself in defiance of a domineering mother, and who meets a man to whom she can respond freely and passionately, Harriet found an imagined self, a screen utopia made to measure.

Cinema attendance during the war was for many women a refuge from the disorientation and dislocation of war—caused not only by the absence of service-aged male relatives, but also by the presence in one's home of billeted strangers. Cinemas were warm in the midst of coal shortages (Stacey 1994; Thumin 1996), and provided the familiar and comforting faces of adored stars. According to the women whose written accounts of the time are analyzed in Stacey's book, the cinema was also a place of community, providing spectators with a "shared group identity," a sense of belonging to an audience that women identified as crucial to the delights of the experience (Stacey 1994: 100). Movies were also an escape from the sadness of war, something stressed in Harriet's recollections, though these memories are at the same time shot through with terms that indicate the looming presence of her father in her life, not unlike that of the controlling mother in *Now,Voyager*:

> You know your family's gone to war, the neighbour's sons got killed or wounded, and you know, it was, it was a garrisoned town where I was living in, so it was very restricted to be going out. The buses stopped running at nine o'clock at night …mind you we was only allowed out once a week if my father felt like it, and this was the local movie place.

Documents in the Mass Observation archives suggest that for young moviegoers during the war, movie theatres functioned much like pubs did, as places to meet others, to obtain relief from the pressures of daily factory and work routines, and to experience a certain amount of privacy (Thumin 1996). For Harriet, movie going provided the added and crucial opportunity for private emotional expression at a time during which the national persona was one of fortitude and restraint:

> That's why you went to those pictures. Why I went to them…and if you wanted a good cry that was allowed but, you know, because my father used to say, "You don't cry. You're strong." But that was allowed.… Well, there's so much sad, the war was on, there's so much sadness, that you didn't want to dwell on the bad things. Because my father was always talking about if the Germans came over what he would do, he would kill his girls, so we was frightened of that, you know, there's all the military around you and you think, it just seemed that you were surrounded. Everywhere you looked there was military.

In these memories, her father's control over Harriet's physical movements and emotional expression is matched and exceeded by the control he claims over her body, her sexuality, and her life. Confronted with the dire prospect of rape by an invading army on the one hand, or murder by her own father on the other, Harriet sought solace in the movies. Her inspiration became Charlotte Vale, the ugly duckling whose mental illness is the result, the doctor declares, of maternal tyranny, and who emerges from her shipboard convalescence as an alluring swan, the camera focusing on her well-turned ankles, shapely legs, and inexplicably beautiful face, shaded by a chic white hat.

Charlotte's achievement of freedom, love, wealth, and beauty in spite of her stifling, limited upbringing seems to have resonated powerfully for Harriet, who never stopped measuring her own marital and familial happiness against that of her favorite film character. This ongoing gesture of comparison is something Annette Kuhn sees as characteristic of women who reached adolescence at the beginning of the war. This group of young women, writes Kuhn, "enthusiastically embraced aspirations for lives very different from those of their mothers," aspirations "informed by their dreams of a better, more beautiful self, dreams nourished and given expression through cinema culture" (2002: 132).

Appadurai also writes about cinema as a field of aspiration that has the power to shape the imagining self, observing that mass media present "a rich, ever-changing store of possible lives, some of which enter the lived imaginations of ordinary people more successfully than others" (Appadurai 1997: 58). His remarks resonate in relation to Harriet's experience of intense and textured identification with *Now, Voyager* and its heroine. In many ways, Harriet's social situation even resembles that of a long-suffering heroine in a movie melodrama. Her powerless position in an authoritarian, patriarchal family, and her class immobility, for example, find an echo in the curfews of a garrisoned city in wartime, constructing her as the damsel beset on all sides by threat and limitation. Harriet has so consistently connected the film to major and traumatic events in her life that her deep responsiveness to it seems to spring both from the initial circumstances in which she viewed it, and from her desire to shape her life according to the affective plan offered to her by the film and Bette Davis' star performance.

Though *Now, Voyager* never directly acknowledges the war, in one notable sequence the force of conflict's presence in the extradiegetic world seems to dictate the terms of the scene, what Robyn Warhol describes as the technologies of affect (2003: 41). In this sequence, Charlotte runs into Jerry at a party by accident, some months after their initial separation, and they arrange to meet later that evening. Charlotte returns home to wait for him in the drawing room of her immense family mansion. A cut to a clock shows the passage of time: it is now almost midnight. Charlotte is suddenly summoned by a phone call from Jerry, who is at the train station. He is determined not to interfere with her engagement to another man, and is about to leave on the last train without seeing her. Rushing into the night, Charlotte reaches the station moments before the train leaves, managing to speak to and embrace Jerry before they part once again. As she stands on the platform in the centre of the medium one-shot, moving toward the camera for a close-up, the light spilling from the windows of the departing train plays across her grief-stricken face, illuminating it in a pattern reminiscent of the lighted centers and black frames of a film strip, before the camera tilt pans down to reveal her corsage of camellias, a secret sign of love, wilted and ruined. The setting of their separation is emotionally overdetermined for anyone having lived through World War II, when good-byes to soldiers departing by trainloads were a common experience for Harriet, her family, and her friends. This scene was one that inevitably brought her to tears as she remembered the deaths of local young men, and her own separation from a young Canadian soldier with whom she began a pen-pal relationship, and whom she eventually traveled overseas to marry in 1946.

"All emigration is based on misapprehension; so is every welcome," writes short story author Mavis Gallant in her introduction to the book *The War Brides*. Gallant worked as a journalist in 1944 and traveled with several war brides on a train from Halifax, Nova Scotia, gathering their first impressions of Canada for publication in *The Montreal Gazette* (Hiebert 1978: xvi). Gallant elaborates not only on the nature of the shock that awaited many of these women as they confronted unfamiliar climates and distances, but the related shock of the new in-laws and extended families that received them (Hiebert 1978: xv). Confusion, hostility, misunderstanding, and homesickness were common, and Gallant marvels not that so many of these marriages failed, but that so many survived, especially given the tensions created when young couples had to share living space with often intolerant in-laws (Hiebert 1978: xvi). Many of the trials described by Gallant, and by other women interviewed in similar collections, were shared by Harriet, who, at the age of 19, married a Canadian soldier in England, and soon thereafter immigrated to Winnipeg, Manitoba. Harriet found her new life on the Canadian prairies very trying. She stayed for one year, and then returned to Britain in 1947, discontented with her new home and with her new mother-in-law, whom she remembers as forever dictating how and where the young family was going to spend their holidays. As a young mother dealing with a difficult and hypercritical relative, Harriet turned to *Now,Voyager* once again for validation and comfort, recognizing another commonality between her own life and Charlotte Vale's:

> …And the, the way her mother was, her mother treated her. My mother was good to me, but my mother-in-law wasn't. And I can relate with her with my mother-in-law because I could do nothing right with my mother-in-law, and it took me back. And I thought, "Oh, I'm her," you know. Just with a different life style. But it was there, you know, because I wasn't happy with my mother-in-law at all. She didn't agree with me, so it was a hard life.

Harriet eventually returned to Canada in 1953 with her two children, but continued to express her unhappiness at living in Canada. From time to time, Harriet saw *Now, Voyager* on television, and each time she would cry over the film, even though viewing it gave her immense pleasure. Recalling her final move to Canada, Harriet said this about her husband and her life here in relation to her favorite film:

> And that's the way I feel. Even now I feel I've been cheated, you know? And yet he's, he's a good man. But my heart's not in it. So when I get down I put a movie on and that comes on and away, I'm way away. It's just a movie. But it's not. It's because I didn't want to come back to Canada.

For Harriet, a screening of *Now, Voyager*, in her words, "brings it all back," the fear and promise for her of 1942. Memories of wartime deprivation, of her family's poverty, of class discrimination, and of her powerless position within her family are mixed with imaginative constructions of herself as Charlotte Vale, the woman who, through the adoring attention of a soft-spoken lover, one day learns to stand up for herself, and becomes the beautiful woman she never thought she could be. Davis's star turn as Charlotte Vale in *Now, Voyager* has become part of Harriet's emotional canon of endlessly meaningful films, a reservoir of images to be consulted for advice and turned to for both inspiration and consolation. The life-long endurance of Harriet's loyal fandom embodies the mobility of both cultural products and people, as well as the emotional exchanges that take place between regionally located viewers with often complexly transnational pasts and identities, and an industrial vehicle of the global imaginary: Hollywood film.

The image of Bette Davis striding across the screen in *Now, Voyager*, cigarette held in a stylish hand, is for Harriet now so evocative that it has almost managed to detach itself from the rest of the film's narrative. Nostalgia, regret, desire, and admiration mingle in her response to the film and to the actress, creating a surplus of feeling that can be summoned up just by closing her eyes, "Because," as she said to me, "I can think about Bette and that, and I can just sit there and the tears will come."

ACKNOWLEDGMENT

My thanks to the Social Sciences and Humanities Research Council of Canada and to the University of Manitoba Centre on Aging for support in the preparation of this research.

REFERENCES

Affron, C. (1995) Star Acting: Gish, Garbo, Davis, New York: E.P. Dutton.

Appadurai, A. (1997) *Modernity at Large: cultural dimensions of capitalism*, Delhi: Oxford University Press.

Belton, J. (2005) *American Cinema, American Culture*, 2nd ed., New York: McGraw-Hill.

Bennett, T. (2001) "Culture, Power and *Mission to Moscow*: film and Soviet-American relations during World War II," *The Journal of American History*, 88.2, Online. Available HTTP: <www.historycooperative.org/journals/jah/88.2/bennett.html> (accessed 26 October 2004).

"Bette Davis" (8 January 1939) *Life*, 53–58.

Biesen, S.C. (2005) *Blackout: World War II and the Origins of Film Noir*, Baltimore: Johns Hopkins University Press.

Clifford, J. (1992) "Traveling Cultures," in L. Grossberg, C. Nelson, and P.A. Treichler (eds.) *Cultural Studies*, New York: Routledge.

Conekin, B., Mort, F. and Waters, C. (eds) (1999) *Moments of Modernity: reconstructing Britain 1945–1964*, London: Rivers Oram Press.

Dyer, R. (1993) "Entertainment and Utopia," in S. During (ed.) *The Cultural Studies Reader*, London: Routledge.

Gomery, D. (1986) *The Hollywood Studio System*, New York: St. Martin's Press.

Hiebert, J. (ed.) (1978) *The War Brides,* Toronto: PMA Books.

Higham, C. (1975) *Warner Brothers*, New York: Scribner.

Kuhn, A. (2002) *Dreaming of Fred and Ginger: cinema and cultural memory*, New York: New York University Press.

Lant, A. (1996) "Prologue: Mobilizing Femininity," in C. Gledhill and G. Swanson (eds) *Nationalising Femininity*, Manchester: Manchester University Press.

LaPlace, M. (1987) "Producing and Consuming the Woman's Film: discursive struggle in *Now, Voyager*," in C. Gledhill (ed.) *Home is Where the Heart is: studies in melodrama and the woman's film*, London: British Film Institute.

Richards, J. (1984) *The Age of the Dream Palace: cinema and society in Britain 1930–39*, London: Routledge and Kegan Paul.

Sperling, C.W. and Millner, C. (1998) *Hollywood Be Thy Name: the Warner Brothers story,* Lexington: University Press of Kentucky.

Stacey, J. (1994) *Star Gazing: Hollywood cinema and female spectatorship*, London: Routledge.

Thumin, J. (1996) "The Female Audience: mobile women and married ladies," in C. Gledhill and G. Swanson (eds.) *Nationalising Femininity*, Manchester: Manchester University Press.

Warhol, R. (2003) *Having a Good Cry: effeminate feelings and pop-culture forms*, Columbus: Ohio State University Press.

Part III

The culture of film and the production of history

11 Alterity, activism, and the articulation of gendered cinemascapes in Canadian Indian country

Kathleen Buddle

INTRODUCTION[1]

Marrying art and social change, documentary filmmaking in Canada by Native women provides an important confluence of cultural *action* and feminist accountability. Beginning with the assumption that people engage with media in ways that are both socio-culturally embedded and idiosyncratically meaningful, this anthropologically informed analysis of Native film contextualizes the social practices pervading the sites of Native women's media production, and theorizes the "habitus" emerging from these practices (cf. Bourdieu 1990, 1993). The aim is to provide a more nuanced understanding of film work as a form of cultural action that is comprised by deeply politicized "contact zones" (cf. Pratt 1992).

Directorial virtuosity in the Aboriginal film world is expressed in a certain kind of agency—one that is informed by a relational consciousness. The renditions of womanhood that are performed in film production settings, for example, are in no way arbitrary, but are "creatively contingent on a field of preconditions which constitutes a set of references" (Hughes-Freeland 1998: 7). The collective recognition of value that occurs in the interstices where film and other fields meet is contingent upon conditions that exist in each of the intersecting spheres. These spheres consist of the institutions, discourses, narratives, and practices of "locality."

Among other cross-hatchings, filmmaking fields interpolate with multiple spheres of women's work and knowledge. The aesthetics and forms of prestige and proficiency that are esteemed in these areas serve as referents to which agents in emerging contact zones creatively gesture. These interstitial fields represent new contexts which both exceed the conceptual and material boundaries of "communities," and which generate new conditions for the "production of locality" (Appadurai 1996: 179).[2]

Examining film production sites sheds light on the ways that new political subjects and practices are articulated with and against older hegemonic formations. Aboriginal filmmaking thus "distinguishes" itself not in abstract oppositional terms, as against other filmmaking traditions, but rather, in terms of the relationships that are established between film praxis

and other Native institutional, individual, and family patterns of production and frameworks for labor—in the ways filmmaking becomes newly
embedded in, and produces, specific social contexts.[3]

Perhaps because filmmaking has been incorporated across Indian Country into broader projects of "cultural production" from which both cultural products, including films and local subjects are derived, there is a
tremendous emphasis on the *mode of participation* with which Native films
are brought off. Filmmaking, however, seems to require more than meeting the minimum requirements for engaging legible cultural practices—the
"habitus," or regular reproducible patterns of action of a cultural world
(Bourdieu 1977). As an inter-cultural training ground, there is a strategic
and expressive dimension to the articulation of cultural practice that is best
encompassed by the notion of "performance" (Schieffelin 1998: 199).

In what follows, I advance the argument that filming itself is an important form of performative action that has illocutionary rather than representational power in the arena of Aboriginal gender relations. Fields of film
labor delimit places where women are able to organize their gendered and
"culturalist" projects and to perform selected versions of their selves. These
expressive practices serve to consolidate values from other fields and enable
women to work out the ways social categories, political change, and subjectivity are connected "as they are actually lived and felt" (Williams 1977:
133). I show that in attempting to organize systems of knowledge, meaning,
and affect, women's filmic action shares with other forms of Aboriginal
aesthetic expression the pragmatic goal of re-establishing an ethos of "balance." While the finished film texts may do their work on a more expansive
even, world stage, production practices are oriented toward reconfiguring
the social dynamics of the groups of people in whom "locality" is relationally anchored. Emphasizing the practices of production rather than filmic
representations invites reflection on a sphere of activity in which social
actors perform their cultural competency for fellow "insiders."

In making films, Native women may both appeal to and challenge dispositions associated with "traditional" womanhood. Their documentary
practices seem to represent at once a negotiating of urges toward identification and community, and a critique of those dominant integrationist
methods of modern nation-building that colonialism continues to under-
write (Buddle forthcoming). Their defiant accommodations draw attention
to the ways that access to symbolic resources is stratified among members
of urban and reserve Aboriginal populations.

FILMIC ACTION AND THE
PRODUCTION OF LOCALITY

I take it as axiomatic that Aboriginal peoples' identifications are respon-
sive to a constantly shifting context. This assertion supports a version of

community that is closer to Appadurai's concept of "locality" (1996: 178) than it is to constructions of cultural collectivities that take for granted the congruence and stability of cultural, political, and geographic boundaries. The notion of locality as a relational achievement is especially relevant to this study of women's filmmaking sites which addresses Aboriginal women's multiple but material, scattered, and often disconnected contemporary working conditions. I argue that women's provisional engagements in filmmaking have implications for their capacities to act socially or to embody locality, and to position themselves within socially and spatially defined groups.

This analytic strategy serves as a critique to scholarly approaches that treat Aboriginal territorial formations such as reserves as if their "locality" were given. Disrupting, rather than protecting Aboriginal forms of sociality, the Canadian reserve system erected arbitrary boundaries around multi-First National populations and between the members of extended kin groups; relocated and reconfigured previously functioning work units, radically redirecting trade and communication routes; barred Native people from urban areas and from incorporating the potentialities they afforded into their existing socialities; and dramatically transformed the ways Native peoples would engage in socio-cosmological and political practices.[4]

State efforts to *localize* "Indianness" at certain historical moments as oppositionally remote and insular or "too far," and at others as failingly integrated, or "too close," reveal an uncanny convergence of interests between Aboriginal social formation and state policy for regulated public life. They tell little, however, about Aboriginal peoples' actual associations, commitments, attachments, involvements, and movements. The relative ability with which Aboriginal and non-Aboriginal Canadians are able to determine boundaries for others, to shape others' lives by exerting control over the production, circulation, and consumption of signs and objects and over the making of subjectivities and realities is an enduring social fact. Its recognition ought to serve as a powerful incitement against adopting facile models of Aboriginal sociality that fail to take into account the ways supposedly "traditional" social formations may be implicated in the discourses of colonialism itself.

Not necessarily imagined as a cohesive system of beliefs, values, and behavior (Clifford 1988), nor a tangibly bounded geographic locale in which the social form of these traits becomes realized, the concept of "locality" more appropriately denotes something relational, contextual, and partial (Appadurai 1996: 178).

Attending to social interaction and sociality rather than nationalism and identity allows for a consideration of the ways social engagement and action themselves provide the basis for identifications—the most powerful among them not necessarily being with spatialized and totalized "communities." Non-Natives often erroneously assume that specific tracts of Aboriginal territory are the preeminent frames in which Native peoples make their lives. Without elucidating the actual social relations in which the idea of an Aboriginal community is realized, however, it is difficult to account for the emotive power territorial constructions call forth (Buddle 2005). As Amit suggests, in order to apprehend how it is that people *realize* locality, we must explore "the visceral nature of community, that these are not coldly calculated contracts, but embodied, sensual and emotionally charged affiliations" (2002: 16). With regard to Native women's filmic practice, this requires attention to the conditions, politics, and meaning of production. This includes investigating contested processes for producing locality and history and for achieving cultural competency. Because it denotes a meaningful reconfiguring of complex strategies of alliance and of cultural capacity production, community filmmaking has important implications both for Native women's nascent subjectivities and for Native sociality more generally.[5]

"SKIN" FLICKS: THE CONTINGENCY OF AESTHETIC POWER[6]

Edmonton-based Cree, Chipewyan visual artist, Jane Ash Poitras exhibits her paintings in prestigious galleries, museums, and in international art shows. She does not sign her video work, however, nor does it traffic through the circuit of Aboriginal film festivals that are held annually in most major Canadian cities. Instead, she organizes screenings of her videos for Edmonton Police Services. The aesthetic she shoots for is a clear enough picture to yield an identification under what are usually poor lighting conditions. The footage consists mainly of the automobile license plates and partial profiles of the johns who pick up under-aged Aboriginal prostitutes in Poitras's neighborhood. Although she rarely succeeds in capturing an "event," Poitras never fails to establish her presence. That who, how, and why Poitras is filming, involves extensive prior negotiation and requires the recognition and ongoing approval of fellow members of certain urban Aboriginal polities. It is this improvisational capacity to provisionally achieve a recognized form of sociability that is what counts in evaluations of Aboriginal cinema in Native circles. And, the stakes associated with meeting such standards are high, for as Leuthold rejoins, "aesthetic expression and assumptions about the aesthetic help keep native communities together" (1998: 1).

Insofar as it answers a call to engagement or "activism," Poitras's video work is not unlike that produced by Native women who make documentary films professionally. She uses visual recording devices to enact a particular rendition of unity with which other analogously positioned individuals are compelled to identify. She expresses her own "oneness" in the process, thereby providing a measure of her commitment not merely to interpreting the world, but to active involvement in it. Although Native film contexts are profoundly intercultural places, the grounded, practical, or embodied orientation that characterizes Aboriginal women's filmmaking provides a degree of "distinction" rendering it unique from other sets of cultural practices (cf. Bourdieu 1993).

The style of politically engaged filmmaking that characterizes Native women's documentary praxis, reveals a greater concern with tangible manifestations of social change than with the aesthetic dimensions of finished film products. The attention to the experiential in Aboriginal women's filmic practice diverts attention away from the finished film products, toward the practices of production (cf. Ginsburg 1993). This is evinced in the almost invariable presence of a second and sometimes a third film crew whose role is to document the "making of" process.[7] Shirley Cheechoo[8] (Cree) performs her vision of sociality by deploying filmmaking as an opportunity to train youth on reserves. On her sets, each crew member is shadowed by at least one Aboriginal youth, who is able to learn "by watching and by doing." Film production contexts such as this create new symbolic realities not simply by transmitting an argument, description or commentary via the film text, but rather by socially constructing a situation in which participants experience symbolic meanings as part of the process of what they are actually doing.

What filming means in First Nations contexts is likely to be obscured if films are approached merely as "representations" that can be abstracted from film *texts* and analyzed apart from the identity projects and discourses in which their meanings develop. In a field where aesthetic power is evaluated in terms of the artist's capacity to provide compelling *enactments* of collectively recognized status-appropriate forms of knowledge, an examination of the stories apart from the *way they are told* is more likely to reproduce the very structures and practices which impede Aboriginal peoples' capacities for intercultural engagement, than to yield any valuable insights into Indigenous film. Failing to interrogate the universality of dramaturgical categories, or presuming the nature of actors, audiences, agency, and events, in "other" cultural settings risks placing under erasure the very people and places in which meanings are relationally embedded.

Elsewhere I discuss the notion that the circumstances of modern life for Aboriginal people do not always allow for relationships to be sustained through ritualized gestures of sociability that invoke "local" norms such as kinship proscriptions, age and gender appropriate manners of address, and other protocols for contact in a face-to-face context (Buddle 2005). I show that communications media, however, may endow the symbolic content of tradition with some degree of temporal permanence, sustaining cultural continuity despite the distance traditions are made to travel from the places in which they originated and in spite of the diversity of contexts in which they newly take root (Buddle 2005).

Activities surrounding the production and consumption of Aboriginal media have become one means through which Aboriginal people perform locality or a "sense of" community. In terms of filmic production, the heads of Native film units effectively socialize film crews and film subjects when they provide, or themselves enact, identifications with which the latter are able to affectively attach. Filmmaking sites provide controlled contexts in which individuals learn to embed certain practices, dispositions, protocols, and forms of cultural action in new types of relationships—as the fictive kin groups that often arise in these settings would evince. As transitory communities of practice or interest, filmmaking units pry open the state-mandated legal enclosures of community, vesting in ephemeral situational formations more enduring types of relatedness. This represents a powerful form of involvement that validates a competency of action rather than mere geographic or genealogical locatedness. These relationships facilitate a specific quality of interaction in order that people may collaboratively restore the "structure of feeling" with which locality is commonly associated in Native settings.

There are currently a handful of Native women who make a living producing documentary films in Canada. Despite the artists' class, age, and cultural differences, their work, collectively, is governed by a logic of its own—one that provides a pragmatic rationality for the "way things are done" (Schieffelin 1998: 199). What they have in common is an approach that emphasizes the nature of interaction rather than the efficacy of communication. Derived from attempts to understand certain qualities of social relationships and experiences, women's filmic practice appeals to an alternate cultural hypothesis—one that queries: "knowing who" and "knowing how." This orientation, Dwight Conquergood suggests, contrasts markedly with the dominant "view from above approach" that informs propositional or official knowledge: "knowing that, knowing about" (2004: 331).

To achieve Aboriginal community recognition requires, according to Algonquin filmmaker Monique Manatch, the capacity to bring filming off "in a good way." However, while the Native women who make documentaries ground their creative processes in traditional forms of knowledge, they are mindful of the mainstream film conventions for artistry and may desire to be recognized in those terms as well (cf. Thomas 1997: 264). Women directors have seen how the bestowing of public value on certain types of accomplishment translates into real financial capital with which project goals might be realized. Consequently, they often endeavor to acknowledge both registers. This is accomplished by dividing the filmic labor in such a way as to allow them to focus on negotiating interactions, while delegating others to take on the tasks of imaging. Whether or not they achieve critical acclaim outside their spheres of influence, Native women's films may be said to be consequential when they initiate a continuing process of social criticism in the public sphere—when they engender and inform practice and when they model change.

In the actual provision or practice of liberated subjectivities for Aboriginal women, the women who head Native film units deploy strategies that often rupture the very notions of womanliness that are ennobled both in First

Nations "traditionalist" discourses and in Canada's popular imagination.[9] Thus, the very practices that are able to elicit collectivity may also evoke other expressions of unity or difference that belie *cultural* affiliations.

Filmmaking and screening provide opportunities for Native women to create social spaces that valorize erstwhile underrated registers of social action. Filmmaking serves to encode forms of Aboriginal women's agency with value, and allows participants to make sense of the particular circumstances in which they find themselves. The fields these activities create may serve as the only spaces where women are able to achieve recognition for performing specific adaptations of their selves. Enabling these performances and calling new subjectivities into being in the process accomplishes a certain kind of work—namely, the modification of contemporary Aboriginal femininity.

LIFE-GIVING AND TRADITION-KEEPING: WOMEN'S INDIAN ACTS

From the time of the earliest encounters between Natives and newcomers, Europeans sought to socially engineer in Indigenous settings their own versions of a gendered sociability—one premised on a hierarchical model of familial relationships (Etienne and Leacock 1980; Cruikshank 1994, 1990; Commaroff and Comaroff 1992; McClintock 1995; Thomas 1994). Missionaries, model farms, reserves, and residential schools provided the early models for reconfiguring Aboriginal domains of labor (Carter 2001; Fiske 1996; Miller 1996). The morality of feminine domesticity and male public culture informed the performance of newly inhabited "Christian" space throughout the nineteenth century (Carter 1996; Albers and Medicine 1983). Later, legal discourse would reinforce Euro-Canadian gendered expectations for women's performance, as well as race and class hierarchies (McGillivray and Comaskey 1999; Sangster 2001).

That the moral place Native women occupy is ostensibly "domestic" is a performance that is now policed by Aboriginal peoples themselves with clearly punitive consequences for those who fail to measure up. Domesticity as a gendered *identity*, rather than simply a form of gendered labor (Lloyd and Johnson 2003: 8) currently provides an important measure for the general judging of "women's lives" (Kline 1995). The ideal of domesticity also connects with the fantasy of "Aboriginality'" as a perennial legacy of habits and understanding accumulated from the past, and constituted within a small-scale, wholly integrated, unchanging, usually northern group. Both notions maintain a purchase in the popular imagination and in Canadian nationalist discourse. Yet, the ongoing movement *en masse* of Native women from northern reserves to cities[10]—a pattern not matched by Aboriginal men—points to a wide scale dissatisfaction with so-called 'traditional' social policy on reserves. It suggests, moreover, that urban areas, which are habitually misrecognized as "non-traditional," may actually afford Native women access to pre-Christian (so-called "modern") freedoms or what Saskia Sassen refers to as greater capacity to emerge as subjects (1998).

Despite the plurality of contemporary Aboriginal cultural traditions and the changing socio-cultural context, the hegemonic (domesticized) narrative of "traditional womanhood" continues to play up the ontological and the "natural" in the gender hierarchy. Beatrice Medicine submits that in the sphere of re-vitalized tradition, in particular, attention to male social agendas, is dominant (2001). Women are life-givers and tradition-keepers in "neo-traditional" gender arenas. Consequently, in these spheres, Aboriginal women are availed of subject positions or symbolic participation in public political space principally by harnessing their productive energy toward reproducing people and "tradition." This poses problems both for those whose identification with womanhood does not exclusively entail producing children, and for those who affirm different relations with "tradition."

The hegemonic narratives of traditional women's work that pervade scholarly, popular, and Aboriginal discourse nonetheless provide women with constraints as well as grounds for resistance. In many instances, regional and local variations on "traditional" schemes conflict with more unified national conceptions. These may allow among other things, for women to confer positions of leadership; to speak and act for the water and for children; and to occupy a political or ceremonial office, or to own certain songs, dances and stories. The indeterminacy of these latter roles seems to allow for a greater degree of creativity in their interpretation and enactment. It is significant that women's media making endeavors are often organized so as to achieve work that is amenable to these more indeterminate categories, even while they simultaneously appeal to selective components of an essentialized traditionalism.

MIMESIS AND MOHAWK GIRLS

Tracy Deer's filmmaking is embedded in and attends to the ways social processes call "traditional" and "modern" women into being at the Kahnawake reserve near Montreal. The strategies she deploys in filming show that simply engaging in non-conventional activities creates possibilities for new historical ideas, new images, new subjectivities, and new cultural practices. After completing a university Film Studies degree and a number of student film projects, Deer, a twenty-something Mohawk, migrated home to Kahnawake. She ventured back to the place of her birth to begin a community process that culminated in a film entitled, *Mohawk Girls* (2006).[11]

Her aim was to create a gendered space by placing girls and women "at the center"—privileging their voices, perspectives, and life experiences.

Deer nurtured relationships with local adolescents who were attending the on-reserve "traditional" Survival School and with girls who elected to attend the Catholic private school in a nearby town. She constructed a space of interaction where participants could form relationships with one another and in which they could dramatize the tensions they experienced concerning the pull toward modern citizenship, characterized by individuation, education, professionalism and prestige (Beck and Beck-Gernsheim 2002; Giddens 1991)—and societal pressures to uphold "traditions." Deer invested considerable time with the girls' families and peers in each of the schools and attended other community events. As a graduate of the private school in town, Deer positions herself as critically engaged in a cosmopolitan zone—a space characterized by many overlapping alliances and multi-locale memberships. Deer used her own experience at the school and film footage she had taken as a teenager as a frame to orient the story and to negotiate the rough terrain of issues the girls in each setting confronted.

Deer resolved to make a film that would have an immediate practical import in community members' lives. In this regard, the aim and scope of her film are at odds with the dominant cinematic model that seeks to amass viewer *numbers*, and to proffer entertainment products. This genre of community filmmaking, both indigenized and feminized, is oriented toward an intentionally social focus. Rather than a straightforward extension of national identity into explicitly political pursuits, however, the filmic strategies are oriented toward *relational* goals: namely they address processes of identification (cf. Schouls 2003) and strategies for socially organizing symbolic power (cf. Bourdieu 1984). Here, filming provides stages for people to testify and persuade, to educate and experience, and to empower the local citizenry to act socially.

In terms of film content, Deer's *Mohawk Girls* takes on contentious issues that are central to local identity politics such as discrimination, language-loss, sexism, and abuse, ostensibly to interrogate the very "laws of recognition" (cf. Povinelli 2002: 7) that have a regulative effect on gender. The community processes she instigates in making the film provided a space for the reconstitution of symbolic repertoires with which Mohawk girls —with different stances toward and investments in womanhood—could think and formulate a unified image of their difference from their others, including a surrounding non-Native public.

In Gramscian terms, Deer's activities bespeak a moral commitment not merely to interpreting Mohawk realities, but to actively re-constituting them. Deer envisaged the community film screening as an opportunity to open a space—a public sphere, as it were —not solely for the deliberating on issues of profound concern to the subjects on screen, but where one might connect with, or be moved by, these intimate realities in an experiential way.

As a community member and a woman, Deer disrupted any straightforward distinction between spectator and producer. As Halleck notes, the term *spectator* itself may have little explanatory power in these contexts and could productively be replaced by "user-participant" (2002: 385). As part of a larger process of empowering younger generations to broaden their repertoires of possible life scripts, the filmmaking process does not merely involve young girls in the selection of themes, but provides in the person of Deer, herself, an alternative model for civic participation. Embodying cultural signs, Deer's performance of womanhood, of community, and of Mohawkness show the plurality of subjectivities that are possible and how they can be accomplished.

The particular community process she engaged, however, showed that many, but not *any*, subjectivities were possible. Indeed, Deer's film succeeded in meeting the conditions bearing on aesthetic excellence in the Kahnawake context not simply because Mohawk people made the film. Rather, the film accomplished its aesthetic goals for the reason that over the course of the artistic process, its producers acknowledged locally recognized ideas of selfhood and performed local behavioral regularities aptly. Gesturing at structures or fields of preconditions, the filmmakers played with and against these practices rather than simply inventing new structures out of the blue.

Deer's approach to filmmaking builds on the strategies of the women who have preceded her. Alanis Obomsawin's presence in Deer's community in 1990 to document the confrontation between Mohawk peoples and Canadians (in the films *Kanasatake: 270 Years of Resistance* and *Rocks at Whisky Trench*) would have profound implications for Deer's life course. Deer's family appears in the latter film, in a car that a white mob attacked with rocks. She learned from Obomsawin to film these events for evidentiary purposes. Through filming, Deer is able to experiment with "imaginative" practices that are increasingly influenced by transnational movements of goods, peoples, and images, while asserting a place for, and at once constituting the collective memory of, her fellow Kahnawake residents.

BUSH FILM: MAKING THE PERSONAL POLITICAL

Native women's community rooted filmmaking is embodied in real individuals. However, in drawing on the affective elements of consciousness and relationships it may become nationally emblematic. In provisionally engaging with local social practices and local subjects, women's filmmaking has the effect to prepare places for cultural producers to perform their localities and to achieve community recognition. In sharing stories with and in revealing various aspects of their selves to one another, community members interweave selective elements to mobilize specific forms of interactive continuity.

Cat Cayuga (Mohawk) a formerly Six Nations, Ontario-based filmmaker is one of the founders of the Aboriginal Film and Video Arts Alliance (AFVAA, Ontario), an artist run coop that worked productively with the Centre for Aboriginal Media (CAM) and V-Tape to encourage the distribution of films and videos by Aboriginal peoples. V-Tape and CAM organizes imagineNative, the largest annual Aboriginal film festival in the country. Cayuga maintains that it is conceivable for community film and video projects to foster regional identifications.

In the mid-1990s, Cayuga, along with project mentors and fellow documentarians, Bernelda Wheeler, Alanis Obomsawin, and Wil Campbell, initiated an Aboriginal media training project entitled, "Elder Voices." Ten culturally and experientially diverse Native communities on reserves and in cities throughout Ontario participated in the project. According to Cayuga, although it involved teaching community members how to develop scripts, use video equipment to tell stories, and market the final product, the principal purpose of the project was to promote the idea of a "collective process":

> It was our understanding to try to work in what we thought was...an *Aboriginal* way.... What does that mean to us? How do we work with each other?... It will be each individual's point of reference within themselves, within the group, within their community, and how it relates to them within their community.... And the idea of strengthening our cultural ground...you strengthen this ground in Moose Factory or in Toronto. At some point all our ground is going to meet. (12 December 1996)

The screening of the final product, a video comprised of 10 treatments on the subject of local elders, enabled an embedding of the notions of elders from a multiplicity of locales, in the imagined territorial unit of Ontario. At the opening screening for the film, Cayuga introduced the film by providing the story of its making. The showing also served as a recruitment zone hailing individuals from the audience to become involved in filmmaking.

The story highlighted the point that the criterion applied to women's filming evaluated the very qualities that are held to mark off accession to womanhood in Ontario Aboriginal circles: namely a concern with the future generations; the capacity to work under duress; to accomplish a extraordinary feats with minimal funds; to promote harmonious social relations; a desire to advance the community rather than oneself; and the willingness to serve as a model showing others what they can do. These dispositions, rather than the message or content of the film in exclusion, provided the aesthetic and practical values according to which the Aboriginal audience assessed the film's success.

To assess the content of Native documentaries on their own terms would entail an intensive study into each locality's conventions for the narration of historical subject matter, which is beyond the scope of this paper (see instead, Leuthold 1998; Buddle 2004b). In very general terms, however,

Native documentaries offer interventions that ultimately seek to alter the oppressive power relations that are encoded in the name of race and empire, and to replace these lingering discursive vestiges of colonial times with their own preferred articulations of Aboriginal history.

In terms of performance, I would submit that this shifting of boundaries around gendered work practices has concrete implications for the processes of cultural formation. Namely, this form of social action valorizes novel forms of involvement, identification, and cultural affiliation putting into play a wider repertoire of meaningful associations. In gendering the productive practices of film, women are combining their ongoing corporeal projects with the production of broader collective sociabilities. These processes are inevitably caught up with local cultural politics for the reason that both have cultural survival as their end.

Alanis Obomsawin (Abenaki) is well known for the documentary films she has made with communities other than her own. Documentary is a genre that is uniquely well-suited to the realm of Native women's work, where "telling others' stories" enables one to engage in public labor while upholding the values of humility, modesty, and submission to community service that Native womanhood ideally extols. National Film Board of Canada (NFB) Director Gil Cardinal[12] claims that in filming dramas, the voice of the Director is everywhere apparent. Dramatic films are auteuristic in that they tell the Director's story. He insists, however, that only those who are willing "to give up control" are able to make successful documentaries on Native issues, "[the] work demands that you're constantly conscious of your values, your ethics, your humanity, your spirit; which is [what] leads you to the stories, to the issues that are important to you—that you can give yourself over to" (2003).

Indian Country is a place where different eras seem to co-exist. In some contexts women are expected to be seen and not heard. Elsewhere, women are outspoken and authoritatively participate in public political space. When women filmmakers work as outsiders in others' communities, it has the effect of disembedding them from the structures governing "traditional" gender roles. Outsiders are not held to the same rigorous standards for social comportment. And, as Angela McRobbie posits, "as the overwhelming force of structure fades so also does the capacity for agency increase" (2004: 261). Still, to distinguish oneself from non-Native outsiders, and to have their films recognized as "authentically Aboriginal" in community contexts, it is nonetheless incumbent on filmmakers to competently reference the structures they are rejecting. In this sense, there is no free-floating agency, even for those whose sociability requires that they master capacities for flexibly affiliating.

Once an established recording artist, and still more at ease being heard than seen, in addition to her documentary work Obomsawin is a passionate advocate for Aboriginal radio. Her documentary filming begins with long visits where she simply spends time in the company of her film subjects, sometimes listening to community members while audio tape-recording their stories. Visual documentation enters relatively late into the creative process (2003). Obomsawin insists that documentary film is foremost, "a place where First Nations people can talk to each other about their losses" (2006).[13]

Obomsawin began her filmmaking career to fulfill her responsibility as a woman to her community—"to make the world a better place for the generations to come." Working outside the home, but in a traditional-ist domain (Pink 1998: 136), Obomsawin strategically dissociates herself from feminism, but aligns with local contingents of "strong women" in the communities whose stories she documents. She does this to create a social field in which local forms of cultural capital may be recognized. Cultural capital, as it is employed here, refers not to the realm of "restricted produc-tion" that is "high art," as is denoted in Bourdieu's *Distinction* (1984), but rather to forms of low, but still selectively shared, "grass roots" competen-cies and dispositions that flow from a cultural knowledge that is *of* the people, but that is not *for* all people.

Under their Challenge for Change Program in the 1970s, the National Film Board of Canada sponsored Obomsawin to facilitate storytelling workshops through pictures, slides, film, and sound among members of the Manowin reserve in Québec. Her first films were tri-language educational kits designed for use by teachers in classrooms with Native students so that children would learn about themselves and their ancestors (1996). She insists that screening community films is a way of creating new forms of rec-ognition that are crucial to the social health of Aboriginal communities.

Her films have an impact that extends beyond realms of Aboriginal rel-evance, however. In Alberta, screenings of the Richard Cardinal story are not simply "spectator" events. These gatherings—where hats are passed, networks take shape, and political actors are mobilized—form part of the broader film process of engendering political change. It is commonly known in Aboriginal circles that Obomsawin's public screening events in Alberta, which spurred massive protests at the social services office, effec-tively shamed the Department of Social Services into revising its policies concerning Aboriginal foster children.

Obomsawin's aims are instrumental, namely she seeks to convey what oppression, injustice, and racism "feel like." For her, the personal emo-tional toll of filmmaking renders it every bit as much a repeated corporeal, as it is an intellectual or representational process. In her films the stories of forsaken foster children, homeless city dwellers, and demoralized defenders of the land are irrevocably interpolated with broader cultural structures and politics. Making a film that alters social circumstances and creates the reality it proclaims is an act of cultural production that both reveals *and* accomplishes something.

In general, Aboriginal women's filmic agency is primarily performa-tive—it consists of women acting on the margins of conventional womanhood, teaching others either to appreciate and recognize the legitimacy of alternative forms of competency, or conversely, about the limitless contexts for traditional forms of competency. For Obomsawin, documentary filmmaking ensures that Aboriginal "voices are heard," that traditions will thrive, and that Native children will lead more livable lives.

CONCLUSION: DIS-MEMBERING DOMESTICITY, RE-MEMBERING TRADITION

The tendency in studies of Aboriginal film has been to privilege explicit notions of linear communication delving into textual analyses of film plots, camera shots, and authorial intentionality (Bataille and Silet 1980; Friar and Friar 1972; Kilpatrick 1999; Wollen 1992; Worth and Adair 1972). The shift to reception studies (cf. Morley 1992) merely reproduces this paradigm by maintaining the text and its interpretation as the locus of meaning making (Pederson 2005: 386). This chapter situates complex technologies of social engagement within: the personal life trajectories of individual women; the history of "modern" Aboriginal political movements; and the history of colonial projects which created both some of the needs for, and many of the limits on, Aboriginal media initiatives. Looking to the place of filmmaking in the poetics of everyday life, I have sought to theorize embodiment, event and agency, focusing on the way filmmaking performance raises questions about the framing of reality, the production of action, and the shaping of selves.

The members of women-headed Aboriginal filmmaking units seek to proffer acknowledged forms of skill or artistry *interactively*: through participatory, not straightforwardly communicatory modes. The film production contexts, therefore, create symbolic realities by enabling participants to experience symbolic meanings as they are actually lived and felt in interactive relation with particular social categories, historical moments, and self-positionings.

Determining how to perform the self and one's heritage, to be a childless life-giver, an iconoclastic tradition-keeper, to become a filmmaker, an urbanite, a culture-critic, and remain appropriately womanly and Native requires the capacity both to enlist and to validate certain relevant registers of cultural knowledge and action. This negotiating of new modes of Aboriginal femininity entails engagement in ongoing corporeal acts that occur primarily behind public screens, in "hidden transcripts," and in shadow dramas that are played out in others' homes. These are spatially rooted, relationally anchored performances, therefore, that are grounded in the places and predicaments in which Native women find their selves.

The performative nature of the women's filmic production represents an important form of social action, providing a stage for the playing out of territorial, cultural, gender, and identity politics. Women's filmic performances create particular visions of community and popular memories that both honor preferred versions of Aboriginality and womanhood and help them to endure. Insofar as they stress the validity of alternative registers of social competency, these performances ultimately contribute to the subversion of more "official" efforts to govern public culture and to set the terms on which discourse on civic participation and public citizenship will occur.

In making films locally and transporting them to international Indigenous film festivals, women filmmakers are asserting their place in an other than domestic space and in a larger than local social sphere. This represents an assertive rejection of the regulative effects of both tradition and individualization on Aboriginal women's capacities for participatory parity beyond spaces historically reserved for them by local and state authorities. The film practices women enlist provisionally organize their culturalist projects by restructuring "traditional" feminine subjectivity and by re-channeling its circulation. Finally, in privileging the interactive over the communicative and situating their work in others' homes, Native women perform a transformative sociability. These documentarians generate a semiotic milieu that exceeds the boundaries of the site of the "real" action of modernity—the public sphere—productively "respatializing"[14] culture, power, womanhood, and work in the process.

NOTES

1. Research for this paper is derived from ongoing ethnographic research in collaboration with members of the Aboriginal media community in Canada. I am very grateful to: Monique Manatch, Shirley Cheechoo, Tracey Deer, Cat Cayuga, Alanis Obomsawin, and to Gil Cardinal for their contributions. I would like to thank the Social Sciences and Humanities Research Council of Canada and the University of Manitoba for funding this research. The article has profited from suggestions by Tina Chen and David Churchill and from fellow authors at the "Film, History and Cultural Citizenship" seminar in Winnipeg.
2. I mean here to invoke the idea of a property of social life, or structure of feeling, rather than a substantive social formation (cf. Appadurai 1996: 199).
3. I prefer to avoid the construction of "pre-textual" for the evolutionary trajectory it suggests. Anthropologists and film theorists pursue different questions surrounding the relationship between "texts" and film which, while complementary, take them to different destinations. Analyzing filmic narrative texts is not the end toward which media anthropological research into Native film necessarily progresses. This is not to say anthropologists have no concern for texts. Clifford Geertz, and other proponents of hermeneutics, for example, have argued that cultures might be examined as an assemblage of texts (1973: 452), thus, one might speak of the obviously symbolic: songs, rituals, speeches, as well as the more mundane: meals, clothing, buildings, and conversations as texts, and the competency with which one performs with them as a form of literacy. Cruikshank (1990) and Basso (1984) contend that landscapes are viewed in various Native cultures as texts in so far as sites

are named and mapped, and are productive of signs which are subsequently read by competent Native interpreters (see Buddle 2004a).The mode of analysis I am advocating herein following others, begins with the assertion that the meaning of the medium of film is not inherent to the screened text, but must be sought in the social relations of production, distribution, and consumption. I, therefore, seek not merely to bring the circumstances of a film's production to bear on the finished text, but to elucidate the ways that valued forms of women's competency in Aboriginal circles become valorised during the production phase, not as is generally assumed, in subsequent discussions about the screened film product.

4. To make matters worse, in order to be recognized as warranting social entitlements and thus to access Aboriginal rights, Indigenous subjects are called on both to identify with and to perform a "domesticated nonconflictual "traditional" form of sociality and intersubjectivity" (Povinelli 2002: 6), that is grounded in the impossible ideal of an immemorial "authentic" difference.

5. In general, the field of anthropological inquiry has shifted from a concern with what were once thought to be either spatial or scalar, bounded social entities existing in relative isolation from a modern world system, to more complex populations that are (and likely always have been) embedded in wider social and cultural constructs. An oppositional alterity, in other words, is not the only, nor necessarily always the principle, narrative in terms of which Native women frame their lives in Canadian cities. Indeed, if "community" is found to hold purchase as a collective symbol in the lives of Native women, it is incumbent upon researchers to interrogate our received notions of the term and to consider the multiple modes in which "community" may operate: methodologically, theoretically, phenomenologically, politically, and legally (Amit 2002).

6. Something like the "n..." word for Blacks, "skins" is a reclaimed and re-signified version of the term redskins and has come into wide usage in Aboriginal circles. I use it here to reference the activity "out of place" that nominally "low cultural" films structurally occupy. Hence, Native, melodramatic, and pornographic films are structurally analogous. Aboriginal women's documentary filming not only takes women out of home, but "Indians" out of the bush.

7. Generally comprised of young trainees, their presence lends a pedagogic component to women's filmic labor. This is in keeping with Aboriginal women's "traditional role" to culturally produce the next generation and to show by doing.

8. Some of Shirley Cheechoo's other films include: Silent Tears (1998), an autobiographical film about her experiences with her parents on the trapline as a small child; Bear Walker (2000), the story of four sisters who struggle to overcome oppression, violence, and police corruption; and Shadow in Deep Water (2004), which documents Shirley's healing journey which takes her to Peru.

9. It should be stressed however, that among Canadians and traditionalists, multiple gender models exist.

10. Statistics Canada Census, 2001.

11. Tracey Deer co-directed her first film with Neil Diamond. One More River: The Deal That Split the Cree (2004) follows Grand Chief Ted Moses' 80-day campaign to convince James Bay Cree communities to officially approve a deal with the Province of Québec that would dam the Rupert River resulting in monumental changes to the local environment.

12. Gil Cardinal (Cree/Métis) has made over thirty films. Some of his better known works include: Totem: The Return of the G'psgolox Pole (2003), David with F.A.S. (1997), Tikinagan (1991), and The Spirit Within (1990).

13. In over thirty years of filmmaking she has now made more than twenty films including: Richard Cardinal: Cry from a Diary of a Métis Child (1986) which addresses the failure of the Office of Social Services to properly care for Native children. No Address (1988) confronts Aboriginal homelessness in Montreal. Incident at Restigouche (1984) chronicles an historic raid on a Micmac reserve by the Quebec police. Kanasatake: 270 Years of Resistance (1993) documents the standoff between Mohawk people and the Canadian Army. The Crown at War with Us (2002) investigates the clash between Micmac fishers and the federal government Department of Fisheries.
14. Cf. Marcus (1997).

REFERENCES

Albers, P. and Medicine, B. (eds.) (1983) *The Hidden Half: studies of plains Indian women*, Washington, D.C.: University Press of America.

Amit, V. (ed.) (2002) *Realizing Community: concepts, social relationships, and sentiments*, New York: Routledge.

Appadurai, A. (1996) *Modernity at Large: cultural dimensions of globalization*, Minneapolis: University of Minnesota Press.

Basso, K. (1984) "Stalking with Stories: Names, Places, and Moral Narratives among the Western Apache," in E.M. Bruner (ed.) *Text, Play, and Story*, Berkeley: University of California Press.

Bataille, G. and Silet, C. (1980) *The Pretend Indians: images of Native Americans in the movies*, Ames: Iowa University Press.

Beck, U. and Beck-Gernsheim, E. (2002) *Individualisation: institutionalized individualism and its social and political consequences*, Cambridge: Polity Press.

Bourdieu, P. (1977) *Outline of a Theory of Practice*, New York: Cambridge University Press.

—— (1984) *Distinction: a social critique of the judgment of taste*, trans. Richard Nice, Cambridge, MA: Harvard University Press.

—— (1990) *The Logic of Practice*, trans. Richard Nice, Stanford, CA: Stanford University Press.

—— (1993) *The Field of Cultural Production*, New York: Columbia University Press.

Buddle, K. (2004a) "White Words, Read worlds: authoring aboriginality through English language media," *The International Journal of Canadian Studies*, 30: 121–58.

—— (2004b) "Media, Markets and Powwows: Matrices of Aboriginal Cultural Mediation in Canada," *Cultural Dynamics*, 16: 29–69.

—— (2005) "Aboriginal Cultural Capital Creation and Radio Production in Urban Ontario," *Canadian Journal of Communications*, 30: 7–40.

—— (forthcoming) "Transistor Resistors: Native women's radio in Canada and the social organization of political space from below," in M. Stewart and P. Wilson (eds.) *Global Indigenous Media: cultures, practices, and politics*, Durham, NC: Duke University Press.

Carter, S. (1990) *Lost Harvests: prairie Indian reserve farmers and government policy*, Montreal: McGill-Queen's University Press.

—— (1996) "Categories and Terrains of Exclusion: Constructing the 'Indian Woman' in the Early Settlement Era in Western Canada," in Ken Coates and Robin Fisher (eds.) *Out of the Background's Readings in Canadian Nature History*, Toronto: Copp Clarke.

—— (2001) "First Nations Women of Prairie Canada in the Early Reserve Years, the 1870s to the 1920s: a preliminary inquiry," in C. Miller, and P. Chuchryk (eds.) *Women of the First Nations: power, wisdom, and strength*, Winnipeg: University of Manitoba Press.

Clifford, J. (1988) *The Predicament of Culture: twentieth-century ethnography, literature and art*, Cambridge, MA: Cambridge University Press.

Comaroff, J. and Comaroff, J. (1992) *Ethnography and the Historical Imagination*, Boulder, CO: Westview Press.

Conquergood, D. (2004) "Performance Studies: interventions and radical research," in H. Bial (ed.) *The Performance Studies Reader*, New York: Routledge.

Cruikshank, J. (1990) *Life Lived Like a Story: life stories of three Yukon Native elders*, Vancouver: University of British Columbia Press.

—— (1994) "Claiming Legitimacy: prophecy narratives from Northern Aboriginal women," *American Indian Quarterly*, 18: 147–67.

Etienne, M. and Leacock, E. (1980) *Women and Colonization: anthropological perspectives*, Toronto: Bergin and Garvey.

Fiske, J. (2001) "Gender and the Paradox of Residential Education in Carrier Society," in C. Miller and P. Chuchryk (eds.) *Women of the First Nations: power, wisdom, and strength*, Winnipeg: University of Manitoba Press.

Friar, R. and Friar, N. (1972) *The Only Good Indian: the Hollywood gospel*, New York: Drama Book Specialists.

Geertz, C. (1973) *The Interpretation of Cultures*, New York: Basic Books Inc.

Giddens, A. (1991) *Modernity and Self Identity*, Cambridge: Polity Press.

Ginsburg, F. (1993) "Aboriginal Media and the Australian Imaginary," *Public Culture*, 5: 557–78.

Halleck, D. (2002) *Hand-Held Visions: the impossible possibilities of community media*, New York: Fordham University Press.

Hughes-Freeland, F. (1998) "Introduction," in F. Hughes-Freeland (ed.) *Ritual, Performance, Media*, New York: Routledge.

Kilpatrick, J. (1999) *Celluloid Indians: Native Americans and film*, Lincoln: University of Nebraska Press.

Kline, M. (1995) "Complicating the Ideology of Motherhood: child welfare law and First Nation women," in M.A. Fineman and I. Karpin (eds.) *Mothers in Law: feminist theory and the legal regulation of motherhood*, New York: Columbia University Press.

Leuthold, S. (1998) *Indigenous Aesthetics: Native art, media and identity*, Austin: University of Texas.

Lloyd, J. and Johnson, L. (2003) "The Three Faces of Eve: The post-war housewife, melodrama, and home," *Feminist Media Studies*, 3: 7–25.

Marcus, G.E. (1997) *Cultural Producers in Perilous States*, Chicago: University of Chicago Press.

McGillivray, A. and Comaskey, B. (1999) *Black Eyes All of the Time: intimate violence, Aboriginal women and the justice system*, Toronto: University of Toronto Press.

McRobbie, A. (2004) "Post-Feminism and Popular Culture," *Feminist Media Studies*, 4: 255–64.

Medicine, B. (2001) "Indian Women: Tribal Identity as Status Quo," in B. Medicine and S. Jacobs (eds.) *Learning to Be an Anthropologist and Remaining "Native": selected writings*, Urbana: University of Illinois Press.

Miller, J.R. (1996) *Shingwauk's Vision: a history of Native residential schools*, Toronto: University of Toronto Press.

Morley, D. (1992) *Television Audiences and Cultural Studies*, London: Routledge.

Pederson, M.A. (2005) "Performing Media: toward an ethnography of intertextuality," in E.W. Rothenbuhler and M. Coman (eds.) *Media Anthropology,* London: Sage.

Pink, S. (1998) "From Ritual Sacrifice to Media Commodity: anthropological and media constructions of the Spanish bullfight and the rise of women performers," in F. Hughes-Freeland (ed.) *Ritual, Performance, Media*, New York: Routledge.

Povinelli, E. (2002) *The Cunning of Recognition: Indigenous alterities and the making of Australian multiculturalism*, Durham, NC: Duke University Press.

Pratt, M.L. (1992) *Imperial Eyes: travel writing and transculturation*, New York: Routledge.

Sangster, J. (2001) *Regulating Girls and Women: sexuality, family and the law in Ontario, 1920–1960*, Toronto: Oxford University Press.

Sassen, S. (1998) *Globalization and Its Discontents*, New York: New Press.

Schieffelin, E.L. (1998) "Problematizing Performance," in F. Hughes-Freeland (ed.) *Ritual, Performance, Media*, New York: Routledge.

Schouls, T.A. (2003) *Shifting Boundaries: Aboriginal identity, pluralist theory, and the politics of self-government*, Vancouver: University of British Columbia Press.

Thomas, N. (1997) "Collectivity and Nationality in the Anthropology of Art," in M. Banks and H. Morphy (eds) *Rethinking Visual Anthropology*, New Haven, CT: Yale University Press.

Williams, R. (1977) *Marxism and Literature*, London: Oxford University Press.

Wollen, P. (1992) "Cinema's Conquistadors," *Sight and Sound*, 2: 23.

Worth, S. and Adair, J. (1972) "Navajo filmmakers," *American Anthropologist*, 74: 9–34.

Interviews

Cardinal, G., *Personal Interview*, October 2003.

Cayuga, C., *Personal Interview*, April 2006.

Cheechoo, S., *Personal Interview*, June 2005, November 2005.

Deer, T., *Personal Interview*, March 2006.

Manatch, M., *Personal Interview*, October 2001–2005

Obomsawin, A., *Personal Interview*, March 2006, October 2003, September 1996.

12 *The Battle of Algiers*
Pentagon edition

John Mowitt

The message is that there are no knowns.
There are things we know that we know.
There are known unknowns. That is to say,
There are things that we now know that we don't know.
But, there are also unknown unknowns.
There are things we don't know we don't know.—Donald Rumsfeld

ESTABLISHING SHOT

The much ballyhooed "theory wars" took a decidedly ugly turn in October of 2004 when the US paper of record, *The New York Times*, in reporting the death of Jacques Derrida, indulged in an unmistakable bit of *Schaden-freude* proclaiming that with Derrida's demise, the theory of everything could now "rest in peace." In effect, the theory wars had become personal. Of course, the deepest cut was not the aggressivity of the *Times*' editorial cluelessness, but, as always, the bait. That is, the implicit invitation for theory partisans to rise to this provocation by accepting the notion—popularly thought to be denied by deconstruction—that Derrida, like Socrates, was a subject after all and therefore mortal. For reasons it would take too long to detail, the *Times* appears to have felt certain that Derrida had always already been so irrelevant, that no opportunity—not even his obituary—could be allowed to pass unexploited in the inexplicably urgent labor of nailing his coffin shut.

In a rare feat of prescience, film studies had beaten the *Times* to the proverbial punch in proclaiming a full decade earlier the death of what David Bordwell and Noël Carroll called "grand theory." To be fair, "grand theory" was not exactly what the *Times* meant by "the theory of everything," but the stakes were similarly grave. For Bordwell and Carroll the issue concerned the more narrowly disciplinary or professional matter of whether one studied film in order to, as is still said, "do theory," or whether one studied film, well, as film: not exactly as was once said of art, *le film pour le film*, but similar. The bald tendentiousness of this position did not prevent Bordwell and Carroll from deploying it as something of a litmus test for sorting among those who deserved to have academic careers in film studies and those who did not. It was perhaps not a matter of life and death, but certainly one of livelihood.

Many commentators have pointed to the performative contradiction at work within any theoretical repudiation of theory (even a mid-level, neo-formalist, cognitive psychological one), and if it is worth raising these issues at the outset of a re-reading of Pontecorvo's *The Battle of Algiers* this is because the recent reception history of this film invites us to think at least twice about the articulation of cinema and theory. The temptation is strong to invoke here Deleuze's brilliant passage from *Cinema 2* on the solicitation of theory by the cinema—a solicitation so intimate that the ontological distance between the medium and its conceptual mediation vanishes—but I will settle for a more modest point. If it is possible for the foreign policy of the United States, indeed the prosecution of a military campaign, to orient itself through discussions prompted by the screening of a film, *The Battle of Algiers*, then are film scholars not thereby directly confronted with the disciplinary task of deciding what it means, in such a situation, to advocate, indeed to champion studying film in the absence of some sort of general account of their relation to their object of study? My point is not to establish, indeed re-establish, that it is impossible to avoid "doing theory" while analyzing the cinema, but to acknowledge this impossibility and pose the obvious follow-up question; that is, what complicity, even if unintended, might there be between the current foreign policy of the United States and the claim that film studies should concern itself with the study of film and stop thinking about the conditions of possibility for doing so, in short, stop thinking about theory. The mid-level theory advocated by Bordwell and Carroll, to the extent that it submits such conditions to cognitive profiling—that is, to the extent that it reduces all films to exemplifications of fundamental cognitive processes—would be one among several perspectives implicated in such a question.

Put this way the question is unfair, if only because it solicits a response that is a tad too obvious. To complicate matters, consider that to break the link between theory and the cinema, so as to locate where film properly starts and stops, is to separate the cinema from the social order of which it is a part. Theory, after all, is not simply detached mentation. It is, among other things, one of the discursive practices that circulate in and around what Marx and Engels once called, "ruling ideas." Indeed this is what prompted Althusser's confection of "theoretical practice." Whether we insist that the cinema is art, information, or entertainment (or all three) we are situating it in the social field where the cinema stimulates and is stimulated by the effort to make sense of it. As such, it belongs to the struggle over the process of social reproduction or its breakdown, and different positions or tendencies can be read in terms of their effects within this process. Recognition of this state of affairs could be said to lie behind Horkheimer and Adorno's decision to recast the relation between theory and critique as a pleonastic one. The general effect that concerns me here is not that of alignment, but of compromise, not in the sense of selling out, but in the sense of sacrificing one's ability to take advantage of the questioning that the cinema may provoke as the result of the pressure placed upon it by the history of a specific film. Especially, I hasten to add, a film such as *The Battle of Algiers* that can be read to pose—in both its statement and its enunciation—the question of the very historicity of the cinema.

My effort to respond to the provocation of the Pentagon's screening of Pontecorvo's film will seek to address four related issues. First, there is the matter of the situation of the cinema in the field of historical experience. To what extent is the latter accessible today without essential reference to the cinema? Second, there is the issue of the conditioning of historical experience as a result. To what extent has the cinema played an essential role in the rendering of historical experience both as a field of repetition, but also as an endless supply of "teachable moments?" Third, there is the issue of the troubling relation between cinematic representation (its irreducible indexicality) and violence. To what extent can the cinema teach historical lessons without twisting the truth? And fourth, given the intimacy of history and cinema, the problem of how this relation is to be thought must be raised. In other words, to what extent can history now be understood in the absence of film studies, and, conversely, to what extent can film studies now be understood in the absence of history? If the Pentagon's screening of *The Battle of Algiers* raises such issues it is not because its employees or their counselors are especially thoughtful. Instead, these issues are provoked by this screening because of what becomes legible on the surface formed between the film and the Department of Defense's interest in it.

Although I am not entirely sure I understand what he means by the distinctions, my invocation of historicity explicitly recalls Phil Rosen's discussion in the introductory chapter of *Change Mummified: cinema, historicity, theory*. There, Rosen contrasts the titular historicity with both history—the "real pastness" that the historiographer seeks to reconstruct—and historiography—the "text written by the historian" for the present. Historicity is then, "the particular interrelations of the mode of historiography and the types of construction of history related by it" (Rosen 2003: xi). In a subsequent paragraph, his insistence upon his interest in the history of both history and the theory of history suggests that historicity seeks to bring to unity the manifold of impressions that arise at the join where, like the navel of the dream, "real pastness" and the conventions of its representation dance around a clearing, a spacing that is neither history nor historiography. Or, so it seems to me. In any case, this is precisely one of the more remarkable questions posed by *The Battle of Algiers*, a question that if *not* addressed in one's reading of the film makes it impossible to learn what is perhaps its most disarming lesson. That is, the lesson regarding the stakes involved in engaging the past as a "teachable moment."

My recourse to the rhetoric of pedagogy is a calculated one. On the one hand, it is meant to invoke a term that surfaced repeatedly in the public discussion of the Pentagon's screening of the film. For example, when *The Nation*'s Stuart Klawans covered this story for *The New York Times* he titled his piece, "Lessons from the Pentagon's Favorite Training Film" (Klawans 2004: AR 26). On the other hand, and in accord with a certain colloquial, even disciplinary logic, "lesson" was the theme by which the topic of history often slipped into this debate. Consider in this light the language of the flier circulated within the Pentagon about the screening: "Showing the film offers historical insight into the conduct of French operations in Algeria," where "historical insight" condenses the entire thematics of historical repetition and the need to learn from history precisely so as to fend off those repetitions deemed undesirable; in the stated preoccupations of the flier, winning "a battle against terrorism, but los[ing] the war of ideas." Given that the historiographic notion of historical repetition would appear to be one of the ideas at war in the battle against terrorism, one wonders whether the Pentagon's "lively discussion" as reported by Michael Kaufman addressed the fundamental pedagogical conceit that organized its reception of the film? Let me suggest that one sure sign the "terrorists have won" is that the Department of Defense was, already in 2003, in deep denial about a war that had already set the very ideas organizing its screening of Pontecorvo's film ablaze.

To be sure, the most provocative dimension of this pedagogical rhetoric has not yet been detailed. Doing so requires some detailing of the "real pastness" of summer 2003. Here's what we think we know: on 16 September 2001 Bruce Hoffman, director of Rand Corporation Washington, published a piece in *The Los Angeles Times*, calling for some "out of the box" thinking about the attacks that had taken place in New York and Washington only days before. As if on hold, this call was picked up in the summer of 2003 when the Directorate for Special Operations and Low Intensity Conflict at the Department of Defense (a group whose "non-military" component gives it a potentially eccentric perspective on policy) proposed a screening and discussion of Pontecorvo's film.[1] To stir interest among the wonks and wonkettes a flier announcing the screening was prepared. The portion of it released to the press reads:

> How to win a battle against terrorism and lose the war of ideas. Children shoot soldiers at point-blank range. Women plant bombs in cafes. Soon the entire Arab population builds to a mad fervor. Sound familiar? The French have a plan. It succeeds tactically, but fails strategically. To understand why, come to a rare showing of this film. (Kaufman 2003: Sec. 4, 3)

Stories covering this screening appeared first in US papers (*The New York Times* and *The Washington Post*), but they soon appeared abroad as well. In November of 2003, Secretary Rumsfeld was interviewed by the French weekly, *Paris Match* where he is asked about the screening, which he confirms. In fact, one of the most provocative discussions of the screening takes place between Salon.com's Christopher Farah and, of all people, Saadi Yacef, the author of the book that along with Fanon's *A Dying Colonialism* inspired Pontecorvo's film. As if channeling the Pentagon's own framing of the matter, Yacef is expressly asked, "What kinds of lessons do you think the United States should learn from the film?" (Farah and Yacef 2004: 2). His answer zeroes immediately in on the lesson/historical repetition link.

As with the entirety of empiricism, one could go on and on. But what deserves highlighting is what earlier I referred to as the most provocative dimension of this pedagogical rhetoric. One of the important strands of the film's re-reception, that lip of its text that Miriam Hansen, following Habermas, calls its public sphere, is precisely the journalistic discourse that reported it. Recognizing that this textual lip folds back and forth between the press and the university (among other sites), Michael Kaufman titled his contribution to *The Times*' "This Week in Review" section, "Film Studies: What Does the Pentagon See in 'Battle of Algiers'?" What this underscores, if only obliquely, is the structural link between the Pentagon and the university as sites for the study of film. Indeed, virtually every journalistic discussion of this screening at some point reminds readers of a "real past-ness" in which *The Battle of Algiers* was studied either as part of a course on Third Cinema, or debated as a worthy source of tactical insight for militant organizations. Important here is not the appeal to the past per se, but the implicit acknowledgement of a link between various modalities of study. Not to put too fine a point on it, one might say that as with the defense attorneys for the LAPD who used a rigorous form of textual analysis to trouble the testimony of Rodney King, the Pentagon turned, during the Battle for Baghdad, to the techniques of film studies to avoid the strategic disaster of colonial occupation as depicted in Pontecorvo's film. While certainly not necessary, this episode marks a contingent possibility that addresses itself to the very being of academic film study. To restate the matter in the form of a question: what must film studies be if it is always already likely to collude with the prosecution of US foreign policy? The response—film studies is the study of film as film—may be securely post-theoretical, but it is also utterly inadequate.

One could say that this general situation was "heralded" the year before when *The Battle of Algiers* was adduced by Michael Vann as an ideal peda-gogical tool for teaching radical history. Vann's essay appeared in the once renegade now prestigious *Radical History Review* in the recurring section, "Teaching Radical History." Organized by Ian Christopher Fletcher, this special issue of the journal, and Fletcher's contribution to the "Teaching Radical History" section in particular (titled "History and Film") sought explicitly to reflect upon the use of film as historical evidence, especially radical historical evidence. And despite the fact that "radical" and "evidence" were evoked continually by Fletcher (not to mention Vann) film never managed to become anything *more* than evidence, just atypical, and in that rather benign sense, radical, evidence. The cinema never assumed the qualities attributed to it by Rosen, where the very history, indeed the political history, of evidence is made to matter fundamentally to any history venturing to call itself radical. In Vann's discussion of using Pontecorvo to teach Frederick Cooper and Ann Stoler's call for tearing down the wall between the histories of colony and metropole, he never manages to think through the pedagogical problem of teaching what earlier I called the navel of the disciplinary dream, and this despite the fact that Pontecorvo's film explicitly poses—at once as theme and as technique—the problem of how the cinema articulates the wall between the colony (the Casbah) and the metropole (the French quarter), and it does so in a way that makes this precise articulation key to what film has to teach us about both the history of colonialism and history as such.

I will return to the cinematic articulation of this wall, but for such a gesture to be meaningful, how I am proposing to supplement Cooper and Stoler's critique of historiography deserves clarification. In *Tensions of Empire* (1997) Cooper and Stoler pressure the Eurocentrism of historiography by drawing attention to the intellectual compromises that arise when we trust too readily in histories of "contact zones" (to use Mary Louise Pratt's felicitous phrase) that reduce contact to the dominant party's construal of it. In effect, this is an expression of the project of Said's *Orientalism* worked out in historical terms. As important as this type of work is, it too often or too quickly settles for an inversion of perspective where instead of posing the problem of the discourse of Eurocentric historiography, its epistemology as well as its rhetoric, it struggles over the matter of who is the subject and who is the object of a given history. Avoiding this would mean recognizing "evidence" (as word, as value, as effect of a certain procedure, etc.) as part of historiographic discourse, and examining what happens to the discourse of historiography when the displacement of the subject/object relation occurs. There is, in effect, a discursive equivalent of the phenomenon of what Fanon called the *évoluées*, the comprador class that arises within the colonial situation to re-construct the relation between the colonizer and the colonized in the postcolonial relation between the state and civil society. Phrased in terms of Cooper and Stoler's figure of the wall, its breakdown accomplishes little if the significance of doing so is already determined within the historiographic rhetoric of the metropole. One might think here of Marx's famous turn of phrase in *The Manifesto of the Communist Party* where commodities are described as the means by which capital "batters down all Chinese walls" (Marx 1974: 71). What this highlights is the rather obvious need to think theoretically about both the rhetoric of articulation within historiography, and the task of situating critique in a critical location, a task which has only become more insistent as globalization—the condition of presumed total articulation of, in

Marx's terms, the formal as well as real subsumption of all substance by capital—has taken hold.

But here again, film studies appears to be anxiously avoiding the work of "doing theory," thereby confusing the redemption of the cinema with its sacrifice. In essence, it is fruitless to protest Vann's lack of disciplinary dedication because there is finally little difference between his reduction of film to evidence and the terms of film studies' repudiation of this very status. It is not, of course, that the cinema is ignored as a source of evidence about itself—one sees this everywhere one looks in the field—instead, it is that the question of what is evidenced by the cinema, or how film studies colludes to protect "evidence," is foreclosed.

TORTURED LOGIC

The question posed by Kaufman, "what does the Pentagon 'see' in *The Battle of Algiers*?" is one we must now answer, not necessarily for the Pentagon, but for ourselves. Only then can we evaluate the telling dead space of the Defense Department's otherwise "lively discussion." Contrary to what several have claimed, the Pentagon did not fail to respect the radicality of Pontecorvo's achievement. Or, put differently, it cannot be faulted for being any less respectful than the hagiographic left, a left that has itself failed to articulate the radicality of *The Battle of Algiers*.[2] As Žižek impishly put the matter with regard to Abu Ghraib, the problem is not what Washington claims not to know, but "what Secretary Rumsfeld Doesn't Know that He Knows" (Žižek 2004: 1), or, rephrased in my terms, what the Pentagon doesn't see that it sees in *The Battle of Algiers*. My answer, put succinctly, is that it does not see that it sees the irreducibly cinematic articulation of our relation to the "real pastness" of the present. Fair enough, but in what sense does it make sense to say that Pontecorvo's film confronts its viewer with precisely this articulation?

As is well known, *The Battle of Algiers* was censored in France for five years. As Saadi Yacef explains in the interview referred to earlier, this had precisely to do with the fact that the film, strictly speaking, traumatized French public opinion, making it impossible to get past the humiliation of its complicity in precisely the barbarism France, especially in the wake of the occupation, defined itself against. Because much of the flack in France was stirred by the resident *pieds noirs* and the Association of the Repatriated, Pontecorvo felt it crucial to clarify that none of the footage in the film was actually from French television, and this despite the enormous technical pains taken to achieve precisely this effect. In an interview Pontecorvo explained that he shot in black and white because, "an image seems most true…when it resembles those furnished by the media" (Solinas 1973: 167). Indeed, he describes in some detail (and his biographer, Irene Bignardi, has corroborated this) how carefully the technical conditions—the lens, the film

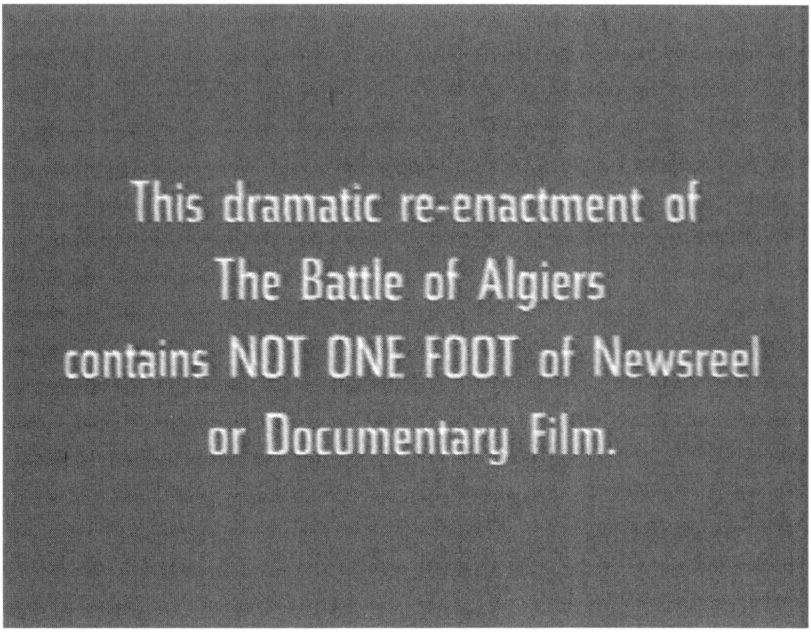

Figure 12.1

stock, the lighting—necessary for realizing this resemblance were sought out. When discussing the possible US distribution of the film under such circumstances, "friends" suggested that he add a one sentence disclaimer at the beginning of the film (see Figure 12.1). Sensing that this might help both at home and abroad, Pontecorvo agreed. However, he might just have well have written: "This is not a pipe," because if this disclaimer manages to do anything it twists, and in the strictly etymological sense, tortures the logic of representation by alerting all spectators to the need to be vigilant during every foot of the following film less he or she be confused about the epistemological status of what then appears in the ensuing 10,760 feet of film. In effect, the disclaimer tints every foot of film with a fundamental question: what is the status of what you are seeing, implicitly establishing that the disclaimer was necessary because one always might be taken in without it. Moreover, this disclaimer-effect captures in one 15 second shot the entire fetishistic aspect of cinematic spectatorship. As it was famously put by Christian Metz, yes, I know very well that it is just a movie, *mais quand même*....

There are two additional points that must be stressed here. First, the disclaimer effect achieves a certain reflexive apotheosis when the film stages what clearly accedes to the status of documentary footage within its own diegesis. I am thinking of that arresting scene (number 73 in the published scenario) in which Colonel Mathieu is screening what is, from the spectator's point of view, a scene recorded earlier as part of the police surveillance conducted at checkpoints between the Casbah and the French quarter. We recognize the "bomber's" face. Here the film and with it the cinema as a mode of representation, is caught up in the torturous logic of the liar's paradox. To wit: the very film in which you are seeing a scene that really did appear earlier (indeed we watched the actress/character prepare for her part) has also told you that you are not seeing the scene you know you have seen. All epistemological mysteries aside, what this foregrounds is the entire thematics of the telecommunication of historical experience. That is, the fact that the evidence of "real pastness," is modeled on and rooted in the collection, storage, and retrieval systems of the modern archive, in this case, the cinema as a documental medium.

Second, as the work of both Rosen and his colleague Mary Ann Doane attests, we are dealing here with the vexing problem of indexicality, again not simply as a semiotic enigma, but as a fundamental condition of historicity as such. In other words, if "real pastness" is both the cause and the effect of the index, that is, the fact that something before, by virtue of its contact with the medium of representation (in this case photosensitive celluloid), is captured in an ever renewable present, in effect, in the technological condition of a certain mediated form of representation, then what it means to unleash the disclaimer-effect on every subsequent foot of film is to posit and withdraw, in an indiscernible flicker, the documental, and in *that* sense historical, dimension of the cinema: not simply the cinema as a medium through which to encounter either accurate or inaccurate representations of history—in this case the Battle of Algiers—but the cinema as a medium in which history and representation adjust themselves to one another. If this is accurate, then what is to be seen in Pontecorvo's film are not simply potential lessons about winning battles and losing wars, but the way the very pedagogical concept of the cinema belongs to a historical perspective the cinema cannot, at the same time, avoid lobbying for. Put crudely, the film does not represent a history which can either be repeated or not, but the representational articulation of cinema and history. Treating the film precisely as that which teaches one about history, the Pentagon cannot see that it sees this more far reaching and metacritical point. But, and this is important, it knows that the cinema is the right place to look.

As Rosen has demonstrated, Bazinian ontology was never simply about cinematic realism, the fidelity between events and their celluloid inscription. It was also always about history, the very notion not simply that a "before" matters to an "after," but that the latter is obliged to be faithful to the former. Expressed through the concept of precedent it is not hard to see how a sixteenth century jurist and theorist of political sovereignty, Jean Bodin, might matter fundamentally, as some have argued, to the crucial Western innovation that separated history from historiography. But, as so often is the case, is there not more here than meets the eye? Could the precedent setting structure of the index also be implicated in torture? And if so, can the representation of torture both as narrative event and narrative gap (in scene 112 Colonel Mathieu is finally obliged to drop the euphemism, "interrogation") in *The Battle of Algiers* belong to what the Pentagon doesn't see that it sees in the film? To answer in the affirmative it suffices to recall the powerful link forged by the classicist Page duBois between torture and truth.

A full summary of her intricate argument would take us far afield, so I will settle then for some relevant highlights. Read in terms of its narrative arc duBois's analysis moves us from a literal to a figurative deployment of the Greek word *basanos*. Not uninterestingly this arc also traces a movement from test to torture. Literally, *basanos* refers to basalt, that is, an igneous rock used to test the existence and quality of gold. By scraping the basalt with that whose metal is being tested, the quality and value of the latter was determined by the mark left on the basalt. What is meant by the concept of the "touchstone" derives from this procedure. From here duBois underscores two diachronic developments. First, this notion of testing the value of something begins to frame the way Athenians, precisely during the process of democratization, discuss testing for loyalty, in effect, for determining friends and enemies, a test that more often than not took the form of pressuring someone to act or not act in a certain way at a given time. She notes that playwrights in particular exploited this innovation. Secondly, and for our purposes most importantly, *basanos* comes to designate the test applied to witnesses in juridical proceedings. In effect, here the touchstone becomes the body of the witness whose testimony is either provoked or tested by being marked with what even today's *Army Field Manual* would recognize as the implements of torture. The second development to some extent subsumes the first in that torture is used to elicit the truth from slaves and non-citizens, that is, those whose loyalty is suspect. Although duBois makes less of this than she might, what happens as the touchstone becomes more figural is that its use intensifies in its literal violence, not because figurality hides this, but because it conditions it. In other words, truth is no less torturous than torture is truthful. Well and good, but what precisely does this have to do with *The Battle of Algiers*? I will confine myself to two points. First, as anyone who has seen the film remembers, it opens with a scene of torture (see Figure 12.2).

Immediately following the disclaimer we are shown a room in which several French *paras* surround an Algerian man. He is trembling and, as the *paras* offer him some coffee, it is obvious that we are witnessing the immediate aftermath of an act of torture. His scarred left breast is clearly presented as the touchstone upon which his metal has been tested. As the very first diegetic scene, this shot punctuates the film so as to place its beginning, the place at which the film begins and the profilmic world ends, precisely at the join between the before and after of torture. Indeed, the disclaimer could be said to veil the off screen space where, in classical fashion, an unpresentable act of violence has taken place. As this scene concludes, the more standard punctuation device—the credit sequence—

Figure 12.2

begins in earnest. In effect, the beginning of the film is immediately re-presented.

The credit sequence concludes as the *paras* and the torture victim arrive at the camera obscura of Ali La Pointe, a hiding place we see being constructed later in the film but here serving as the tiled screen on which the director's name is projected. Clearly, the beginning of the film and the beginning of the plot are articulated through torture. Moreover, this mere contingency has been supplied with necessity by virtue of the disclaimer-effect, which, like the touchstone, marks every subsequent foot of film with the question: is this true? As if to intensify this, Pontecorvo and Solinas structure the film's plot as a flashback. However, the film is not simply the re-counting of a "real pastness" (how Ali came to be where "we" find him), it is an enactment of the distinctly cinematic articulation of the relation between the past and present, the here and now/there and then. Specifically, the flashback is enunciated through an audiovisual plunge where the audience enters not simply Ali's "head," but the past of colonial Algeria (see Figure 12.3).

It cannot be insignificant that this plunge, the deliberate loss of focus, is shot in precisely that film stock (note the grain) that in simulating the documental confusion warned against in the disclaimer, links this fusion of plot and film technique to the vexed theme of returning to the past, in effect, to history but history now scored with the telling traces of historicity (see Figure 12.4).

Figure 12.3

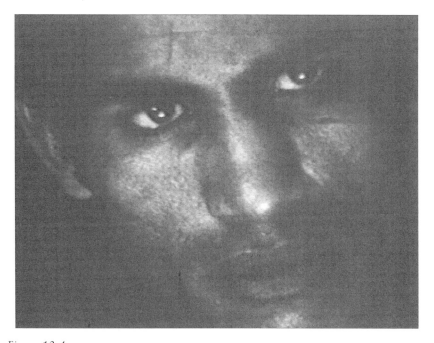

Figure 12.4

Coupled with the deliberate alternating of shots inside and outside the hiding place—an alternation so endemic to the cinema as to show its very code in operation (see Figures 12.5 and 12.6)—followed by an equally endemic left to right pan that in literally articulating the border between the Casbah and the French Quarter joins our impossible point of view within the hideout to our fluid craning over this very border, the entire gesture of crossing into the diegesis of the film is staged so as to associate, and associate intimately, the event of torture and the problem of filmic truth (see Figures 12.7 and 12.8).

As I said before, we are dealing here with a torturous logic, one summoned beautifully in Foucault/Magritte's phrase, "this is not a pipe," or as it makes more sense to say at this juncture, "this is not a film."

My second point is even more perverse, but no less important. If the touchstone functions literally to test one's metal, and it does so by virtue of leaving a mark that determines value, then it is important to recognize in this mark precisely what Charles Sanders Peirce would call an index (Peirce being both Rosen and Doane's source), that is, a sign defined by a real contiguity between it and its object. In other words, beyond the bullet hole and the personal pronoun—both examples of what Peirce included among indexical signs—one would have to add here the forensically significant marks left in the wake of torture. And, if this is so, and if indexicality stands as the minimal pre-condition of historiography—the inscription of

Figure 12.5

Figure 12.6

Figure 12.7

Figure 12.8

a before in an after that remains loyal to it—then regardless of whether Pontecorvo is seeking to make a theoretical point about the entwinement of history and torture—where a "real pastness" is obliged to surrender its secrets—*The Battle of Algiers* confronts its spectators, then and now, with precisely such a provocation. In other words, the anti-colonial history it "re-enacts" is one in which torture stands at the threshold of both the film's past and present (the flashback displaces what in the diegesis is the future—the death of Ali la Pointe—by locating it within the past of the film) as well as, by extension, the threshold of the indexical sign, that is, the space time of the sign's representation of its object. One might say, with only slight exaggeration, that the film is the confession wrested from Algeria when put to the test by the French. As such it is not simply a mark, but a re-marked mark, that is, one that gives voice to the unspeakable conditions of its speech in what it has to say.

Frankly, I take this to be the unruly irony of the scene referred to earlier where Colonel Mathieu is lecturing his officers while screening footage putatively shot earlier at one of the checkpoints between the Casbah and the French Quarter (see Figure 12.9).

For those watching the film we see and hear not just that precisely as the French speculate as to whether they are seeing what they need to see, they fail to, but that in the film this not only takes the form of watching what we recognize to be a "clip" from *The Battle of Algiers*, but as the sequence

Figure 12.9

unfolds, the screen within the frame becomes, in shot seven, the frame and all conceivable spectators of *The Battle of Algiers* are positioned as French soldiers straining to see (see Figure 12.10).

In other words, the film shows itself being studied and the studious spectators failing, in that very act, to see what they need/desire to see. Indeed, the film showed this to the Pentagon, which, of course, could not see that it saw this. Of the many commentaries on the Pentagon screening, the only one not to avoid the significance of this most unsettling scene was Stuart Klawans of *The Nation* writing for *The New York Times*. Alas, as I will argue in closing, he draws the wrong conclusions.

At the heart of Klawans's analysis stands the insight expressed in the sensible phrase, "but it's just a film." What he tries to show both by suggesting (along with numerous others) that certain historical facts of the re-enactment are misrepresentations of the "real pastness" of the battle in Algiers, and by raising epistemological doubts about cinematic representation as such, is that the Pentagon doubtless overlooked the fact that, at best, Pontecorvo's film might show one how to win over an *audience*, but that it could not, as a matter of principle, show one how to win either a battle or a war. Sensible indeed, but I take this to be yet another articulation of the view Žižek objected to in his *In These Times* piece on Abu Ghraib. In other words, Klawans is resisting the notion that the Pentagon doesn't see that it sees, and sees precisely in turning to a film to think the martial strategies of the present. In short, the crucial point is not that it is *just* a film, but that it

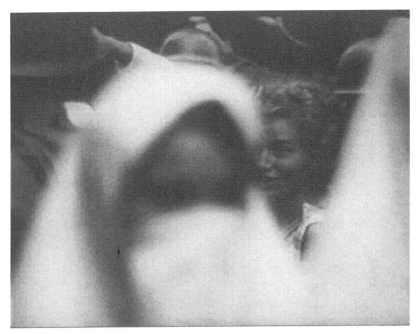

Figure 12.10

is film that says, 24 frames per second, "this is not a film." It says this not to efface its articulation of our relation to history whether past or present in order to let the truth shine forth unobstructed, but to insist on the tangled role of the cinema in the articulation of this relation, to draw out the deep, perhaps even torturous, affinity between the cinema and what Rosen called historicity.

To clarify, if briefly, what this might contribute to both film theory and the public reception of the Pentagon screening, I turn to Derrida's taped dialogue with Bernard Stiegler, *Echographies of Television*. There, in response to a query about the contemporary resurgence of ethnocentrisms of all sorts, Derrida proposes that these belong to a "powerful and violent technological expropriation" (Derrida and Stiegler 2002: 80), one that links democratization and delocalization in a way that clears the field for the accelerated return of petty nationalisms, in effect, everything from the preemptive unilateralism of US compassionate imperialism to the sectarian fundamentalisms walling off Palestine, and now inciting civil war in Iraq. In other words, the accelerated diffusion of cultural reception conditioned by the mode of technological reproducibility once consummately embodied in the cinema but now best exemplified in so-called real time, continuous broadcast television, provokes a deep anxiety about both home and identity. We are constantly exposed to the identities of others and live our own identities as now shared with them—so much so, in fact, that the very concept of identity becomes an indefensible border. Is this not key to the Bush

White House's resentment of al Jazeera? To the extent that history and historiography (whether national or not) secure these identities, they fall prey to this unsettling anxiety. Indeed, never more so than when historicity is localized, to whatever extent it can be, in the very tele-technological and ever accelerating diffusion of cultural reception and encounter.

What makes *The Battle of Algiers* the revolutionary achievement that it is, is the fusion it effects between a historical struggle and the struggle for history, a struggle now indissociable from the very medium of their articulation. In screening this film the Pentagon, in effect, saw that film, perhaps even this film, could allow it to see how winning the war of ideas might well include thinking through, among other things, the left to right pan whereby, in the film, the West and the rest are made to matter to each other, not simply as adversaries, but as locations caught up in an uneven but nevertheless shared process of radical delocalization. Doubtless, it did not see that it saw this. The tragic thing—and this is not a word I use lightly—the tragic thing is that film studies is similarly blinded by the anti-theoretical insight struggling to assert itself in the field. While this tendency may well prevail in the current disciplinary battles, in the end it will have lost the war of ideas, not because it traffics in bad or even feckless ideas, but because it has no idea what the cinema has become.

NOTES

1. In his article, "Terror's Aftermath: A Counterterrorism Policy for Yesterday's Threat," Hoffman invokes the now proverbial "box" in order to draw attention to the fact that Rumsfeld's Department of Defense is perhaps the first since the US withdrawal from Vietnam, officially dedicated to the proposition that military strategy need no longer wring its hands anxiously over the "Vietnam Syndrome," the notion that Americans are reluctant to fight unpopular wars, especially when those wars are undeclared or mendaciously justified. Indeed, the Defense Planning Guidance document drawn up by Paul Wolfowitz, Dick Cheney's aide Scooter Libby, and Benjamin Netanyahu essentially presumes that the belligerent spread of democracy through permanent war (revolution) requires us to, in effect, forget Vietnam. This said, Hoffman's proposition resembles Žižek's in suggesting that Rumsfeld's Pentagon, once faced with its own bogeyman (the post-Cold War enemy-to-come, now "global terrorism"), is inclined to forget, not Vietnam, but that it was responsible for producing the historical meaning of overcoming the Vietnam Syndrome. One must be careful not to go too far here, but Hoffman's suggestion would appear to focus, however unwittingly, on the sore spot between the "real pastness" of Vietnam and the historiographies deployed to represent it.
2. Allowing for a certain bagginess in the concept of the Left one can trace a persistent, very intense interest in Pontecorvo's film. This may have been triggered by Pauline Kael's early review of the film in which she famously warned that Pontecorvo was the most dangerous kind of Marxist because he was a Marxist poet. A good overview of this history is to be found in Mike Wayne's *Political Film: The Dialectics of Third Cinema*, but certain highlights are worth drawing attention to here. One thinks, for example, of Francee Cov-

ington's probing essay "Are the Revolutionary Techniques Employed in *The Battle of Algiers* Applicable to Harlem?" where she explores the relevance of the film's "lessons" for the US civil rights movement. More recently of course there is Edward Said's essay/interview with Pontecorvo, now collected in *Reflections on Exile*, where he characterizes *The Battle of Algiers* as one of the "greatest political films ever made" (a point he reiterates in his film on Pontecorvo). And, one would have to include here as well, the long discussion of *The Battle of Algiers* found in Ella Shohat and Robert Stam's *Unthinking Eurocentrism*. I hasten to add that this all too brief list refers only to works written in English and published in the Anglophone world.

REFERENCES

Bordwell, D. and Carroll, N. (eds.) (1996) *Past-Theory: reconstructing film theory*, Madison: University of Wisconsin Press.

Derrida, J. and Stiegler, B. (2002) *Echographies of Television: filmed interviews*, Trans. J. Bajorek, Cambridge, UK: Polity Press.

Farah, C. and Yacef, S. (2004) "I Killed People. I Did It for My Country," Salon.com, Online. Available HTTP: <http://www.salon.com/ent/feature/2004/01/09/yacef/print/html> (accessed 12 January 2004).

Kaufman, M. (2003) *The New York Times*, 7 September, Section 4, p. 3.

Klawans, S. (2004) "Lessons from the Pentagon's Favorite Training Film," in *The New York Times*, 4 January, AR 26.

Marx, K. (1974) *The Revolutions of 1848: political writings, volume one*, D. Fernbach (ed.) New York: Vintage.

Pontecorvo, G. (1966) *The Battle of Algiers* [VHS] Santa Monica, CA: Rhino Home Video.

Rosen, P. (2002) *Change Mummified: cinema, historicity, theory*, Minneapolis, MN: University of Minnesota Press.

Solinas, P. (1973) *Gillo Pontecorvo's Battle of Algiers*, Trans. none given, New York: Charles Scribner's Sons.

Žižek, S. (2004) "What Rumsfeld Doesn't Know That He Knows About Abu Ghraib," in *In These Times*, 21 May, Online. Available HTTP: <http://www.inthesetimes.com/site/main/article/what_rumsfeld_doesnt_know_that_he_knows_about_abu-ghraib/> (accessed 10 June 2004).

13 *Jacob the Liar* and historical truth in Berlin and Hollywood

Cheryl Dueck

The anthropologist Jan Assmann defines cultural memory as the "outer dimension of human memory" (1992: 19), and includes two distinct concepts within it: "memory culture" (*Erinnerungskultur*) and "reference to the past" (*Vergangenheitsbezug*). In films and books about the holocaust, the memory cultures in which they are produced are at least as informative to the work as their references to the past. In two filmic versions of a story set in a Jewish ghetto in Poland, one produced by the socialist, state-owned production company DEFA in the German Democratic Republic in 1974 (Beyer), and the other by Robin Williams's American-based Blue Wolf Productions in 1999 (Kassovitz), memory and historical truths are contingent on the ideological perspectives of their producers. Ultimately, by means of their differing approaches to the same subject matter, the films of *Jacob the Liar*[1] support the founding myths of their countries of origin. For the GDR, the antifascist foundation of the state in 1949 remained a rhetorical cornerstone throughout the regime. The DEFA production foregrounds the hope for liberation of the ghetto by Soviet troops and, by extension, for a socialist collective that addresses the needs of all. The United States, on the other hand, relies rhetorically on faith in the individual to rise above adversity, learn from the lessons of the past, and support liberty, diversity, and equality. For the American public, the protagonist Jacob is revealed as an individual hero who resists the malevolent Other to bring hope to future generations for a freer and more humane society.

While the 1974 film was the first and only East German film to be nominated for a Best Foreign Language Film Oscar, and received the Silver Bear at the Berlin Film Festival, the 1999 version met with little critical or public success, partly due to unfavorable comparisons to the previously released film, *Life is Beautiful*. In the two films of *Jacob the Liar*, the approach to the authenticity or truthfulness of the story is entirely different, and is shaped largely by the ideological contexts in which the films are produced. Furthermore, the viewer response to the films, by critics and the general public, hinges on the manner in which the nature of the memory and truth are framed. The framework of the story in the Beyer's version allows him, for the first time ever, to use humor as an effective strategy in telling a story of a Jewish ghetto on film, whereas Kassovitz's remake is marred by flaws in its attempt to do so. Both writers of the screenplays, Becker and Kassovitz, draw on some personal memories for the images in the film, but they are mined in different ways. Consistent with American memory culture, individual personal memories of the filmmaker's own life give shape and authenticity to the American film, while the East German memory culture would place more value on considerations of collective memory. Becker's own memories serve as a general background for the film, and lead him to question the reliability of individual memory. Through the use of fantasy flashbacks and a narrative framework that place aspects of the story in doubt, Becker and Beyer establish a dialectic of memory and imagination. Kassovitz and Williams, on the other hand, merely contrast truth and fiction, while they underline the importance of truth and authenticity of memory, and represent Jacob's lies as part of a heroic survival story.

Jurek Becker, the screenwriter of the original film, was himself a concentration camp survivor. Born in the Polish city of Lodz in 1937, he was sent together with his mother from the Lodz ghetto to Ravensbrück/Sachsenhausen in 1944, where his mother died. Jurek was one of very few children to survive the camps. His father was sent to Auschwitz at the same time, but survived and was united with his son by the workers at a Red Cross children's camp after the war. Father and son moved immediately to East Berlin rather than back to Poland or to Israel, and worked hard to be integrated and accepted in Germany. Perhaps in part because of the predominant silence between father and son on the topic of the holocaust, Jurek later took up Jewish themes in his writing, and became the most important Jewish literary voice from the GDR. He began writing the script for *Jacob the Liar* in 1963, in collaboration with the director Frank Beyer. Just before filming was about to commence in Poland, Polish authorities refused access to studios for filming in Krakow—in Beyer's view, due to prevalent anti-Semitism (Beyer 2001: 187). Becker then decided to write a novel with the subject matter instead, and when it was published in 1969, it was both critically acclaimed internationally and widely read. Following the success of Becker's novel, and in a period of cultural thaw in the GDR, the East German film studios (DEFA), again expressed interest in proceeding with *Jacob the Liar*, with Beyer as director. It was the first film anywhere to use humor and laughter to represent the Jewish Shoah.

The seed of the story began with an anecdote told to Becker by his father about a man in the Lodz ghetto who had had a hidden radio and shared BBC news with the community. Jurek Becker, who became one of the best known writers of East Germany after he wrote *Jacob the Liar*, had no memories of his early childhood in the Lodz Jewish ghetto in Poland. In Becker's screenplay and novel, a tragic-comic treatment of life in the ghetto, he makes the significant change that the radio is fictional. Set during the war in an unidentified ghetto, where people face starvation or deportation on a daily basis, the story focuses on the protagonist Jacob. One evening, he is sent to Gestapo headquarters for violating curfew. In the office, he overhears a radio report that the Russians are 20 km from Bezanika, not far from the ghetto. Since no one emerges from Gestapo headquarters alive, Jacob's story is not believed. In order to make the good news credible, he lies, and tells his friend that he has a radio. When the word gets out, Jacob is constantly probed for news, and is compelled to invent more and more news reports to keep those around him both "informed" and entertained.

Information found for Gilman's biography of Jurek Becker suggests that Max Becker himself may have been the man in the anecdote. In his file with the Berlin Jewish Community, says Gilman, "his deportation from Lodz is attributed to his having owned a radio and having spread 'oral propaganda' (read: rumors) against the Germans. How accurate this claim was is open to question" (Gilman 2002: 25). Responding to questions about his past, Max became quite a storyteller, and many of his stories were helpful for survival in a difficult environment. Because members of the resistance were loved, it would have been useful to him to be seen as a resistor. In any case, in Max's later version of the anecdote, the man with the radio was betrayed to the Germans and shot. Becker's father considered him a hero, and wanted his son to tell the story of the hero. Becker, in speaking about this anecdote in Toronto in 1983, says that he had no desire to tell this story about the hero (Becker 1983b: 272). He did come back to the story years later, but made one notable change: his protagonist Jacob does not actually have a radio. This change allowed him to avoid the heroic storyline, and to motivate the story with questions of the present:

> For example, I had the desire to meditate upon the question of what role hope plays in the lives of people. Whether it is sufficient for survival, or whether it is only helpful when it spurs people into action. For example, into resisting. (Becker 1983b: 272)

The question of hope is particularly significant for the East German context at the time. A pressing question for writers and filmmakers was whether they could hope for the socialism with the human face that was proposed during the Prague Spring, and what role their stories played in generating hope for the people of the GDR.

Throughout both filmic versions of *Jacob the Liar*, Jacob Heym debates with himself about truth and lies. In the novel, the narrator is a witness who knew Jacob, and who repeatedly reminds us that his memories are not exact and are sometimes invented, and he leaves it up to us what and how much we want to believe. He even provides us with two endings, one of which corresponds with historical events, and the other that he considers "incomparably more satisfactory than the real ending" (Becker 1990: 189). The question of truth and lies is therefore central to the story, but it is handled differently in the films.

The opening sequences of the two films reveal a fundamental difference in the narrative approach. Beyer's 1974 version sets up a dialectic of truth and fiction, which is carried through the body of the film with the use of fantasy flashbacks, set off by brighter color than is used in the rest of the film. The opening sequence establishes one of the main themes of the film, which is the shifting and problematic nature of truth and authenticity, specifically with regard to the events of the holocaust.

> The tale of Jacob the Liar is not true.
> Honest.
> But maybe it is true after all.

In theory, truth could be equal to the narration of the story, but in reality, it is not. The silence of the sequence, as well as the textual frames, serve as tools of distanciation, borrowed first, from silent movies, and second, from Brecht's *Verfremdungseffekt*. This narrative interjection is external to the action, and suggests from the outset that the story has been related to a third party after the fact. The memory of the events may or may not be reliable, and even the events themselves are called into question. When I asked Beyer about the tensions between truth and memory in the film, as represented by the narrative structure, he responded by saying that he and Becker conceived more of the tensions between memory and imagination (Dueck and Boyer 2003). "To be precise," he said, "Jacob the Liar is written in a quest for childhood memory."[2] Becker had no personal memories of the ghetto, and interestingly, remarks that he could not have written the story if he had. It was necessary to be able to fictionalize the events. His father had a completely different relationship to the story, and would not speak to his son for two years at the time that Jurek wrote and published the novel (Becker 1983a: 288).

Peter Kassovitz, a Hungarian born Jew and concentration camp survivor, living and working in France, purchased the rights for Jakob the Liar and, based on the French translation of the novel, wrote a French screenplay for the story. He tried for years unsuccessfully to make the film in Europe. Eventually, one of his co-workers in Los Angeles brought the screenplay to Robin Williams, who then starred in and served as executive producer for the film. It is clear from Kassovitz's commentary on the DVD that the focus on Jakob as the reluctant hero was important to him. The Kassovitz/Williams collaboration begins with a voiceover in which Williams tells a joke:

> Hitler goes to a fortune teller and asks, "when will I die?" The fortune teller replies, "on a Jewish holiday." Hitler then asks, "how do you know that?" And she replies, "any day you die will be a Jewish holiday."

Jakob goes on to speak of humor as survival, as the camera pans the ghetto and then zooms in for a close-up on his face, alternating with a view of the sky from his point of view. As his introductory monologue ends, the music swells. This establishes the main theme of this version of the film, which is the triumph of the individual spirit in the face of adversity. It also sets up Jakob as the hero, a perspective absent from the GDR version. The narrator *is* Jakob, which lends to the story an autobiographical authenticity. A question is asked and answered at the beginning of the film: "How could you tell a joke like that at a time like that? That is how we survived." The narrator, by extension, defends the use of humor in a film about the holocaust. Since humor was used by the Jews themselves, it is permissible, for reasons of authenticity, to depict events with humor. The audience is also permitted laughter as distanciation from horror, therefore allowing them to confront the holocaust obliquely.

In both versions of the story, Jacob is hiding a child, Lina, whose parents have been deported. The child represents innocence, and naïve acceptance of illusion as reality. Lina finds out about the radio, and begs to hear it. Of course, Jacob has no radio, but since the child has never seen one, Jacob pretends to play it for her. What is played on the radio differs in the two versions. Specifically, a fairy tale is told in the GDR version that is omitted in the remake. Kassovitz states in his commentary on the DVD that he had to cut the fairy tale to trim the length, but it was clearly not a key to the narrative for him. In the original, Jacob plays the role of the fairy tale uncle, and tells the story of a princess who is very ill. The king does everything he can for his treasured daughter, to no avail. When the visiting gardener hears that the princess wishes for a cloud, he asks the princess what a cloud is made of. She replies that it is made of cotton, and is as big as her pillow. The gardener returns with a piece of cotton, as big as her pillow, and the princess is cured. As the fairy tale is told, the film cuts to a colorful fantasy sequence, in which Lina is the princess in her imagination. Because Lina has never seen a radio, even when she peeks around the screen to see Jacob's performance, she is not sure what to think. She partly feels very clever in having discovered the ruse, but she also partly believes that the radio *is* Jacob and that the story is true. This is a key to the larger story: just as the princess's health is restored by the false belief that her wishes can be fulfilled, the psychological health of the ghetto is buoyed by Jacob's lies or fantasies.

In the remake, we hear Williams do a clever impression of Winston Churchill and then he dances with Lina to the Beer Barrel Polka to a record that he puts on a hidden turntable. In this scene, as in several others, Kassovitz draws on his own poignant childhood memories in Hungary. He was hidden by a family in Budapest during the war, and remembers the popularity of the Beer Barrel Polka. The record player and the music it plays in the scene are real, not imaginary, and Lina never looks behind the screen:

there is no ironic break. The child is innocent and her innocence must survive until the end of the film. Although the scene is effective, funny and tender, the choice to eliminate the fantasy element here and elsewhere causes difficulties of credibility and continuity for his fantastic conclusion.

Throughout the earlier film, on the other hand, Jacob himself indulges in a series of fantasies about his past life, filmed in bright, vibrant color that supports the dialectic of memory and imagination. The veracity of these sequences is called into question at various points. For instance, a woman appears in most of the sequences as a happy wife or partner. One of the sequences, however, shifts the truth of the others, since the woman tells him that another man has proposed to her, and Jacob must make a decision. He tells her that he has to think about it, and thereby loses his chance. All memories, then, are consequently exposed as partly imagination. The use of color, says Beyer, was a key change in the film from the first version of the screenplay in 1966 to the eventual production. Previously, Beyer had enjoyed and mastered the black-and-white film aesthetic, and *Jacob the Liar* was his first color film. Paradoxically, the color film was used to draw attention to the *lack* of color in the ghetto. Significantly, it also had the effect of emphasizing the adjusted, transfigured truth of memories:

> We had incorporated the flashbacks from the novel, in which the characters remember the past a little nostalgically. Presumably, the potato pancake shop that Jacob possessed, was a little bit dirtier than it is portrayed in our film. These transfigured memories have a rather kitschy, colorful quality, while the setting in the present has hardly any color—everything is grey, brown, black, dirty-white. You notice that it is a color film almost only by the faces of the people and by the yellow Jewish stars on the clothing. (Beyer in Interview with Dueck and Boyer 2003)

In the color sequences, imagination is linked to alternative pasts and futures; Lina imagines herself being saved by the gardener, while Jacob imagines a successful pancake house and a happy love affair. Every aspect of the film, both in structure and content, draws attention to the fact that the story that is being told is just that: a story that shows both memories and imagined elaborations of them in a dialectic framework.

The fantastic element of the narrative is notably absent from the remake until the film's conclusion, where it is abruptly introduced. The conclusions of the two films are as fundamentally different as their introductions. Beyer's 1974 film concludes with a scene in a boxcar, after the ghetto has been evacuated. Lina looks through an opening at the clouds in the sky and asks Jacob if the fairy tale about the princess is true. Jacob answers, "Of course it's true." Lina says that the boys did not believe her when she told them that the princess got better when she was given cotton balls. Jacob explains that the princess wanted a cloud, and that she just thought that clouds were made of cotton. Lina asks, "Aren't clouds made of cotton?" At this moment, she experiences the loss of a fantasy, and the disillusionment of relative truth. Kassovitz, on the other hand, tags a double-ending to his film, along the same lines as the double-ending in the novel. Jakob is called in to the Gestapo to reveal the location of the radio, and is tortured when he is unable to do so. The officer finally believes that Jakob does not have a radio, and to save face, demands that he confess before the whole ghetto that all of his news was fictional. In a melodramatic scene, Williams as Jakob stands heroically on a platform before the ghetto, bloodied and defiant, and when he refuses to confess, is shot. The ghetto is evacuated, and while the camera focuses on Jakob's mutilated body, we hear the voiceover of Jakob the narrator: "So that's how it ended. I never got a chance to make my big speech. I swear I had a big speech about freedom and never giving in…. And they all went off to the camps and were never seen again." The shot then breaks to the fantasy ending, and he says: "But then again, maybe it was not like that at all…." In the concluding scene, a wide-eyed Lina looks out of the boxcar at Russian tanks, which have stopped the train to liberate them, and at the Andrews sisters on top of a tank, singing the Beer Barrel Polka.

Both directors struggled with the conclusion, and Becker had written several versions. In the first two drafts of his screenplay, Jacob loses hope and attempts an escape from the ghetto and is shot. The final scene shows Russian soldiers liberating the camp and features one soldier leading Lina away by the hand. The first draft was written during a time when Becker had more confidence in the GDR, before the Russian tanks rolled into Czechoslovakia to violently end the Prague Spring in 1968. The Russian soldier as liberator, holding a child's hand, fit well into the GDR's allegiance with Russia and the narrative of the anti-fascist foundation of the state. The *idea* of the Russian troops as potential liberators remains a strong ideological undercurrent in the Becker/Beyer production, but three factors caused them to change the ending. One was Becker's disillusionment with the political situation and the Russian role in it; the second was his de-emphasis of any heroism; and third was the revelation that the Russians had not, in fact, liberated any of the ghettos. The Nazis had beat them to it and had sent the inhabitants either on transports to the West or to the gas chambers. Beyer, who remained a committed socialist until the end of the GDR, says in his autobiography: "We did not want to bring the Russian Army, and the historical truth that they had freed half of Europe from fascism, into discredit with a little lie" (Beyer 2001: 185). The ending that they chose does shed a slightly less glowing light on the Soviets as the bearers of hope. Still, Becker, reflecting back on the film in 1976 at a point when his disappointment with the rigid practices of the GDR state was at its peak, just before he emigrated to the West, was undoubtedly referring to the film's relationship to GDR memory culture when he said that he considered the film "too conventional and too good" (cited from Becker's Stasi files in Gilman 2002: 93).

The Kassovitz/Williams fantasy ending concludes the film on a hopeful note, but the hope of course does not stem from Soviet involvement. The idea that the liberation was by Soviet soldiers would not have registered as very significant for American viewers. The fantasy scene is a conflation of multiple forms of historical liberation, and what dominates in the end is the American jazz band playing a wartime hit song from Europe for a girl who will survive and bear witness to the past. While the fiction of the ending corresponds to Jakob's storytelling in the film, it leaves the viewer with a disrupted sense of the narrative and, since there are no other fantasy sequences, comes as a shock. Kassovitz, in the director's commentary on the DVD, defends it with the following remark:

> This ending with the Russians stopping the train.... We could be accused of doing this Hollywood kind of happy end. But it's not at all this in our mind. It's really a last lie of Jakob. The film is called *Jakob the Liar*. He invents a last lie for the little girl—even he himself is dead—and for the audience. [Pause] Are you shocked by this ending? I think it's great.

In this final scene, the voice of Jakob returns to the role of the narrator and, by extension, he *becomes* the radio; in the voiceover, he speaks as a disembodied subject, just as a radio does, and thus sends a universalized message of hope. This final fantasy scene by Kassovitz is grounded in authenticity, since fantasy for Kassovitz is not the land of a fairy tale, where imagination reigns, but that of his own experience, and his memories of the Beer Barrel Polka playing on the radio in his youth. While the final scene is surreal and fantastic on the one hand, it also comes from an authenticated reality.

In an interview with Marty Fairbairn, Kassovitz agrees with Fairbairn that the story is about "hope in the midst of hopelessness." He says, "Yes, this is the one thing you *can* learn from the Holocaust: you can keep your *humanity* even when the situation is desperate. Actually, there is not really hope. The hope is that you will not lose your humanity" (Fairbairn 1999: 5). The film's ending supports his belief in this message.

One could also speculate about the response to Judaism in the two conclusions of the film. In Max Becker's interpretation of the story of the radio, the courage of the man and his hope for the improbable is the core. By removing the radio, Becker is rebelling against his father, but perhaps also against his forefathers, who set their hopes on God's promise of blessings and land for the Jewish people in the story of Jacob's ladder (Genesis 28:15). Becker never sought out the Jewish community in Germany, and certainly did not practice the faith. Kassovitz's re-reading of the story may, then, continue a conversation about Jakob's history. Jakob dies a heroic death in the ghetto—a Zionist as well as American vision of ghetto life—

but his lie lives on. The little girl benefits from it, as do the Jewish people. If the spirit can triumph in the face of unspeakable horror, there can be hope for Judaism after the Shoah.[3] The muted hope that remains in Becker's version stems from the fact that the Russians are not far away, and will soon help to end Nazi control, not from any expectation that the Jewish faith can endure.

The question remains: given the Hollywood formula of heroism and the triumph of the human spirit, why was the Kassovitz/Williams production of *Jakob the Liar* a success with neither the critics nor the audience? The numbers on box office sales certainly tell us that the cinema audience did not respond well: *Life is Beautiful* had earned $57,598,247 (USA) by 3 October 1999 (the last data available on http://www.imdb.com) and *Jakob the Liar* had earned just $4,956,401 (USA) by its peak on 31 October 1999. Reviews of the film were largely negative, with a few exceptions.

Critics have had an ambivalent relationship with films about the holocaust, stressing on one hand the importance of cultural memory and confronting the past, and on the other, criticizing the holocaust industry and the manipulation of trauma for profit, for political purposes, or emotional catharsis. The early *Jacob the Liar* pre-dates the spate of films about the holocaust that appeared in the eighties, nineties, and beyond, and yet it is clear that the GDR state was able to take advantage of the film successfully to support its own memory culture and identity as a nation that arose from antifascist activists. The later version, on the other hand, was released during a wave of films on World War II and the holocaust, and capitalizes on the particular needs of the American audience to identify with the victims and claim a power of moral authority and resistance. The problem for the film's reception, in my view, is that it professes authenticity, as indicated in the opening clip, but fails to achieve it. Particularly, the casting of Williams in the lead role distances the viewer from the action. Roger Ebert typically compared *Jakob the Liar* to *Life is Beautiful* in his review, and made the important point that he preferred "*Life Is Beautiful*, which is clearly a fantasy, to *Jakob the Liar*, which is just as contrived and manipulative but pretends it is not" (Ebert 1999). In other words, on the promise of authenticity, designed for the American audience, the film fails to deliver, and the consequence is that the audience is not granted the cathartic feeling that they have been witnesses to history and overcome the past.

From the opening and closing sequences of the films, we can conclude that these filmic depictions of the holocaust serve a function that is common to the holocaust industry in general: that is, the films re-validate the founding myths of the countries which produce them. The Nazi society functions as the Other, against which the society in question defines itself. In the case of the East German film, the founding mythology is that of antifascism. One of the gestures that Becker made to the cultural policy of the GDR in the script was to indicate in the first radio report that it was

Russian soldiers who were advancing towards the ghetto. These Russian troops would bring about a liberation that, as the audience knows, resulted first in Soviet occupation of Eastern Germany and then the German Democratic Republic under the leadership of the Socialist Unity Party. In the GDR, the state representation of World War II history primarily emphasized the socialist resistance, the heroism of socialists in Germany and in exile, and the antifascist foundation of the German Democratic Republic as a nation. The extermination of the Jews was frequently mentioned only in combination with a recognition of political prisoners in the camps. A novel and a film about a Jewish ghetto, *without* a socialist resistance story, were therefore an important contribution towards addressing a gap in the official rhetoric. While Becker managed to have the film made without the requisite socialist realist hero, the positive image of the Russian liberators is nonetheless important to the film. In the final sequence, the narrative shifts from fantasy to reality, as the little girl is forced to confront the terrible reality of her existence. This opens the space for the new socialist way; the Soviet occupation will introduce equality and social justice. Despite the removal of the image of the Soviet soldier with the little girl at the end—a scene that the authorities had liked very much—the film was recognized as important and was supported by the culture ministry: its debut was on GDR television during primetime on the Sunday evening before Christmas. It was seen by millions of viewers and became an important part of the GDR film canon.

The Hollywood (Columbia TriStar) version, on the other hand, celebrates the triumph of the individual spirit and freedom of expression, both in the heroism of Jakob's death, and in the musical liberation fantasy. I talked to Beyer in 2002 about the Kassovitz/Beyer remake of his film. He emphasized that it was a great compliment to Becker's screenplay and to the film to have someone buy the rights to remake it, but he was quite bemused to discover that the remake did exactly what he and Becker predicted it would when they talked about it in the early 1970s. A passage from his autobiography reports the conversation he and Becker had about how an American version of the story would go. They imagined it as a thriller in which the Gestapo searches dramatically for a radio that does not exist, and there is a "long showdown." Jacob is found and tortured, but the truth that he has no radio is at first not believed:

Frank: So they gather the ghetto together and demand of Jacob that he tells the people that he is a liar and doesn't own any radio after all?
Jurek: For example. But Jacob refuses, of course, to take the hope away from his people. And so they beat him to death or shoot him.
Frank: The Americans wouldn't make any film about the red army as the carriers of hope for people in a Polish ghetto.
Jurek: You don't know that. They would in any case make a happy ending, and the Russians could drive up to the ghetto with American

> tanks and trucks. They brought the Russians plenty of supplies
> during the war, after all....

Thirty years after we talked about such variations of our material, the
Americans did in fact do a remake of Jacob the Liar with a showdown
and a happy ending, just as we had sketched it out.

And they went even further. They made Jacob into the leader of an
armed insurgent group in the ghetto. And the happy ending with tanks
that stop the evacuation of the prisoners is as if the American cinema had taken over the traditions of socialist realism from the Stalinist
period.(Beyer 2001: 195f.)

The details of this conversation can more likely be considered an amus-
ing anecdote than an exact rendering of the conversation, but the passage informs us that the ideological reception of the film was a factor that
Becker and Beyer considered carefully. The resulting American approach to
the conclusion is similar to that of Roberto Begnini's film, *Life is Beautiful*.
Sander Gilman has compared the approaches of various comic films about
the Shoah, and points to a shift towards heroic narrative in the period after
Spielberg's film, *Schindler's List* (Gilman 2000). He points out that the
driving plot motivation in *Life is Beautiful* is for the father to heroically
save the life of his son through the sustaining game that he plays with him.
In the end, the father is randomly shot as he steps out in front of his son,
and one of the American tanks that is liberating the camp comes and takes
the child to be reunited with his mother. The promise of a rescue and a
happy ending is what allows us to laugh in this movie. Gilman takes issue
with both *Life is Beautiful* and *Jakob the Liar* (Kassovitz) as "part of a
rereading of the Shoah as the place of heroic action" (308). What Gilman
does not explain, however, is why *Life is Beautiful* received an Oscar for
its efforts while *Jakob the Liar* foundered on every level. Alvin Rosenfeld
looked at a series of studies done by the American Jewish Committee in
several countries to investigate the differences in what people know about
the holocaust. The study showed that, among the populations studied,
Americans know least about the events of World War II, but paradoxically
care about it most, deeming it something essential to understand (Rosenfeld 1997: 120). Rosenfeld identifies popular culture as the source of most
Americans' knowledge of the holocaust, and explains the way this knowledge is processed:

> It is part of the American ethos to stress goodness, innocence, optimism,
> liberty, diversity, and equality. It is part of the same ethos to downplay
> or deny the dark and brutal sides of life and instead to place a pre-
> ponderant emphasis on the saving power of individual moral conduct
> and collective deeds of redemption. Americans prefer to think affir-
> matively and progressively. The tragic vision, therefore, is antithetical

to the American way of seeing the world, according to which people are meant to overcome adversity and not cling endlessly to their sorrows. [...] The Holocaust has had to enter American consciousness, therefore, in ways that Americans could readily understand on their own terms. These are terms that promote a tendency to individualize, heroize, moralize, idealize, and universalize. (Rosenfeld 1997: 123)

Given the false promise of authenticity in Williams's *Jakob the Liar*, we can see in retrospect that there is no way that the predominantly American audience for this picture could process the content of the film in the manner to which they had become accustomed. The film failed both in its attempt to address the questions of truth, memory, and imagination of the past addressed by the original text, and in its attempt to package a product for the audience conditioned by the Americanization of the holocaust to expect a heroic narrative of resistance.

As we have seen, memory cultures in the contexts of both films of *Jacob the Liar* are nationally determined—for the first, by the myth of antifascism, and for the second, by the myth of individual freedom. In the novel, Jacob's attempt to escape from the ghetto and the Red Army liberation are told as the narrator's fantasy, but this is immediately debunked by the "pallid and depressing, the true and unimaginative" ending (Becker 1990: 199), whereas Kassovitz significantly concludes the film with the fantasy. An essential element of the novel is the narrator's role as a witness who tells us Jacob's story as one of doubtful memories. He takes us aside for "just a few words about doubtful memories, a few words about the carefree life; we're going to whip up a cake with modest ingredients, eat only a mouthful of it and push the plate to one side before we've lost our appetite for anything else" (Becker 1990: 19). Despite his doubts, the narrator feels compelled to tell the story. He chooses details from his memory that suit his purpose, and fills in the rest as it *should* have happened—to bake a good cake—and then leaves it up to the reader to accept his improbable story or be resigned to the grim truth. Multiple layers of untruths or lies make up the narrative structure of the novel and the 1974 film, including the untruths of the state, the deliberate imaginings of the storyteller, and the unreliable nature of memory anecdotes. The doubts constitute an important part of memory work; we cannot simply heroize and memorialize without acknowledging the fragmentary and elusive nature of historical memory. In the 1999 film, no room is left for doubt, and the collective memory is founded on a claim of the authenticity of the narrator's memories. While Becker may have considered his version of the film "too conventional and too good," Kassovitz's version, which ends with a tidy dialectic of grim truth of a dead hero with an alternative fiction of an American-style liberation, is too simple.

NOTES

1. Jacob is the spelling used for the English translation of the original novel and film, while the 1999 film uses the German spelling, Jakob. The latter is viewed perhaps as the more authentic option by the filmmakers in the United States, and befits their approach to the story. When both films are referenced together, I have used the spelling Jacob.
2. Translations from this interview, as well as from Beyer's autobiography, *Wenn der Wind sich dreht*, are my own.
3. I am grateful to Dr. Ben Baader at the University of Manitoba who, in response to an earlier version of the paper, pointed out the possible Zionist message.

REFERENCES

Assmann, J. (1992) *Das kulturelle Gedächtnis. Schrift, Erinnerung und politische Identität in frühen Hochkulturen*, München: Beck.
Becker, J. (1983) "Answering Questions about *Jakob der Lügner*," *Seminar*, 19.4: 288–92.
—— (1990) *Jacob the Liar*, Trans. Leila Vennewitz, London: Pan Books.
—— (1983) "Resistance in *Jakob der Lügner*," *Seminar*, 19.4: 269–73.
Beyer, F. (1999) *Jacob the Liar* [DVD] Massachusetts: DEFA.
—— (2001) *Wenn der Wind sich dreht: Meine Filme, mein Leben*, München: Ullstein.
Dueck, C. and Boyer, S. (2003) "'Ich habe mich immer zunächst dafür interessiert, eine gute Story zu finden...'—Sophie Boyer und Cheryl Dueck im Gespräch mit Frank Beyer," *Glossen*, 18, Online. Available HTTP: <http://www.dickinson.edu/glossen/heft18/navigation18.html> (accessed 5 April 2006).
Ebert, R. (1999) "Jakob the Liar," *Chicago Sun-Times*, 24 September, Online. Available HTTP: <http://rogerebert.suntimes.com/apps/pbcs.dll/article?AID=/19990924/REVIEWS/909240305/1023> (accessed 15 April 2006).
Fairbairn, M. (1999) "The Ethics of Representation: A review of *Jakob the Liar*; An Interview with Peter Kassovitz. Report from the Toronto International Film Festival 1999," *Film-Philosophy*, 3.41, Online. Available HTTP: <http://www.film-philosophy.com/vol3-1999/n41fairbairn> (accessed 15 April 2006).
Gilman, S. (2000) "Is Life Beautiful? Can the Shoah be Funny? Some Thoughts on Recent and Older Films," *Critical Inquiry*, 26: 279–308.
—— (2002) *Jurek Becker*, Chicago and London: University of Chicago Press.
Kassovitz, P. (1999) *Jakob the Liar* [DVD] Culver City, CA: Columbia Pictures.
Rosenfeld, A.H. (1997) "The Americanization of the Holocaust," in A.H. Rosenfeld (ed.) *Thinking about the Holocaust: After half a century*, Bloomington and Indianapolis: Indiana University Press.

14 Abderrahmane Sissako

Les lieux provisoires of transnational cinema

Michelle Stewart

As globalization has effected a greater awareness of the Eurocentric frame through which scholars have gazed at Africa, critics have labored to "[find] a new discourse for the historical experiences of African societies" (Bakari 2000: 15). In the postcolonial context, the political discourses of modernization, development, and even structural adjustment dictated both the spatial and temporal orientation of African politics, pushing governments to emulate northern teleologies of progress before fully addressing the historical, cultural, and political ruptures of colonial violence. African film criticism has approached these forces from either a Nativist or Afroradicalist framework (Mbembe 2002). While the entirety of Mbembe's critique of African studies does not apply, the two tendencies he identifies have dominated debates about African film. Despite their seeming opposition, both paradigms tend to reify identity: the Nativist approach by equating authentic African (national) experience with the oral tradition (in indigenous languages) and the Afroradicalist by promoting national culture as the key to postcolonial consciousness. In this essay, I will concentrate on the way that director Abderrahmane Sissako (Mauritania/Mali) points African cinema away from a nationalist paradigm and eschews both the didacticism of an earlier national liberationist cinema, as well as the more recent concern with the potential commercial appeal of national popular forms.

Abderrahmane Sissako's cinema does not uncritically adopt a pan-Africanist rhetoric that would reverse the Eurocentric gaze by projecting an "authentic African experience." Instead, his work elaborates the positioning of African experiences in relation to transnational cultures, ideologies, and economies. In response to those disenchanted by the failures of post-independence states and the recalcitrance of capital in the form of neocolonialism and cultural imperialism, Sissako wants to retrieve and recalibrate a de-centered humanism that does not take "Europe as its point of reference" (Mowitt 2001). Through filmmaking, Sissako creates a transnational dialogue that subtly maps the relationship between Africa and Europe.

At first glance, *Rostov-Luanda* (1997), Sissako's sole documentary, seems to follow an emerging form of African filmmaking that uses the autobiographical to illuminate the historical, elaborating a personal history to excavate a national one. Rachel Gabara has noted the growing importance of autobiographical and mixed documentary modes in recent African cinema (2003). Earlier African film critics once dismissed reflexive storytelling as "umbilical" and self-indulgent artistic forms born of western psychologism (Boughedir 2000: 113). Gabara (2003) works to reclaim the genre of autobiography as relevant to African cinema and to underscore the ways in which certain contemporary African directors, particularly David Achkar, Jean-Marie Teno, and Sissako, use self-presentation to elaborate the historical brutality of the authoritarian post-independence state. Gabara describes Achkar's *Allah Tantou* (God's Will, 1991) as a film that "slips back and forth between personal and historical narrative, telling a piece of the history of a postcolonial West" (2003: 331). Sissako approaches the personal and the local with different ends than Achkar. His films are less about retrieving a suppressed or untold history, than they are about discovering a "usable present," evoking and eliciting a reflection on the varied experiences of Africans today. Sissako's interpretation of the *porte-parole* (spokesperson) means neither ventriloquizing the other, nor allegorically standing in for the silenced African.[1] In fact, Sissako's style prevents an easy assimilation of his films as representative of a single unified African experience. His filmmaking is unique for a personal, essayistic style that defies the generic expectations of documentary and narrative. His improvisational style involves family and friends in what he characterizes, in the case of *Rostov-Luanda,* as:

> a project of staging my own situation of discovery, along with a confrontation between imaginary and visible realities.… From the very outset, this self-staging will allow for the inscription of the differences that make this story possible: the difference that separates French- and Portuguese-speaking Africa, the difference of a man living in exile, of one whose aim is to render visible to himself [the] first of all [the] realities which have remained invisible. (Sissako 1997)

It is "an invitation to the freedom of the other" (Sissako cited in Barlet 2003). Stressing the role of chance in filmmaking, all of Sissako's films evince a preference for historical contingency and possibility over chronology or causality (Barlet 2003). In *Rostov-Luanda*, Abderrahmane Sissako sets out to find an Angolan friend, Baribanga, whom he hasn't seen in 16 years. They met by chance on a train traveling from Moscow to Rostov-on-Don in 1981, where they would study Russian for a year before beginning their training in the USSR: Baribanga in state administration and Sissako in cinema at VGIK, the state film school in Moscow. Sissako's two journeys—to the Soviet Union (1983–1991) and then to Angola in 1997—trace the effects of global politics on Africa. To Sissako, Angola represents "a destiny common to many African countries": the failure of independence to bring peace, freedom, and prosperity to African peoples, and an emblematic site of Cold War conflict in decolonized Africa. In this regard, the search for the former revolutionary, Baribanga, serves as a significant frame, even though he appears only briefly before the credits roll. Though we do not see the encounter, in the final voiceover of the film, Sissako indicates that Baribanga is considering returning to Angola, which leaves Sissako ambivalent: "I heard him pronounce in the language we learned together in the name of an old illusion, the word 'return' just like an accomplishment"; having achieved the purported goal of his journey, the problem of return, of rebuilding, remains. Without the certitude of revolutionary ideologies (now seen as youthful illusions), Sissako wonders what will serve as the philosophical and practical grounds for rebuilding war-torn African societies. For Sissako, there can be no simple return to previous remedies or hopes. In *Rostov-Luanda*, he does not attempt to reconcile past motivations with the needs of the present; rather, Sissako uses the process of filmmaking to forge a "place of common memory where individual destinies meet" (1997). Thus, he eschews the projects of national history and autobiography, instead focusing on the personal choices of Angolans—to stay, to leave, to return. In this manner, *Rostov-Luanda* presents an open-ended exploration of how Angolans (and many Africans of Sissako's generation) imagine the future after decades of violence and destruction (1997).

The focus on Angola remains significant as an extreme example of the failure of revolutionary aspirations in African struggles for independence, as well as of the catastrophic effects of factionalism, militias funded by the extraction of natural resources (diamonds and oil), and the interference of external powers (apartheid South Africa, United States, USSR, Cuba) in fueling a devastating multi-decade conflict that left many Africans dead or displaced. Sissako leaves this history to be read off the shell-scarred buildings of Luanda. Some facts about the conflict do emerge in interviews with Angolans who fought for one of the liberation fronts, with children who lost parents, with parents who sent their children abroad, with those who are still looking for friends or family (as is Sissako). But Sissako's questions aim at eliciting the shared destiny of Africans in the present, a destiny he constructs in all of his films as linked to a deterritorialized identity. It is for this reason, perhaps, that Sissako chooses to interview many middle-class mestizo Angolans in *Rostov-Luanda*, emphasizing the multiethnic character of African nations (Sissako 1997). Most of the interviews take place at a bar called The Biker, a crossroads convening Angolans of various ideologies, as well as foreigners. Sissako further highlights travel and border crossings between African states by beginning his own journey in Mauritania with family to whom he must explain his need to travel as one of discovery. In relating these disparate views of Africa's future, Sissako pushes toward a revised pan-Africanism, one that refuses to offer essentialized versions of nation or Africa as antidotes for the suffering of Africa. It is in this sense that Sissako promotes the role of filmmaker as a kind of mobilized exile, who can, with the aid of a technology that might itself be deterritorializing, explore shared experiences of diaspora and migration as conditions of African experience, at the same time pointing to the legacy of different phases of globalization on African peoples.

Sissako also chooses Angola to hint at how post-independence African nations have been conscripted by more powerful players in global politics for economic and ideological reasons. In the early years of the Cold War, the US, the USSR, and European nations saw cinema as both economic and cultural inroads into African nations.[2] Along with other prominent African directors (notably Ousmane Sembène and Souleymane Cissé), Sissako's studies in Moscow were underwritten by the Soviet state as part of a larger agenda meant to "promote the state sector to the detriment of private enterprise," and to foster African socialism in post-independence states by training an indigenous intelligentsia and by forging new political, economic, and cultural ties to the USSR (Kovner 1971 cited in Woll 2004: 224). While the Soviets provided scholarships and followed the development of African cinema with great interest, they invested more readily in other kinds of development, particularly training in political leadership, science, and industry.

By contrast, France's investment in post-independence Africa appears most prominently in its construction of cinema as national patrimony, an emphasis that was reflected in the creation of the Ministry of Cooperation and Development, whose Cinema Bureau (1963) was charged with supporting African film production (mostly Francophone West African) in the postcolonial era. Manthia Diawara and others point out that French colonial policy did not support the training of African directors or the development of an indigenous film industry. Yet, in the post-independence landscape, film training, production, and distribution became an important industry for building and maintaining ties between African nations and those nations jockeying for global position.

For many years, French support for Francophone sub-Saharan African cinema ensured it the strongest production on the continent, at least until the recent growth of the South African film industry and the Nigerian video industry. Roy Armes (1996) and Teresa Hoefert de Turégano (2004) trace the emphasis on the value of cinema for national culture to colonial and neocolonial policies, arguing that these hindered the development of a viable commercial industry in Francophone West Africa. Hoefert de Turégano's careful study of the development of Burkinabé national film culture demonstrates the extent to which most Francophone sub-Saharan states patterned their film policies on the French model conditioned by the Cinema Bureau (2004: 76–95). On this model, states tended to emphasize the cultural and educational value of cinema at the expense of developing both the infrastructure and the demand for African cinema on African screens.[3]

Some critics contend that European involvement has not simply steered African states away from developing a more viable commercial film industry (or more successful private–public partnerships), but that the nature of funding[4]—often requiring the participation of European producers, technicians, and post-production services, with reception tied to European festivals, television networks, and thus European audiences—subtly affects the kinds of films that African directors create (Armes 1996; Diawara 2000; Hoefert 2004).[5] Olivier Barlet notes in his review of FESPACO 2003 (Festival Panafricain du Cinéma et de la Télévision de Ouagadougou) that the question of audience dominated the festival, particularly when Abderrahmane Sissako's "difficult" film, *Heremakono* (Waiting for Happiness, 2003) took home the Etalon de Yennenga (top prize), upsetting two genre films popular with African audiences: Moussa Sene-Absa's *Madame Brouette* (2002) and Flora Gomes's musical comedy *Nha Fala* (My Voice, 2002) (Barlet 2003). Calling the film "a provocation in itself," Barlet distinguishes *Heremakono* from more familiar African cinema in its improvisational style, its symbolism, its nonlinearity, and its "[focus] on uncertainty in a cinematic tradition dominated by the overt stating of messages or morals" (2003). By foregoing the didactic social realism of the 1970s and 1980s and repackaging national allegory into commercially successful generic forms, both *Madame Brouette* and *Nha Fala* represent a major trend in African production over the last decade. Yet Sissako departs from this new trend as well: *Heremakono* resists the formulae of national cinema and established genres. How then does he position his cinema in relation to his presumed audience? Are these "umbilical" works of international art cinema, born of European financing and intended for a European audience?

Sissako finances his films, as do many West African directors, by pooling funds from several governmental and commercial sources (European and African). Sissako has benefited from the French Ministry of Foreign Affair's *Fonds Sud* ("southern fund") and its aid to developing cinema (*ADC-Sud*),[6] in addition to funding from French and European television, notably the French-German cultural channel, ARTE.[7] Many critics argue that funding provisions have tended to separate directors from African audiences. For example, although *Fonds Sud* requires directors to film in "southern" countries, other French funding mechanisms provide more support if directors have production companies in France,[8] and more still if they are in French or an approved language (Hayward 2000; Hoefert 2004). Most importantly, African directors have had much difficulty getting their films exhibited on African screens. According to Versi and Dalby, "African films comprise only 3% of Africa's film market, as opposed to 70% for US films and the rest mainly Indian or Arab" (2003: 39). Even in Burkina Faso, which features the strongest state sponsorship of cinema in West Africa, local audiences are said to return to commercial fare once FESPACO has ended (Barlet 2003). And by some estimates (Badenhorst 2000: 159), only about 2 per cent of the African population goes to the cinema.

African directors have long sought a solution to the problem of reaching African audiences. In the immediate postcolonial era, African directors embraced filmmaking as a crucial means of healing the wounds of colonialism, rebuilding African society, and supporting new national cultures.[9] From its inception in 1969, the Pan-African Federation of Filmmakers (FEPACI, Federation Panafricaine des Cineastes) called for the formation of strong national cinemas to address local needs and to foster national and continental liberation.[10] Yet by the 1980s, FEPACI directors had recognized the reality of repressive states and weak economies. They began to argue against national censorship by increasingly authoritarian regimes and opted for regional circuits of production, exhibition, and distribution to ward off neocolonialism (most visible in foreign distribution networks) *and* state control (Diawara 1992; FEPACI 1996). Yet today, film scholar Manthia Diawara laments the increasingly nationalist tone of FESPACO:

> Even the awards emphasize the movement towards nationalism as the winning films become symbols of national pride and signs of cultural superiority over the countries that did not win. This situation has unwittingly created the basis for ethnocentrism, not to mention tribalism, in a region that is desperately in need of larger markets for the films than the ones celebrated by the nation-state. (2000: 89)

While states may hail festival awards as national victories, contemporary African filmmakers seem less allied with state rhetorics of national development than the first generation of African cineastes. In the wake of the failed modernization schemes of the 1970s and the disastrous consequences of structural adjustment in the 1980s and 1990s, directors are calling for new cultural strategies that take both postcolonial African history and global trends into account (Diawara 2001). Some directors have sought to create a commercially viable national-popular cinema, built upon the oral tradition, indigenous languages, popular music, and local theater traditions, in dialogue with popular international genres. Sissako's filmmaking, though featuring local languages and music, does not resemble either older African political-allegorical filmmaking or more contemporary national popular forms. Uniquely reflexive and poetic, his style draws from all of international art cinema, most notably, African and Soviet lyrical realisms. As Gabara has made clear, African directors evincing reflexive and experimental styles are often accused of self-indulgence or pandering to European tastes (2003: 334). Yet Sissako's filmmaking reflects in style and content a complex view of cultural inheritance and creation. Sissako does rely upon transnational cultural forms and economic networks (in financing, promotion, and distribution), but he does so in a manner that allows him to address the ways in which these transnational forces affect Africans. If Sissako's films do not squarely address the nation, it is because he recognizes both the global reach of cinema and that the nation can no longer be depended upon to guarantee the rights and well-being of Africans in Africa and the diaspora.

In fact, the consistent deterritorialization of film financing, production, and exhibition belies the tidy labels of national cinema and national film policy. Though the language of French aid for African filmmaking emphasizes national cinema and cultural specificity, national film culture and policy (in France and Africa) reflect a necessarily elastic conception of national identity that must adapt in relation to changing regional (European, African) and global forces. The neo-colonization of post-independence African film industries forced an earlier realization of the need for regional and transnational support for film production. Taking account of the temporal and spatial dislocations of the global economy, Sissako's filmmaking gives a nuanced picture of the possibilities for African cinema, culture, and philosophy in a global world. Citing Aimé Césaire as his greatest influence, Sissako rewrites earlier pan-African aspirations and liberationist philosophies for contemporary Africa, underscoring the particularity of African experiences, without strictly opposing them to European civilization. He acknowledges the significance for Africans of the devastation wrought by colonialism—the catastrophic modernity experienced by Africans—but does not substitute an Afrocentric vision for a Eurocentric one. Speaking from his position as traveler, adventurer, and exile, he suggests both the arbitrariness and fatal ramifications of the policing of borders by holding internal, regional, and international migration as a fundamental human right. His poetic style points to the necessarily hybrid forms of contemporary experience, subtly mapping out the way individuals traverse and produce subnational, national, and transnational networks, thus making Sissako a contributor to dialogues on globalization and culture.

Seen in this light, cinema constitutes a significant model of the workings of multinational capital: it merges those flows of ideas, images, finance, and people described by Arjun Appadurai (1999) as marking the distinct cultural terrain of globalization. With the restructuring of capital on a global scale, national cinema has become the chief medium for the transformation of culture into profitable export. In this context, national cinema becomes a brand name requiring the jealous protection of its market share, while, at the same time, maintaining its ambiguous status as generic referent, academic specialization, and purveyor of ideologically coherent identity. As such, the nation has not become irrelevant in the global distribution of cinema, film policy, and film economics; rather, as Saskia Sassen describes it, transnational policies, institutions, and temporalities are often 'domesticated' or 'operationalized' by state actors (2000: 227). Thus, while globalization of the film industry appears to have contributed to the "unbundling" of national sovereignty, as nation-states negotiate cultural, and specifically, national film policy, they participate in the creation of "a zone of politico-economic interaction where new institutional forms take shape and old forms are altered," and, in so doing, such institutions come to reflect "national idiosyncrasies" (Sassen 2000: 227). National film policies assuage national anxiety in the face of supranational and transnational networks (as with France in the EU), concomitantly refiguring the boundaries and symbols of the "nation" represented by its national cinema.

Against hegemonic visions of national cinema, Hamid Naficy (2001) poses global independent cinema, calling it an "accented" cinema, which encodes differential relations to nation, origin, home, and place. Diasporic, exilic, and ethnic cinema—all forms of accented cinema—can reinforce alternative forms of national belonging by relocating "home" elsewhere, or they can challenge both mainstream and marginalized national identities. Mirroring the conditions of African film production, accented cinema relies on alternative funding and distribution networks in order to reach a displaced audience. Because the realities Sissako seeks to render visible do not conform to the visions of national identity offered by cultural nationalists of the North or South, his cinema is perhaps best understood as a form of accented, diasporic cinema. While national cinematic policies capitalize on transnational trade agreements in the name of protecting presumably coherent national cultural identities, Sissako's improvisational style enacts a mode of address and a mise-en-scène that force reflection on unequal experiences of transnationalism and migration.

Throughout the body of his film-work, Sissako stresses Africa as a point of departure and return, one marked by various kinds of internal and external migration and immigration. In so doing, he insists upon making visible the interrelations already obtaining between Africa and Europe— Africa and a world marked by overlapping cultural influences. By treating each film as an opportunity, a provisional space for asking participants and spectators to consider contemporary Africa, he enacts a transnational ethics of listening. By drawing on a range of filmic styles, Sissako's filmmaking promotes reflection on the capacity for technology (and film by analogy) to produce intercultural dialogue, though one he presents as unequal, born neither of ideal speech acts nor of equality of access.

Speaking of the figure of the telephone in *Life on Earth* (1998), Sissako intimates that the fact of technological connection signals the "intention" to communicate, which he holds as:

> more important than communication itself. When one decides to speak to the Other, the gesture of love is complete. If someone seeks to speak to me, I exist for him. At any moment, one hears the response of the Other. With the radio, it's the same: RFI [Radio France International] need not believe that we always understand them; it's the gesture of listening that matters. And that shows to what extent African culture is universal and proves it at each moment. (cited in Barlet 2003)

One need not imagine that all forms of mass media present the same potential for promoting a sense of national belonging. Indeed, whereas Benedict Anderson (1991) argued that the novel provided the means for imagining national affiliation in an era of print capitalism, global independent cinema might not merely challenge official nationalisms, but also contribute to emergent forms of identification. Sissako, in this interview and in his filmmaking, is describing uneven kinds of affiliation and communication born of global media networks. In his view, connection without understanding already constitutes the brute fact of a relation—whether it goes acknowledged or not—and, as such provides the basis for affiliation. This is the ethics of listening he elaborates throughout his work.

ETHICS OF LISTENING

In *Life on Earth*,[11] one of 10 works commissioned by La Sept/ARTE for its "2000 Vu Par" series to celebrate the millennium, Sissako plays and films himself in the process of returning to his father's village in Mali (Sokolo) as the basis for his millennial meditation. Following a silent scene of Sissako lifted from Supermonoprix by an escalator, a letter announcing his return is read in voiceover. On the soundtrack, Salif Keita sings "Folon."[12] "Folon" is already transnational Afropop, but with a decidedly national meditation on the institution in 1992 of multi-party democracy in Mali just a few years prior to the release of the album (*Folon*, 1995). Sung in Bambara and mostly acoustic, the melancholic refrain is accompanied by a European-style ensemble of synthesized strings. Excerpts from Césaire's *Discourse on Colonialism* are punctuated by radio broadcasts of the millennium as it arrives at the Tour Eiffel. Though Africa has been incorporated into the imagined community of "La Francophonie," relations in this network are uneven, ambivalent, and ambiguous. The sonically evoked experiences of Paris in no way correspond to the scenes of Sokolo. As Sissako has often suggested in interviews, though the villagers have the radio on, they do not necessarily receive the message: "life in Sokolo [will not be] 'Y2K compliant'" (CA Newsreel).

To highlight the ambiguous relation between "sender" and "receiver," Sissako often employs sound bridges that leave once-diegetic sounds echoing over empty spaces. It is significant that the local radio station, the "Voice of Rice," broadcasts readings of Césaire *and* serves as the principal conduit of French experience (via the simultaneous broadcast of the French millennial celebration). Pointing toward the colonizing force of technology, the broadcast of Césaire instructs us to keep an ear to the ground and wait for tomorrow to pass as a static camera shows the empty space of the radio station. While the "voice" of the radio must be made diegetic—the radio announcers are shown reading Césaire—the later scene of the emptiness of the radio station begs the question of the fate of Sokolo's "Voice of Rice." Indeed, at the end of his letter to his father, Sissako rhetorically asks his father if the coming millennium will bring any real change to Sokolo.

Though France (with RFI as intermediary to the world) offers Sokolo a monologue, Sissako suggests the potential for dialogue. But this is a dialogue that is contingent on the functioning (or malfunctioning) of technology. The postal worker who operates the one phone in the village gives a detailed explanation of the various kinds of cross-transferring (obligatory, partial, and optional) that sometimes help forge a connection. Sissako crosscuts to a tailor who dictates a letter to his brother in France explaining why he didn't respond to his letters: "We needed your money to survive. Can't live here without assistance." Nana waits at the post office for a call that doesn't come. Though technology has the potential to keep far-flung communities in affective contact, positive change for Africa requires an ethical framework exceeding the boundaries of national affiliation and encouraging the recognition of global interdependence.

In *Heremakono: Waiting for Happiness* (2003), Sissako's first major feature fiction, he homes in on the connection between migration, technology, and affiliation. As with *Life on Earth*, Sissako generates an ethical structure of listening in both style and theme. In the earlier film, the epistolary voiceover, music, and technologies of communication serve to draw the European audience into relation with Sokolo. With *Heremakono*, Sissako elaborates upon these strategies, marshalling language, music, and silence in careful relation to the montage and the moving frame.

In this film, Sissako strives to bring to life the experience of waiting and departing for a host of characters. Though dialogue is less prominent than music and naturalistic sounds in *Heremakono*, the language politics of the limited dialogue do matter: the police, the Chinese migrant, and the black Mauritanian characters all speak French (a hint of the racial politics in a society where black Africans occupy the lowest social stratum and those claiming Moorish descent the highest). The character of Abdallah restages a moment in Sissako's own life. Though born in Mauritania, Sissako had grown up in his father's village in Mali. Thus, Sissako, like Abdallah, had forgotten how to speak Hassaniya (Mauritanian Arabic), the local dialect. The film recalls the moment before Sissako's own departure from Mauritania for Moscow, his struggle to relearn his mother tongue, as well as the kind of observation and attachment permitted by silence. For instance, Abdallah's female cousins make fun of the faulty Hassaniya he has learned from Khatra, the young electrician's apprentice, while shared French creates a bond between Abdallah and Nana, a local woman who works as a prostitute. Shot in super-8, Nana's story recounts her journey to France to tell her lover Vincent that their daughter has died: "some things must be said face-to-face." Sissako sets Nana's memories off from the rest of the diegesis, not only by the graininess of the home movie gauge, but also by using faster cuts of static images, framed so as to suggest snapshots of memories from which Vincent has been pushed to the edges.

The mnemonic technology of the home movie permits a kind of intimacy in absence more acute, perhaps, than the novel of print capitalism. Yet as a public medium, circulating and being seen, it is also a technology based on mobility and absence, migration and exile. At once national, transnational, and global, cinema is a stateless medium produced between nations.

In the rest of the film, technology serves as a slightly more direct metaphor for temporal and spatial disjuncture between Africa and the West. Nouadhibou does have TVs, radios, and the occasional car, but the technology is unreliable and, perhaps, not necessary. For example, the scene in which Abdallah sits alone in the saloon with the TV, watching an absurd French game show called "Letters and Numbers," humorously evokes the enormous gulf between the "here" of the spectator and the "there" of the culture that produced the show.

Maata is the old electrician who buries his radios and misses his days as a fisherman, and he best symbolizes ambivalence to technology. In a rare scene with direct dialogue, Maata asks whether people really need electricity, signaling the social necessity of interrogating the function of technology in our lives rather than dismissing technology *tout court*. Tellingly, the scenes in which Maata and his apprentice, Khatra, walk through the desert evening with an illuminated light bulb and a cord trailing behind them are perhaps the most beautiful of the film. Maata cares for Khatra as a son, assuming that Khatra will become an electrician when Maata dies. "Light," then, alternates between its narrative valence as technology/progress and between its formal function, as a key element of cinematography, and as metaphor for the vocation of cinema. Potentially unnecessary or ineffective, Sissako chooses the poetics of light as the best means of forging connections.

Song, too, fleshes out human relations, as it traces cultural memory and multiple paths of and motivations for migration—love, work, freedom, security, curiosity, adventure. Relationships exist in song, as performance or rehearsal. In *Heremakono*, the Chinese migrant woos a beautiful African woman by singing karaoke in Mandarin, yet the melancholic mode and the lyrics commemorate lost friends and lost freedom. Sissako loosely structures *Heremakono* around three pairs of inter-generational relationships: Abdallah and his mother; Khatra, Maata; and, an older woman (played by traditional singer, Nema Mint Choueikh), who is teaching a young girl to play the ardin, a kora-like instrument played by women in Mauritania. Yet, it is the relationship founded on musical training that Sissako presents as the most joyful. With a rich voice beyond her years, the young girl learns Mauritanian nomadic music by echoing the older woman's florid verses of love and lament. It should be remembered that African music, traditional and popular, does reach African audiences, in fact, much more reliably than African film. However, these scenes do not function as a simple stand-in for a reified conception of "tradition" or of the national-popular. The music is not just "live" (diegetic), but constitutes scenes of counsel and care, a reminder that consumption alone does not reproduce cultural forms. Further, music and voice function as critical structuring devices. As the film nears its end, and the three pairs of relationships are juxtaposed, it is this music, now made extra-diegetic, which underscores the silent departures of Abdallah and Maata. By shifting music (and voice) from diegetic to non-diegetic, the voice of one character always comes to support the scene of another.

DIASPORA AND EXILIC SUBJECTIVITY

In interviews, Sissako has explained his style as whispering rather than shouting. And in *Life on Earth*, he whispers the complexity of relations between those living in Sokolo, those who have left Sokolo, and those in his audience who will only know these few scenes. "My objective is not to engender guilt. I consider myself a citizen of the world, and it's to the world that I address myself" (Garbarz n.d.).[13] Sissako cuts to a series of shots of Sokolo residents battling the birds for the rice crop, as he begins to read from *Retour au pays natal* again: "We are standing now, my country and I," he reads, as Folon begins again: "For centuries Europe has fed us lies and sent us plagues. And it is not true that man's work is done. It has only just begun." The voice announces (the one that pierces the night with the sting of an apocalyptic wasp), "Man has to conquer the forbidden fervor stilled in his soul. No race has the monopoly on beauty, intelligence, and strength. Everyone must find his place...."

Having staged his own return, Sissako finds the state absent. In response to the needs of the villagers of Sokolo, who were, in fact, battling the agricultural crisis depicted in the film, the state is conspicuously silent (Daddesio 2004). Who, then, will answer the appeal? Ending his film with "my country and I," casting the locals and his family to play themselves, Sissako offers more than a portrait of a small village in Mali. Stylistically, thematically, and poetically he engages transnational materials to present both a local and a global critique. His camera attends to the specificity of Sokolo, showing us what he misses when he leaves, but without romanticizing the struggle for life there. He situates Sokolo within the political history of Mali only via Keita's reflection on Mali's struggle to maintain democracy (thus only obliquely raising questions about African governance). But by improvising and fictionalizing his own experience of return, he displaces the nation as the center of African experience. Sissako leans on Césaire to resuscitate a critical anti-nationalism—one that Edward Said characterizes as rejecting the "exclusivism and *ressentiment*" of philosophers of *negritude* who would have Africa invert Europe's racist hierarchy (2000: 426). In its place, Sissako constructs a critical pan-Africanism that acknowledges shared conditions of displacement, migration, and exile.

In *Life on Earth*, there is a way in which the letter stands in for Sissako's larger filmic strategy of staging an encounter and creating a dialogue via the journey and the work of the filmmaker. Much like the epistolary films of the accented, exilic cinema described by Naficy, here the letter grants readers "direct access to the characters' subjective viewpoints and emotional states and [readers] are affected by the intimacy, immediacy, and intensity of their interiority" (2001: 102). The letter, as another technology that may be heard or ignored, sent but not received, offers the possibility, but not the promise of understanding and affiliation. In many interviews, Sissako links the letter to the "chain of aid," the ethos of giving and sharing that he sees as the lifeblood of African society. The scenario of dependence and interdependence between family members, and, by implication, Europe and Africa, is made clear as the brother begins to deliver something of a benediction and a quiet appeal for the coming year: "May next year be better if only for the children. I know living in exile is difficult, but it is different." Though not necessarily critically empowering, for Sissako, like Naficy, exilic subjectivity and filmmaking offer up resources and strategies for navigating the temporal and spatial disjunctures of globalization.

In a similar vein, Sissako describes *Heremakono: Waiting for Happiness* as conveying the existential experiences of transit, the ways in which exile begins before one has left (Garbarz, n.d.). In Bambara, *Heremakono*—literally "waiting for happiness"—is the term used for temporary housing. In interviews, the director explicitly links exile with filmmaking (Boukhari 2000). The structure of *Waiting for Happiness* traces Sissako's experience of Mauritania (his birthplace and mother's home) as a provisional space, a space he had left as an infant, and to which he returned at age nineteen. Possessing little dialogue and lavishing in its long-takes of the sea and the desert, *Heremakono* conjures the time and the space of waiting in a small port town, Nouadhibou, on the coast of Mauritania, a place from which many Africans leave for Europe.

The relationship between Abdallah and his mother foregrounds the pull of Europe for him. Abdallah's mother laments the amount of time he spends alone and his refusal to participate in local social life. When Abdallah finally yields to his mother by donning traditional dress and visiting his uncle, he is left alone in the salon, only to notice that his outfit has been fashioned out of the same material as the curtains and upholstery. Though he literally fades into the décor (Sissako's visual humor), the scene underscores both Abdallah's alienation and the distance between the social class of his mother and his uncle—she lives off the scraps of her rich brother.

Sound-bridges also accompany the second major formal device Sissako employs to suggest points of contact between different experiences of migration: the match-on-action cut that emphasizes movement and correspondence. The death of Maata is linked to the departure of Abdallah by a match cut, marking two significant passages. Further, Nana's forlorn return to Africa from France is subtly matched to the motion of the Chinese migrant walking along the beach. When Makan refuses to look at the body that he has discovered on the beach, spectators must confront the fact that the body that has washed ashore is indeed the body of Makan's friend, who did not make it to Europe. As the police question Makan his partial answers are heard over static frames of the sea, the treacherous boundary separating Africa and Europe. Though we can only imagine the different motivations for exile and migration, the mise-en-scène cues us to do so, as the juxtapositions urge us to contemplate the consequences of the legalization of some forms of migration and the illegalization of others.

Sissako strives to accomplish what theory has been at pains to do. He does not privilege national belonging, nor does he dismiss it. Rather he emphasizes the way African subjects experience national and continental borders via migration, exile, and political-economic upheaval. Stylistically and thematically, Sissako focuses on portable, transmissible forms crucial for diasporic culture: the letter, poetry (particularly in his short film *Sabriyah*), music, and technologies of communication. Without ruminating on the origins of idioms—filmic or musical—he turns these to the possibility of communication, of transmitting African imaginations to wider audiences.

When Sissako declares that he is a citizen of the world and a voluntary exile, he underscores the particular dysfunction of North-South relations. Rather than considering exile to be either a privilege of cosmopolitanism or "a redemptive motif" (Said 2000: 183), Sissako sees it as "an *alternative* to the mass institutions that dominate modern life" (Said 2000: 184). Sissako elucidates a political and cultural reality that has become global without resolving the contradictions of a world that recognizes rights and subjectivity on the basis of national belonging. He reads Césaire's stinging account of European barbarism not to "engender guilt," as he says, but to elucidate the role of colonialism and racism in producing new global social forms, what Aihwa Ong describes as "global assemblages," which, while remaining unequal, produce new resources for affiliation and action. As Ong argues:

> the elements of citizenship (rights, entitlements, etc.) are becoming disarticulated from each other, and becoming re-articulated with universalizing criteria of neoliberalism and human rights. Such "global assemblages" define zones of political entitlements and claims. Second, the space of the "assemblage", rather than the national terrain, becomes the site for political mobilizations by diverse groups in motion. (2006:499)

By presenting Africans as groups in motion, Sissako points to new potential sources of affiliation based on appeals to universal rights that no longer are the exclusive province of European civilization. In reflecting upon exilic subjectivity, Said suggests that in order to institute a "new universality" against the ravages of nationalism and racism, what is needed is "an acute sense not of how things are separated but of how they are connected, mixed, involved, embroiled, linked" (2000: 430). Sissako's filmmaking does not make a demand for recognition, or a simple plea for aid. Rather he holds up filmmaking as an opportunity for imagining collective futures. Aware of the networks in which his films will circulate, Sissako endeavors to bring Africa into the social imagination of non-African spectators, to realize the long established interrelations that await full acknowledgement.[14]

NOTES

1. In Sissako's description: "I try to say things for those who do not have the means to say them. As Aimé Césaire wrote: 'My mouth will be the mouth of the unfortunate who have no mouth.' There is too much silence and incomprehension between Africa and the countries that led her to the situation in which she finds herself" (cited in Guichard 2003).
2. Thus, even when African markets offered very small profits in terms of the distribution and exhibition of film, the investment of non-African nations held greater ideological significance: explaining US interest in challenging the French in Francophone West African markets, Diawara argues that "the purpose of AFRAM [Hollywood's distribution concern in Africa] is to ensure the American cultural presence with its films" (1992: 110).
3. As Armes succinctly puts it: "[The Cinema Bureau] set out to offer Africans a means of cultural expression, and at the same time to deepen their awareness of the filmmaking process through direct involvement with a professional technician in editing their work. In retrospect, the efforts of the Ministry must be judged as a unique, remarkable and highly controversial experiment in neocolonialism" (1996: 21).
4. About "80% of funding comes from European donors" (Versi and Dalby 2003: 39).
5. Many critics and directors contend that the emphasis on funding works that demonstrate a strong African "cultural identity" ends up promoting a European caricature of African identity and results in exotic, timeless fables, disadvantaging hard-hitting political works. Others point to a second, cottage industry of "development" films that are generally cheaply made catastrophe documentaries meant to air on Western television networks and to raise awareness of problems facing contemporary Africa.
6. These are perhaps the two most important sources of funding for African cinema, with Fonds Sud supplying funds for developing nations (up to 152,449 Euros) and ADC-Sud covering France's "priority solidarity zone" (up to 137,204 Euros). For *La Vie sur terre*, Sissako received support from La Sept ARTE, *Fond Sud*, the French National Center for Cinematography (CNC), and the French PROCIREP (aid for short productions). For *Heremakono*, ADC-Sud, the European Commission's Media Desk, the Intergovernmental Agency for Francophony, the Hubert Bals Fund (Netherlands), and the MonteCinemaVerita Foundation (Switzerland) contributed funds (Ministry of Foreign Affairs). Visible here is a shift in French cultural policy toward producing films with guarantees of aid from EU institutions, and other European television concerns. Diawara (2000) sees this as a French strategy to conceal the neocolonial character of its lingering ties to Francophone Africa.
7. In this regard, the inclusion of some ARTE programming in TV5's satellite package to Africa stands to change an exhibition landscape that has typically eschewed African productions (Sentilhes 2003: 70).
8. Sissako has Cinenomad Productions in Paris.
9. In so doing, FEPACI allied itself with the Organization of African Unity's particular brand of pan-Africanism, which accepted the national boundaries left by colonialism.

10. For example, at the 1985 FESPACO, Burkina Faso's Thomas Sankara called cinema "part of the greater revolutionary struggle of Burkina Faso and Africa. To take up the cause of cinema was to 'stand together with other proud combatants of colonialism, imperialism, apartheid and the exploitation and subservience of the people of Burkina Faso, the land of culture and home of FESPACO (Festival Pan-Africain du Cinéma). And it is to support all those who believe in the power of culture in general and of cinema in particular to unite the people and bring them closer together'" (Hoefert 2004: 70–71).
11. Official selection, "Un Certain Regard," Cannes 2002 and winner of FESPACO 2003
12. "Before, no one asked your opinion, nor mine. That was how it happened. No one in society cared about things. Those who wanted to protest, those who wanted to express joy or again those who were hungry, no matter that these were your feelings, you didn't have the right to express them. Today, one asks your opinion, and one asks my opinion, today, one solicits the opinion of everyone because, today, people are taking care of things" [from the French translation of the original Bambara, posted on Le Portail de Mali (www.maliba.com)].
13. "Mon objectif n'est pas d'engendrer de la culpabilité. Je me considère comme un citoyen du monde et c'est à lui que je m'adresse." In his intelligent discussion of the role of dialogue and monologue in Sissako's films, Thomas Daddesio (2004) reads *La Vie sur terre* as "skeptical" of the potential for dialogue. However, given the emphasis on dialogue in Sissako's interviews, I would argue that it is essential to view Sissako's films through his own continued efforts to open up that dialogue by the encounters he stages as a filmmaker.
14. After the completion of this essay, Sissako attended the U.S. premiere of his new film *Bamako* (2006) at the New York Film Festival. *Bamako* imagines the trial of the international bodies that have enacted neoliberal policies in Africa. According to Sissako, the film offers—in fiction—the response and debate that have never been permitted to the millions of Africans affected by those policies.

REFERENCES

Anderson, B. (1991) *Imagined Communities: reflections on the origin and spread of nationalism*, London: Verso.
Appadurai, A. (1996) *Modernity at Large: cultural dimensions of globalization*, Minneapolis: University of Minnesota Press.
Armes, R. (1996) "The Context of the African Filmmaker," in S. Petty (ed.) *A Call to Action: the films of Ousmane Sembene*, Westport, CT: Greenwood Press, pp. 11–26.
Badenhorst, J. (2000) "Power, Cinema and TV in Africa," in J. Givanni (ed.), *Symbolic Narratives/African Cinema: audiences, theory and the moving image*, London: BFI Publishing, 158–182.
Barlet, O. (2002) "Interview with Abderrahmane Sissako. Cannes, May 1998," *Africultures*, 19 July, Online. Available HTTP: <http://www.africultures.com/index.asp?menu=revue_affiche_article&no=469&rech=1> (accessed 25 March 2005).
——— (2003) "Fespaco 2003: The onus on cinematic creation," *Africultures*, Online. Available HTTP: <http://www.africultures.com/index.asp?menu=revue_affiche_article&no=2807&lang=_en> (accessed 25 March 2005).

Bakari, I. (2000) "Introduction: African cinema and the emergent Africa," in J. Givanni (ed.) *Symbolic Narratives/African Cinema: audiences, theory and the moving image*, London: BFI, pp. 3–24.

Boughedir, F. (2000) "African Cinema and Ideology: Tendencies and Evolution," in J. Givanni (ed.) *Symbolic Narratives/African Cinema: audiences, theory and the moving image*, London BFI, pp. 109-121.

Boukhari, S. (2000) "Directors in Exile," *UNESCO Courier*, (October): 37–38.

California Newsreel (1998) "*Life on Earth*," Online. Available HTTP: <http://www.newsreel.org/nav/title.asp?tc=CN0101> (accessed 25 March 2005).

Daddesio, T. (2004) "*La Vie sur Terre*: Cultural Monologue in the Era of Globalization," *Ancrage*, 3 (Spring), Online. Available HTTP: <http://www.pitt.edu/AFShome/f/r/frit/public/html/ancrage/ThomasDaddesio.html> (accessed 25 March 2005).

Diawara, M. (1992) *African Cinema: politics and culture*, Bloomington: Indiana University Press.

—— (2000) "The Iconography of West African Cinema," in J. Givanni (ed.) *Symbolic Narratives/African Cinema: audiences, theory and the moving image*, London: BFI, pp. 81–89.

—— (2001) "Towards a Regional Imaginary in Africa," in A. Appadurai (ed.) *Globalization*, Durham, NC: Duke University Press, pp. 103–23.

FEPACI. (1996) "Niamy Manifesto of African Film-makers, 1982," in I. Bakari and M. Cham (eds.) *African Experiences in Cinema*, London: BFI, pp. 27–30.

Gabara, R. (2003) "Mixing Impossible Genres: David Achkar and African autobiographical documentary," *New Literary History*, 34.2: 331–52.

Garbarz, F. (n.d.) "Entretien exclusif avec Abderrahmane Sissako," ARTE-TV, Online. Available HTTP: <http://www.arte-tv.com/home/home.jsp> (accessed 25 March 2005).

Gugler, J. (2003) *African Film: re-imagining a continent*, Bloomington: Indiana University Press.

Guichard, L. (2003) "Review: *Heremakono*," *Télérama*, 18 January (2766), Online. Available HTTP: <http://cinema.telerama.fr/edito.asp?art_airs=MAF2105130&vrub=2&vpage=a_la_une&vsrub=1> (accessed 25 March 2005).

Hayward, S. (2000) "France," in G. Kindem (ed.) *The International Movie Industry*, Carbondale: Southern Illinois University Press, pp. 195–205.

Hoefert de Turégano, T. (2004) *African Cinema and Europe: close-up on Burkina Faso*, Florence: European Press Academic Publishing.

—— (2003) "Featuring African Cinemas," *World Literature Today*, (October–December): 14–18.

Martin, M. (2002) "'I Am a Storyteller, Drawing Water From the Well of My Culture': Gaston Kaboré, Griot of African cinema," *Research in African Literatures*, 33.4: 161–79.

Mbembe, A. (2002) "African Modes of Self-Writing," *Public Culture*, 14.1: 239–73.

Ministry of Foreign Affairs of France (n.d.) "Cinema, Media, and the Internet," Online. Available HTTP: <http://www.diplomatie.gouv.fr/thema/dossier.gb.asp?DOS=CINEMAMEDIAGB> (accessed 25 October 2005).

Mowitt, J. (2001) "In the Wake of Eurocentrism," *Cultural Critique*, 47: 3–15.

Naficy, N. (2001) *An Accented Cinema: exilic and diasporic filmmaking*, Princeton, NJ: Princeton University Press.

Ong, A. (2006) "Mutations in Citizenship," *Theory, Culture and Society*, 23.2–3: 499–505.

Said, E. (2000) *Reflections on Exile and Other Essays*, Cambridge, MA: Harvard University Press.

Sassen, S. (2000) "Spatialities and Temporalities of the Global: elements for a theorization," *Public Culture*, 12.1: 215–32.

Sentilhes, D. (2003) "La Médiathèque des Trois Mondes a 20 ans," *CinemAction*, 106: 66–70.

Sissako, A. (1997) "*Rostov-Luanda*: notes for a film," *Documenta XII*, Online. Available HTTP: <http://www.documenta12.de/archiv/dx/english/news/films/n-rostov.htm> (accessed 1 April 2006).

Ukadike, N. (1995) "New Developments in Black African Cinema," in M. Martin (ed.) *Cinemas of the Black Diaspora*, Detroit: Wayne State University Press, pp. 204–38.

—— (2004) "The Other Voices of Documentary: *Allah Tantou* and *Afrique, je te plumerai*," in F. Pfaff (ed.) *Focus on African Films*, Bloomington: Indiana University Press, pp. 159–72.

—— (2002) *Questioning African Cinema: conversations with filmmakers*, Minneapolis: University of Minnesota Press.

Versi, A. and Dalby, A. (2003) "UK showcase for African cinema," *African Business*, 292 (November): 38–39.

Woll, J. (2004) "The Russian Connection: Soviet Cinema and the Cinema of Francophone Africa," in F. Pfaff (ed.) *Focus on African Films*, Bloomington: Indiana University Press, pp. 223–40.

Contributors

Brenda Austin-Smith is Associate Professor of Film Studies and English at the University of Manitoba. Her publications include articles and chapters on Henry James, film adaptation, Patricia Rozema, Lars von Trier, and emotional responses to melodrama.

Kathleen Buddle is assistant professor of Anthropology at the University of Manitoba. Her research interests include anthropology of the media, technology, and cultural mediation. Her current project is on Aboriginal women's Radio Action Networks and the reconfiguration of First Nations domains of difference.

Tina Mai Chen is associate professor of modern Chinese History and co-coordinator of the Interdisciplinary Research Circle on Globalization and Cosmopolitanism at the University of Manitoba. She is the editor of *Globalization and Popular Culture: production, consumption, identity*, a special issue of *Cultural Critique* (Fall 2004), and co-editor (with Paola Zamperini) of *fabrications*, a special issue of *positions: east asia cultures critique* (Fall 2003).

David S. Churchill is assistant professor of US History and co-coordinator of the Interdisciplinary Research Circle on Globalization and Cosmopolitanism at the University of Manitoba. His current research is on the politics of sexual liberation and Human Rights during the Cold War.

Roewan Crowe works as an artist and assistant professor in the Women's and Gender Studies Program at the University of Winnipeg where she is also Academic Director of the Institute for Women's & Gender Studies.

Cheryl Dueck is associate professor of German at the University of Manitoba. Recent publications include a monograph on the work of East German women writers, *Rifts in Time and in the Self* (Rodopi, 2004), and articles on post-unification German culture.

Macarena Gómez-Barris is assistant professor of Sociology and American Studies and Ethnicity at the University of Southern California. Her research interests are cultural sociology, particularly as it relates to Latina/o and Latin American studies, gender and race representations, as well as political violence and its aftermath. Her most recent work, *Where Memory Dwells* (forthcoming, University of California Press) examines the memory politics of representation and culture in the aftermath of Chile's dictatorship.

Sharon Hayashi is assistant professor of Cinema and Media Studies in the Department of Film at York University. Her current research includes a critical history of Japanese pink cinema, a study of Japanese cinema and empire, and a web-based archival project on the uses of new media by new social movements.

Neville Hoad is assistant professor of English at the University of Texas at Austin. He is the author of *African Intimacies: Race, Homosexuality and Globalization* (Minnesota, 2006) and co-editor (with Karen Martin and Graeme Reid) of *Sex and Politics in South Africa: Equality / Gay & Lesbian Movement / the Struggle* (Double Story, 2005).

Peter Kulchyski is professor of Native Studies at the University of Manitoba. His most recent book, *Like the Sound of a Drum: aboriginal cultural politics in denendeh and nunavut*, won the Isbister Prize for best work of non-fiction in Manitoba.

John Mowitt is Professor in the departments of Cultural Studies and Comparative Literature, and English at the University of Minnesota. Author of numerous texts on the topics of culture, theory, and politics his most recent book is *Re-Takes: Postcoloniality and foreign film languages* (University of Minnesota Press 2005). He is also a co-editor of the journal *Cultural Critique*. His current research concerns radio as an object of scholarly inquiry.

Nima Naghibi is assistant professor of English at Ryerson University. She is the author of *Rethinking Global Sisterhood: Western Feminism and Iran* (Minnesota, 2007). Her research interests are in postcolonial feminism and representations of the Middle East

Michelle Stewart is assistant professor of Cinema Studies and Literature at SUNY-Purchase College. Her research concerns film policy, minor cinema, and globalization with an emphasis on the cinematic production of African immigrants in France.

Index

Page numbers in italics refer to figures or tables.

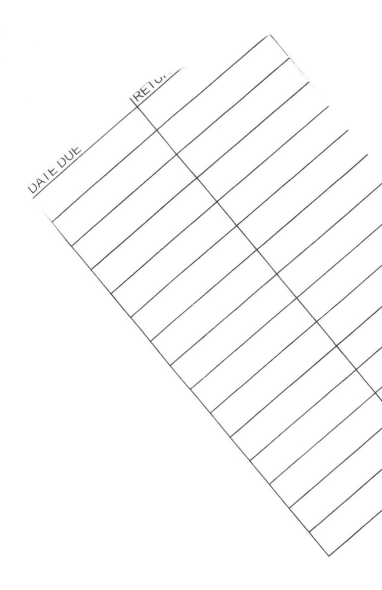

DATE DUE | RETURNED

Printed in the USA/Agawam, MA
March 24, 2014